For Gail

Good wishes

Chris

About the Author

Clive Wilkinson trained as a religious studies teacher and began his teaching career in Surrey. A few years later he went to Rhodesia/Zimbabwe to teach at a mission school, immediately after Ian Smith's Unilateral Declaration of Independence and just as the 'bush war' was starting. Returning to the UK, he attended Newcastle University, where he took a degree in geography before returning to Africa to undertake research on human migration in Lesotho for his PhD. He spent nearly twenty years training geography teachers and environmental studies undergraduates in the UK. After retirement he undertook research on youth homelessness and young people not in employment, education or training, the results of which were published under the title 'The Drop Out Society'. He then worked for several years doing research on rural development in Northumberland. Now fully retired he enjoys walking, gardening, writing, playing table tennis, ceilidh dancing and, of course, travelling slowly.

Dedication

Dedicated to my great-great-uncle, Captain John Wiltshire, and my great-grandfather, Captain William Royan, to whom I probably owe my love of the sea.

Clive Wilkinson

REFLECTIONS FROM THE MONKEY DECK:

CRUISING THE WORLD BY FREIGHTERS

AUSTIN MACAULEY
PUBLISHERS LTD.

A CIP catalogue record for this title is available from the British Library.

ISBN 978 1 78455 589 4 (Paperback)
ISBN 978 1 78455 590 0 (Hardback)

www.austinmacauley.com

First Published (2015)
Austin Macauley Publishers Ltd.
25 Canada Square
Canary Wharf
London
E14 5LQ

Printed and bound in Great Britain

Acknowledgements

Most of the cargo ship voyages on which this book is based, I undertook on my own. On the first two, however, between Australia, New Zealand and China, I was accompanied by my wife and best ever travelling companion, Joan. Since then, although preferring to travel more conventionally with the family, she has very generously indulged my growing passion for this kind of travel, giving me support and encouragement all along the way, and putting up with the long absences such a mode of travel necessarily involves. With her keen eye for detail, Joan has also spotted many errors in punctuation, clumsiness of style, lack of clarity, ambiguities in wording and inconsistent spelling. Her unfailing love and practical support have been invaluable.

I also want to pay tribute to my other travelling companions, all of whose names and other personal details I have changed, for their camaraderie and the fun we had together. On a venture of this kind, you do not know who your companions will be, but you do know that you will be living in close proximity and that you need to get along. The way you deal with this is part of the challenge of the cargo ship experience. I want to thank them all for putting up with me and tolerating my idiosyncrasies.

I need to offer a special word of thanks to the officers and men who work on these ships. I have changed their names too. Theirs is a lonely and often harsh and uncertain way of life, and this is particularly true of the men who live below the deck and who often do not see their loved ones for a year or more at a time. Their pay is very low compared with that of the officers, and pathetically low compared to what most people in the UK are used to. This is one of the factors that make the cost of the goods they bring to us so inexpensive. Often hidden and unrecognised, it is their courage and fortitude that make them the true heroes of my story.

My sister Eileen has also been helpful in drawing on her ever resourceful memory to fill me in on the stories behind the marine experiences of my illustrious sea-faring family. My brother Alan, whose keen literary eye never ceases to impress me, helped me to sharpen up some aspects of my prose and to finally work out what title to give it.

I wish also to thank Polly Shamy, who has been of enormous help researching technical matters in the USA which needed clarifying. Fred Watson, a keen small-boat sailor and a former merchant mariner himself, helped me to name some parts of ships and explained some of the principles of navigation. Thanks also to Ken Branson for helping me to improve my marine vocabulary and understand the mystery of the triple expansion engine.

I am grateful to Graham Stacy for his permission to quote from his unpublished song *Pleiades*, written for the men's folk choir Voicemale.

I would also like to thank Anne Howard for her meticulous editing and helpful comments on the text, and Vinh Tran for dealing so efficiently with my queries in the final stages of publication.

I am a late learner when it comes to this kind of writing and I am therefore particularly grateful to all those people I have met on creative writing workshops who have assisted me in my halting attempts at expressing myself on paper. In particular, I wish also to thank the members of the Arvon workshop on travel writing that I attended at Moniack Mhor. Their encouragement and advice spurred me on when I was tempted to give up.

While I was writing these pages, the members of our local creative writing group have patiently borne with me while I have read out experimental passages, to which they have responded with constructive and helpful suggestions. Thank you Angus Armstrong, Virginia Armstrong, Chrissie Buckley,

Geoff Hoskin, Jeannie Davey, Mags Bell, Pam Moloney, Roger Plummeridge and Katie Scott. A special word of thanks is due to Mary Kemp, who kick-started our creative writing group and so perceptively commented on my work and encouraged me to continue.

To all these, but especially to the courageous sailors who make our consumer lifestyle possible, I offer my sincere thanks.

Contents

CHAPTER 1: The Barque Kilmeny

On a warm late summer's day in 1883 Mary Royan was out for a stroll with her baby daughter in her smart new perambulator. Quite unexpectedly, she saw her husband, Captain William Royan, come out from behind a hedge, peer into the pram, take a long and loving look at his little daughter, smile and then, as quickly as he had appeared, retreat behind the hedge without so much as a word. This was strange because Mary Royan had no idea her husband was at home. They had been married two years earlier, both at the age of thirty-one. In December of the previous year he had set sail from the East India Docks on the barque Kilmeny bound for New Zealand. The perambulator was a leaving present for her and the tiny baby he would not see again until he was due to return almost a year later. She was used to the uncertainties and disappointments that seafaring families were subject to, for her father too had been a Master Mariner, and so also was her brother, Captain John Wiltshire. The members of this large and adventurous family were all used to long absences and the occasional pleasant surprise. This must be one of them.

So, thinking that her husband was playing one of his usual tricks on her, she smiled contentedly and continued her walk in the warm afternoon sun, returning to her comfortable south London home just in time for the unexpected pleasure of tea for two. She half expected he might have left the front door slightly ajar to make it easier for her to get through it with the perambulator, without having to fiddle with the lock and handle. But no, he must have uncharacteristically forgotten. She called out to him as she parked her sleeping daughter in the hallway, but there was no response. He would be in the parlour, she thought, standing upright, as was his way, hands behind his back, waiting for her with his usual mischievous grin. But he wasn't there. The room was empty, as was the kitchen. He must be upstairs sleeping. Of course, he would be exhausted after his long voyage and his little practical joke. She opened the door of the bedroom noiselessly. But the bed was empty. Fighting back a small feeling of irritation at having taken this particular practical joke too far, she put it to one side and attended to her baby's immediate needs. There would be time to talk to him and perhaps even slightly, but lovingly, reproach him. Above all, she wanted his company now.

It had been a very long year and her longing to be with him again was sometimes too strong to bear. She had fought back the usual tears when he had departed for the East India Docks on December 15th 1882. The ship he commanded was an iron barque, the Kilmeny, built under special survey to a higher standard of regulations than normal ships. This was to enable her to withstand the rigours of the regular voyages around the Cape and through the Southern Ocean to which she would be subject. Captain Royan was justifiably proud of his ship. One hundred and ninety-four feet long, her dimensions were impressive. The raised quarter deck measured thirty-six feet long, the fo'c'sle thirty feet. She was thirty-one feet wide by nineteen deep and had three square-rigged masts and one, the aftermast, rigged fore-and-aft. The insides of her steel hull, from the bottom to the upper part of the bilges, were coated with cement. This was the latest innovation in naval architecture designed to keep the lower parts of a ship clean and dry and to act as permanent ballast. Built in 1877, she was listed in the Lloyd's Register the following year. The Kilmeny's anchors and chains had been proved at a public machine recognised by the Committee of Lloyd's Register and licensed by the Board of Trade. Her official number was 76756, her International Code Signal, J.V.S.N. She had last been surveyed at Newport in October 1881, the year before Captain Royan had set off on his voyage to New Zealand. Yes, he was justifiably proud of commanding this magnificent barque.

He had too an experienced and skilled team of stevedores that he could rely on to load his ship correctly and safely. The East India Docks were teaming with human activity. Men were everywhere, hauling on their backs, trolleys or handcarts, everything, from bales of cotton goods to barrels of beer and crates of Scottish whisky, boxes of books, paper and paper goods, bedding, boots and shoes and kitchenware, pallets of furniture. It all had to be carried physically to the ship's side, where the stevedores would take over and position everything carefully item by item and by hand so as to preclude any possibility of its shifting whilst at sea. The Kilmeny had been in port for two weeks, unloading wheat, wool, flax, timber, and other goods from New Zealand, and was now loading up manufactured goods for the return voyage. Like most cargo ships of her day, she spent about as much time in port being loaded and unloaded as she did at sea. It was hard labour-intensive work.

As overseas trade exploded in the nineteenth century, docks throughout the British Isles rapidly grew and provided a powerful magnet for men seeking work. Port areas, particularly in London, Britain's leading port until well into the 1960s, experienced phenomenal population growth as men vied with each other under the casual labour system to find work in the mushrooming docks, warehouses and wharves. The work of dockers was largely unskilled, relying rather on physical strength. If you were lucky you would be picked for a few hours' work, perhaps even half a day or, for the very fortunate, a whole day. Morning and afternoon, the call for labourers would go out and men clambered over each other, desperate to be chosen. Their job was to bring the goods alongside ready for them to be picked up by cranes in slings, or nets or on pallets, or taken up ramps ready for the skilled stevedores to load.

The last rope holding the Kilmeny to the quayside was released on the 15th, a few hours after Captain Royan had bidden his young wife farewell. Under his expert guidance, the Kilmeny made her cautious way down the Thames at the beginning of her long and hazardous journey to the Antipodes. Two days later, on the 17th, she rounded the shoulder of Kent and cast off her tug at Dungeness. On the 21st she passed the Start Point lighthouse. Then heading south-west, she ran into light and variable winds, which soon gave way to a succession of gales and heavy seas from the west. So heavy were they, in fact, that she passed several vessels which had lost both yards and sails and were limping home in dire conditions. The men on board the Kilmeny began to feel uneasy. But their faith in their Captain's skill and judgement was well placed for, apart from the loss of a few of her square-rigged sails, he brought them through these storms unharmed.

The men immediately set about repairing the sails and, having now moved sufficiently far south to take advantage of the light trade winds to carry her westwards, the Kilmeny made good progress, crossing the equator on January 29th. She continued west at least as far as latitude twenty degrees forty-six south and longitude twenty-eight thirty-eight west. Here, her log reports, she "spoke" to another ship, the Rokeby Hall, by flag. The Kilmeny was now very close to the tiny archipelago of Trinidade and Martim Vaz, whose islands lie about a thousand kilometres off the coast of Brazil. Thus far, the trade winds had been good to the ship and at about this point Captain Royan brought her round to a south-easterly direction bringing her past Tristan D'Acunha on 22nd February. His strategy, in accordance with the common practice of the day, was to bring her into the roaring forties to carry his men all the way to New Zealand, assisted by the Antarctic Circumpolar Current which, unimpeded by any land masses, is the world's largest ocean current.

The wind patterns explain why Royan would not have wanted to take the Kilmeny through the Suez Canal, opened just fourteen years earlier. Taking this shorter route would have brought her out into the Indian Ocean straight into the face of the north-east trades, which would have thrust her onto the east coast of Africa. It would be a difficult undertaking to get her down that long coast to the roaring forties, always being thrown uncomfortably close to Africa. It was far easier to take advantage of the long fetch of the Atlantic and the colossal swing to the south that the currents and trades gave her, especially in the southern summer, when the trade wind belt was that much further south.

So, having made good time, Royan was at the Cape of Good Hope on March 6th and soon after he found himself battling with a gale that lasted for two days. After that, the weather was fine until the 27th, when the Kilmeny hit another gale, this one lasting for twelve hours. She came south about on the 11th of April, when she then sighted The Snares, a group of small islands about two hundred kilometres south of South Island, New Zealand. Experiencing very adverse weather up the west coast of South Island, the Kilmeny made it to the Heads, which mark the entrance to Wellington Harbour, at 16:00 hours on the 16th of April. She berthed at the Queen's Wharf the following day, Tuesday 17th, and commenced discharging her cargo on the 18th. It had taken four months and two days to get here. The men were relaxed and in festive mood. They had a kindly but severe Captain. They knew that their lives depended on the rules being obeyed, and that included the way they conducted their personal lives while they were under his command. That morning, the Captain posted a notice saying, "Captain Royan will not hold himself responsible for any debts contracted by his crew without his written authority".

His duties discharged, William Royan now loaded his ship with ballast in preparation for a short voyage across the Tasman Sea to Newcastle, New South Wales. Here he would pick up a cargo of wool, sugar and wheat to carry home for the ever expanding market, in the heyday of Victorian prosperity, for food and luxuries. His mood was buoyant, the men jovial and contented. They were on their way home and soon he would be with his beloved wife and adorable daughter, whom he had scarcely had time to get to know before his duties had snatched him away. With a light heart he left Wellington "in ballast" for Newcastle on the 5th May 1883.[1]

Meanwhile, Mary Royan was feeling distinctly cross with her husband. If this was his idea of teasing her, she was not amused. This was taking the joke much too far. It had been seven months since they were together, but now, having had a tantalising and fleeting glimpse of him, all her carefully practised patience had evaporated and she just wanted to be with him. Having failed to find him in the house after his prank, she could now only assume he was still out walking, something she knew he loved to do after so long at sea. But he could, she thought, surely have just said something to her, told her what he intended to do. With these thoughts tumbling through her agitated mind, she had fed the baby and put her to sleep. Now, putting the kettle on, she set about preparing what she hoped would be tea for two. He would be back by then, she knew. But when after an hour, he didn't appear, and as the late afternoon turned to evening, her annoyance turned to concern, and a cold shiver of fear cut through her. By bedtime she was alarmed and in this state she fell into a fitful sleep.

She woke with a start the next morning and on her way down the stairs saw that the postman had delivered a solitary letter that lay on the doormat. The post mark indicated it was from Glasgow. Ah, she thought, it must be from Kerr, Newton and Co., the owners of the ship of which her husband was Captain.

She began to read the letter as the morning kettle was boiling. It was indeed from the owner. Her husband's ship, it told her, had arrived safely in Wellington on the 16th of April and departed on May the 5th for Newcastle, New South Wales. This voyage should have taken him between two and three weeks, but a certain Captain Holm, of the barque Malay, had reported that he had seen no sign of the Kilmeny when he left Newcastle on the 15th July, some seventy-two days after Captain Royan and his men were known to have left Wellington[2]. Her heart turned to ice and her senses were numbed as she continued to read. One hundred and seventeen days later, the letter continued, there being no sign of the Kilmeny either in London or in New South Wales, the worst had to be inferred. "We regret we have to state," she read, "there is very little doubt that she has come to grief, with all hands lost."

In addition to Captain Royan, my great-grandfather, the following men were also lost: W. M'Kenzie (first mate), B. T. Shaw (second mate), Able Seamen – G. Taylor, T. Roberts, J. Carson, R. Crawford, J. Meegan, G. J. Sansen, P. Jacobsen, J. Tepple, L.Holt, J. Gladstone and W. Hewitt, and two apprentices – C. Osborne, and G. G. Fisher. One man, who came out on the Kilmeny from London, jumped ship at Wellington. He too was someone's great-grandfather, someone by the name of Carolyn, who had been trying to trace him in New Zealand. Other than the fact that he had left the ship and so managed to avoid the fate of his shipmates, nothing more is known about him. Had he too had a premonition?

My sister had a letter from the mother of one of the boys lost on the Kilmeny, sent to the ship's owners, Kerr, Newton and Co. It was an important letter because it told us a lot about the kind of man our great grandfather was. Eileen kept it in her jewellery box and she had read it so often she knew its contents intimately. Then one day, her house was burgled and among the items stolen was that precious letter. But it was so precious to Eileen that she had memorised it.

"Pardon the liberty that I take, but can you tell me if it is true about the Kilmeny? My son was on board and he often told me what a good man the Captain was. It was because of him that my boy gave his life to God."

CHAPTER 2: Typhoon

Tauranga wraps itself round a large harbour at the western end of the Bay of Plenty, in a broad sweep that also takes in Port Maunganui. It owes its origin to some of the very first Maori visitors at the time of the Great Migration across the Pacific from the mythical island of Hawaiiki. These ancient explorers had been drawn to this spot by the distant volcano of Tongariro with its trademark banner of white cloud flying from its peak. They would have been able to see this impressive mountain beckoning them from a great way off, for it dominates the North Island of New Zealand, and it was in this area that they will have drawn their canoes up onto dry land, at what is now the modern port city of Tauranga.

It is likely that the canoes that carried these founding fathers of the Maori nation to their new home, were outrigger canoes. They are still there, these slim, flimsy-looking but utterly stable, streamlined craft. Joan and I came across them on our way to Mount Maunganui (also known by its Maori name Mauao), about five kilometres from the container terminal at Port Maunganui where our ship, the Tasman Discoverer, was waiting to take us to Shanghai. Maunganui is an extinct volcano that lies at the northern tip of a peninsula that forms the eastern flank of Tauranga harbour. Circular in shape, it is the one outstanding feature that catches your eye when you arrive at the port. It guards the entrance to the harbour on its eastern flank. Opposite it, on the west, is the island of Matakana, the south-eastern tip of which almost, but not quite, encloses the bay. All seagoing ships have to navigate their way through the narrow channel between Matakana and Mt. Maunganui. It was near this mountain that we saw the outrigger canoes.

Under the shadow of Maunganui, in a small bay on the western side of the peninsula with a sandy beach where families were playing, two local canoe teams were putting their sleek craft through their paces, one yellow and lime green with six youngsters in it, the other two shades of blue and with one team member missing. Each canoe was equipped with a lime green outrigger. When I first saw them they seemed like two canoes, mother and child, working in perfect harmony, the one watching over the other. In fact, the outrigger serves much the same function as an extra hull for each boat, fixed securely to the parent canoe but about two metres from it, by two curved spars. The extra stability the outrigger gives these sleek craft makes it possible for them to be narrower and longer than they would otherwise be, all this making for greater speed and manoeuvrability.

About half way up Maunganui, there is a delightful track that completely encircles it, grass bank on one side, shady conifers on the other, but widely spaced enough to give a perfect view of the ocean surrounding us. We took this path, in preference to the one that goes to the top. Half way round, we looked down onto an idyllic sandy cove where a couple of young lovers, sitting on either side of a small wooden picnic table, were each totally engrossed with their mobile phones. Further on, we looked out onto the shimmering expanse of the Pacific Ocean and an almost unbroken curve of silver sand stretching away to the south-east as far as the eye could see. As each languid wave came in and washed over the shallow waters of the beach, we watched the aquamarine of the sea slowly transform itself into pure white foam. But before its time was spent, in would come another wave, and then another, forming three, sometimes four sweeping tiers of giant frothy white steps rising out to the Pacific Ocean beyond.

It was time to meet the Captain of the Tasman Discoverer. We admitted to a feeling of anxiety as we prepared for this, our first long voyage on a cargo ship. The much shorter four day crossing from Sydney to Tauranga on the CP Jabiru five weeks earlier, had been more like a taster; this, a nineteen day voyage to Shanghai, would be a major voyage, the real thing. The nervousness began as we approached the security gates. It is the sheer scale of these port complexes that is so daunting; they never fail to intimidate – huge warehouses and marshalling yards, giant piles of timber and steel bars, heaps of coal, acres of containers, forklift trucks and straddle cranes endlessly ferrying enormous loads to and from arriving and departing lorries and waiting ships. It was impossible to work out where we should go and once again, we felt completely lost and ill at ease, dwarfed by the immensity, overwhelmed by noise and the ceaseless flow of heavy traffic. These places were not designed for passengers. We felt out of place in a gargantuan world of metallic automata.

No pedestrians were permitted beyond the barricaded perimeter. All drivers had to stop and produce a photo ID. A security arm was in operation and beyond that was a huge steel wire fence topped with barbed wire, the whole overlooked by video cameras. We found a red button a few metres in front of a small guardhouse and pushed it to announce our presence. Ken, the security guard, phoned the Port Agent, Dirk, to tell him we had arrived. But Dirk had taken a crew member to hospital and so was not available. A stand-in, Joe, was therefore arranged and he took us in the shuttle bus to the Tasman Discoverer. It was a welcoming sight to see the ship that was to be our home for the next three weeks, looming above us, somehow reassuring that in the midst of this alien world, there was a small space for us that we would be able to call ours. We suddenly felt not so out of place. Stepping out of the shuttle bus to make for the gangway, an agitated voice yelled at us from above.

"Out of the way, out of the way. Stand clear, please stand clear."

Looking up, we saw that we were standing immediately below a massive container hovering above us. We scurried away until we were given the all-clear. Not without some trepidation, we climbed the narrow, swaying gangway, clutching a portfolio of documents proving that we were entitled to be on the ship and stepped out onto a green and very wet deck. From there, we were summoned towards a doorway, supervised by helmeted crew members, one of whom led us to the visitor book which we duly signed, for on that day we were mere visitors. We would not board until the morrow. We were issued with security tags, taken along a passageway, and finally ushered through an open door on the right into a well-appointed office.

The Polish Captain, Klimek Popowski, was conferring with the Russian First Officer, Artyom Zykin. They politely greeted us and we introduced ourselves as we handed over our documents. After a brief glance to see that all was correct, the Captain asked us to report to the ship at 10:30 the following day, Monday. It was all very formal and very business-like, but as we were leaving he called after us.

"We will arrive in Shanghai on March 8th, calling at Noumea on the way, in three days."

The MV Tasman Discoverer was a versatile, multi-purpose vessel capable of carrying bulk cargo, such as wood chips or grain in holds on lower decks and, on the Main Deck, thirteen hundred twenty-foot containers, or the equivalent (TEUs). With a deadweight of 21,723 metric tonnes (the total weight of cargo, fuel, oil, water, stores, passengers, etc.) she was a small ship by today's standards. Launched in Germany in 1989, she had subsequently sailed for Singapore where she had been lengthened by sixteen metres at the Jurong Shipyard in 1991. She was on a circular itinerary: Auckland, Timaru, Wellington, Napier, Tauranga, Noumea, Shanghai, Qingdao, Funabashi, Yokohama, Osaka, Busan then back to Auckland.

We had on board a few hundred containers, put in place by the straddle cranes, but nothing like a full load. Just before we departed, the ship's cranes swung into action to take on board what could not be handled by the straddle cranes – half a dozen drums of liquefied gas, several tonnes of timber and, as the day's light began to fade, our last item, a gleaming white yacht, the Makaira, wrapped in an equally gleaming white tarpaulin, was tenderly eased aboard and lovingly nestled in a carefully built nest where three containers had been cleared to make room for her. There she was to be cradled until we reached Noumea.

A burst of soot from the smoke stack accompanied our departure. The Chief Engineer explained how the smoke stacks are cleaned. Ground up walnut shells are injected into the exhaust gases which, when blown through the funnels at high pressure, scour off the soot. It keeps the stacks clean but frees the soot to fall like rain on the deck below.

That night, the first, it was hard to sleep, so just after midnight I went in search of food. Tucked away between the Officers' Mess and the galley was a little annexe, a kind of mini-kitchen about two metres wide and maybe twice the length. I had seated myself at a small well-crafted wooden table positioned snugly against the wall with a couple of solid wooden chairs either side. Above it, an assortment of brightly coloured mugs hung from a row of hooks on a neatly bevelled wooden board. Opposite, a wall cabinet held a supply of tea, coffee, hot chocolate and biscuits and below it, a small cupboard held all the implements necessary for putting a quick snack together, cutlery, plates, cuttingboards. A stainless steel bread bin gave me a choice of white or brown, and a domestic-sized fridge held milk, butter, cheese, cold meats and some fresh fruit. It was perfect. Comfortable, snug, homely. I crept down there from time to time for a late supper or for comfort snacks during occasional restless nights. I was just tucking into a well loaded slice of bread and jam when Captain Klimek Popowski joined me. Making himself comfortable in the chair opposite, he set to and prepared that same delicacy for himself, putting even more jam on his bread than I had done, and I like a lot.

"This is my most difficult ship," he told me. "It is not in good condition."

His hobby was joinery, so in his spare time he used this skill, to improve the ship. He started with the table and chairs where we were sitting. He had made them himself. Like me, he too valued having somewhere where he could sit and snack.

"I like the ship to be homely. I like to see other people sitting here at the table and chairs I made, eating bread and jam. That's what I made them for."

He had also put up wooden shelves in the library to hold the growing collection of books in German, Polish, French and English. He had been at sea for a year but would be going on leave at the end of the current voyage. He was looking forward to being with his wife, whom he clearly adored, and walking his dog again. Also, he had some family matters to attend to, especially as his mother had died a few days earlier.

"Don't mention it to anyone else," he said. "I haven't told the crew or my officers".

At three in the afternoon, Dieter the cook appeared at our cabin door with a large plate of Danish pastries he had just baked. Thinking it was a special treat, we devoured them without demur. The next day he did the same. In fact, so regularly was this tempting plate put before us at that we no longer even tried to protest that we couldn't eat any more. Dieter clearly didn't believe us, and it played havoc with our daily exercise regime. We had optimistically set ourselves a target of walking around the Main Deck ten times a day, hopefully in the afternoon. The final nail in the coffin of that resolution, however, was when the Captain put two very comfortable deck chairs at our disposal on Deck F, just below the bridge and on the starboard side, near the entrance to his own suite. A good time to use these chairs, we discovered, was after we had forced ourselves, out of consideration for Dieter, to devour the pastries. So, having scoffed these delicious items and washed them down with a cup of tea, we needed somewhere we could relax, and we could think of no better place than F Deck and the ideally positioned deck chairs. There the Captain occasionally joined us with a glass of red wine. Ever mindful of the sensitivities of our hosts, we had no option but to go along with these arrangements and forego the exercise.

Dieter was German and, apart from us two, was the oldest member of the crew. He had a Brazilian wife, but he rarely saw her and seemed content with this. In addition to Danish pastries and croissants, he baked fresh bread every other day, white and brown. No bread I have tasted on any cargo ship since then has measured up to Dieter's. Not only was he a brilliant cook, but he was also one of those rare continentals who knew what was meant by the word marmalade, and understood the English weakness for it.

"Look, I've found you some grapefruit marmalade" he said to us one morning, pointing to where he'd put it beside the toaster on the sideboard.

Our first call was Noumea, New Caledonia. The journey took three days, during which we enjoyed relatively calm seas, warm air and sunshine. Just before 19:30 on the third day we saw the pilot's boat ahead of us.

"What speed do you require?" asked the Captain.

"Seven knots," came the reply.

Joining us on the bridge the pilot said, "At least you have a lift, which makes it easier."

The pilot immediately took control of operations.

"Zero forty," he called.

"Zero forty," responded the helmsman.

Manual steering is needed for this kind of delicate manoeuvring. The wheel was disappointing. I had expected the huge wooden classical wheel with spiky bits to hold onto, something marine looking, but it could have been any steering wheel on a small family saloon, and it was square.

And so began our two-hour approach through the channel to Noumea, red lights on the port side, green to starboard.

"Okay, let's go out on the wing," said the pilot.

From that point, all directions were given from the starboard wing. Our approach took us through the Passé De Dumbea and then the narrow channel known as Grande Rade. A tug joined us, a rope was thrown out, our speed dropped to dead slow. We eased ourselves alongside. Ropes were thrown out and secured.

"Tomorrow," said the Captain, "we will look like a box. We are taking more containers on board, piled high."

"How many can you hold?

"About twelve hundred. We have about six hundred at present. Tomorrow they will be piled four high."

As we left the bridge, the Captain asked for our passports and Chinese visas for the port authorities for entry to New Caledonia and for our onward journey to Shanghai. And so tobed, in the expectation of a day ashore on the morrow.

The container terminal at Noumea was surprisingly easy to negotiate on foot. We simply walked down the gangway, set off across the hard standing where the containers were stacked, dodged the straddle cranes as they zigzagged around us, and crossed the road. No one attempted to stop or even question us. A few minutes' walk and we were in the Place des Cocotiers, the central park that seemed to mark the heart of the town. Our plan was to take the local bus to the Baie des Citrons, mosey in the warm sunshine along the promenade, have a coffee and a light lunch, and soak up the atmosphere.

"Be back by 15:00 hours," the Captain had told us.

At the Information Centre in the Place des Cocotiers, we were told where to wait for the Number One bus. "De l'autre côté," the woman told us, "Tous les quarts d'heure". We went to the other side and waited for two lots of fifteen minutes. This was young people's territory, a play area for energetic youngsters. A small circle had gathered round two young men putting on a display of breakdancing. Others were seated in nicely designed bays with wooden benches and small tables for coffee, their heads turned, watching. Children played with balloons. Two young men glided by on skate boards, a couple playing chess looked up.

No bus came. Back to the Information Centre and another conversation. The Number One bus did stop in the Place des Cocotiers but only after it had been to the Baie des Citrons. We should have been waiting at the stop on Rue Anatole France. Here we found another bus stop for the Number One bus. By now, it was almost 12 noon. Two men further along caught my wife's eye. They were seated on a bench waiting for another bus. Joan can never quite resist the opportunity for a quick and easy way to get the information we need. She opened the conversation in French. They replied in broad Australian. This was their sixth annual holiday in Noumea. They used the same hotel and to cut down costs, they did their own catering. To help them in this they had bought a collection of essential cooking utensils which the hotel manager kept in a cupboard for them.

"Look, there's plenty of time for Baie des Citrons," they told us. "Go to Duke's. You can have a good lunch there, and be back here by two-thirty. Nothing to it mate. Do it easily."

I'm always slightly thrown by the way Australians end each sentence with an upward tilt. Were they asking us or telling us? But they were right, there was enough time – to saunter along an avenue of palm trees, in the shade of which six elderly men in baggy shorts and T-shirts were absorbed in a game of pétanque. The talk, the game, the ambience, even the weather, it could so easily have been Provence. To one side of us, the gentle lapping of the ocean on the sandy beach, to the other the quiet hum of traffic winding down for a long lunch and siesta. Over the road was a restaurant where we lunched and looked out on it all. Then a short bus journey back.

We boarded The Discoverer with seven minutes to spare. It was a heavier ship now, with containers piled high. We were fully loaded with twelve hundred TEUs. An officer was checking that the container lashing rods were secure. We stood on the bridge and watched, as we edged away from the quay.

"As we were going round New Zealand I saw that one of the containers was loose," said the Captain. "One of the lashings had not been fitted properly. The officer concerned had tried to cut corners. The whole cargo was at risk. The whole stack of containers was becoming unstable and could have brought down others. We had to put into Wellington, losing one tonne of fuel and sixteen hours. The officer had to go."

Pinned to the notice board was a receipt showing that payment had been received from the crew for $US 50 as payment for two sheets of forty-four millimetre steel lost overboard due to careless handling.

Over dinner that evening as we set off from Noumea, the Chief Engineer opened the topic for the evening discussion.

"I've got a DVD of The Passion of Christ" he said. "Would you like to borrow it?"

He spoke with enthusiasm; it clearly meant a lot to him.

"Thanks," I said, "but I'm not sure I like it. All that emphasis on suffering puts me off."

"But that's how it was," he persisted. "It's an accurate picture of what happened to Christ."

"That's right," agreed the Captain. "The detail is important because we need to understand what we did to Jesus."

This was a conversation I did not want to have. This is what I had fought so hard to leave behind, this dumping of guilt on us all. It was too close to what I had been taught at my first school, St. Joseph's. "Look what you've done to him", the nuns told us. We were given blow by blow accounts of the crucifixion and of the events leading up to it in some kind of grotesque fascination with the physiological details of the suffering of Jesus. As if morbidly turning the pages of a sadomasochistic magazine, the nuns would show us pictures of the Stations of the Cross, with graphic descriptions of brutality for our contemplation. Again and again, we were made to look at gruesome images of this near naked man suspended on an ancient instrument of torture, blood seeping from open wounds, and we found ourselves trapped in an enforced voyeurism, terrified of what we personally had done to him and struggling to purge our guilt. Mea culpa, mea maxima culpa. First, make you feel guilty, then terrify you into belief. And now, here was Mel Gibson trying to recreate those feelings.

I wanted the conversation to end there, but the Chief Engineer needed to tell us about his faith, especially how when he took communion, he really felt the bread taste like the flesh of Jesus. He believed in a literal devil, he told us, in fallen angels and the Bible as the literal word of God. I watched the Captain as he made the sign of the cross and realised that there was a very powerful belief system that these two men shared.

In the morning, Third Officer Emilio showed us how to take readings from the sextant. Captain Klimek insisted that his officers use the sextant every day.

"What would we do if the GPS failed?" he asked.

Every morning therefore, during the forenoon watch, Emilio established three LOPs (Lines of Position) from which he took the mean. That day he was within one kilometre of the GPS position. The Captain was pleased.

From Noumea we continued our north by north-west route, pushing against the south-flowing Australia Current, an extension of the South Equatorial Current, which flows westwards just south of the equator but is diverted south as it pushes against the continental landmass. Our route took us through some of the most isolated island states in the world: through the Coral Sea and Vanuatu, the Solomon Islands, the eastern edges of Papua New Guinea and the Bismarck Archipelago, the Federated States of Micronesia, comprising parts of the Caroline Islands, Marshall Islands and the Mariana Islands, before passing through the Philippine Sea, the Ryukyu Islands, the East China Sea and so to Shanghai. Our first glimpse of land after New Caledonia was when we were making our way through the channel between New Ireland and the Feni Islands, in Papua New Guinea. One after the other they came, these island groups, the Tanga Islands and the Lihir group on our starboard side, and then the Tabar Islands on our port side, all part of the Bismarck Archipelago. Throughout the day they lay tantalisingly close and even their names seemed to draw us, Bougainville, Malendok, Bitbok, Tefa, Boang. If only we could be there, step ashore, feel their texture, meet the people. We watched longingly as they slowly slid past us, wanting to reach out and touch.

Not far to the east of us were the Gilbert and Ellice Islands. They became the separate British colonies of Kiribati and Tuvalu in 1976. I had first come across these islands some forty years earlier when reading Arthur Grimble's delightful book *A Pattern of Islands*. Grimble served as a Colonial Officer in the Gilbert Islands in the first half of the twentieth century. He was a brilliant observer of the people and of their customs. First published in 1952, the exquisite detail of his book transports his story into the present day, bringing to life a culture that is sadly, a century after the events he describes, being absorbed by the uniformity of modernisation and globalisation. There are relics of that earlier culture, however. Tucked inside the pages of Grimble's book there are black and white photographs of outrigger canoes, almost identical to the ones that Joan and I saw under the shadow of Mount Maunganui, old ones of course and entirely homemade, but exactly the same design. They come from this part of northern Oceania and it was from this area that the early Maori settlers made their epic journey to New Zealand, possibly a millennium or two ago.

The story that made the greatest impression on me at the time was the Gilbert Islanders' version of the Fall. I discovered it when as a young man, I was re-evaluating the religious fundamentalism on which I had been raised and was finding it wanting. In the Christian Bible the book of Genesis tells of how the first man and woman found themselves in the blissful Garden of Eden where they disobeyed God, were thrown out of the garden and so condemned the rest of the human race to lives of toil and hardship, pain, suffering and death, all because of one man's sin.

To my astonishment, however, the Gilbert Islanders also had a story of how suffering entered the world, and its interest for me at the time was its remarkable similarity to the biblical story of Adam and Eve and, as in Genesis, a tree occupies a central part in the story. These people too believed that their earliest ancestors had been exiled from a place of peace and beauty in which there had been no sorrow, pain or death, a place known as the happy land of Matang, similar to the biblical Garden of Eden. Here in this paradise, so lush were the trees that they were bowed down by the weight of fruit, fish were abundant, there was no hunger or thirst, no ill wind, and death was unknown. Here Nakaa the Judge planted two trees with strict instructions that the men should gather round the north tree and the women round the south tree. When they kept to this arrangement they were happy and without death or grey hairs. They too had been cast out of this blissful land because they had disobeyed their God, Nakaa. One day Nakaa went on a journey and left instructions that the men and women should remain separate. Predictably, their sexual curiosity overcame them, they disobeyed Nakaa and did what came naturally. But Nakaa found them out, for their sin had left its mark on them in the form of grey hairs. And it was in this way that suffering and death entered the human race.

To soften the punishment about to be meted out to them, Nakaa offered a choice. They could take with them on their journey into exile one of the two trees around which they had traditionally gathered, the men's tree or the women's tree. The men chose the women's tree, the tree of death, and from that moment onwards, Nakaa told them, and forever more, death would always be present in their lives.

In the biblical story of the Fall it is God rather than Nakaa who metes out the punishment for disobedience, but apart from that, the story is much the same. Here, humanity's punishment for the sin of daring to eat from The Tree of the Knowledge of Good and Evil, is perpetually painful childbirth, toiling and sweating for our food, and returning as dust to the ground from which we came. Commenting on the beliefs of the Gilbert Islanders, Grimble said that what we believed was of no account. The only thing that mattered was that their beliefs made them happy, and because they were happy, they were safe.[3]

Trees hold a central position in religious thought, whether it be the one that brought suffering to the human race in the Garden of Eden, the pair of trees in the happy land of Matang, or the Bodhi tree under which the Buddha sat for enlightenment. Our own British and, more generally, European mythology, is richly interwoven with stories of sacred trees, woods and groves. This is hardly surprising given that pretty well the whole of Europe was covered by forest for most of its history. The author, James Frazer, reported that some Germans whom Caesar had questioned, had been walking through the forest for two months and still had not come out of it, so vast was it. From ancient Greece and Italy to Germany and Celtic Britain, trees were regarded as sacred and there were severe punishments for so much as peeling the bark off a living tree or even breaking a twig. Druidic Celts worshipped oak trees. In ancient Sweden, there was a sacred grove in which every tree was treated as divine. Jerome tried to persuade the people of Lithuania to cut down their sacred groves as part of his missionary endeavour, but the people were terrified that in so doing they would destroy the house of God, from which rain and sunshine came. In view of our present concern about the effects of deforestation on global warming, they may have had a point. Dancing round the Maypole or May tree, which is still done to this day in some areas, is a relic of this ancient reverence for trees.[4]

In Buddhism, the tree doesn't bring death or punishment; it is there simply to provide shade and with it an opportunity for contemplation. Siddhartha Gautama sat under the Bodhi tree and found enlightenment. It wasn't a tree of good or of evil, nor did it have any magical powers. It was simply there to provide shade and to offer an invitation to rest under its boughs and meditate on the riddle of life.

After our mealtime discussion with the Captain and Chief Engineer, Joan and I went up onto the bridge wing. It had been a gloriously tranquil day and we could look out across the western Pacific towards the Islands of Tanga and Lihir to witness the ending of the day. We watched the sun sink majestically behind a line of black cumulus clouds towering over the western sky, looking like a parade of giants marching against a background of flaming orange and red as the sun expired below them in a burst of glory. Behind us to the east, another miracle unfolded. On our starboard bow was a parallel wall of even darker cloud, pitch black below, steely grey above, climbing menacingly to some thirty-five or forty thousand feet and reaching into the lower layers of the stratosphere. But their tops were truly magnificent, like huge celestial whirls of candy floss, their anvil heads shimmering in pinks and lilacs as they caught the highest of the sun's rays and threw them back to the west in a defiant paroxysm of splendour.

We stood on the bridge wing looking across the immensity of the ocean, feeling the soft caress of warm Pacific air on our faces and witnessing, to port and starboard, the awesome interplay of light and dark as each tried to outdo the other in sheer spectacle. Directly above us, however, the sky was perfectly clear, and the only sound we could hear was the swish of water as the Discoverer sliced through its inky smooth blackness some forty metres below. It was as if a pathway of the most extraordinary calm had opened up for us between these two cosmic protagonists and I felt enveloped by a feeling of peace and wonder. This was enough for me. I needed no other interpretation of the meaning of life.

In her thoughtful article on the nature of spirituality and its relationship with the world in which we live, Rosemary Hammerton wrote that her deepest spiritual insights had taken place within the family and in the natural world. Her sense of spirituality, she said, came from being connected to the earth and her conviction that everything in it was holy[5]. John Keats put the same thought in his *Ode on a Grecian Urn*: the only thing we need to know, he said, is that truth and beauty are the same thing. That is what matters. Nothing else.

At 05:00 on the following morning, the Captain made a rendezvous with our sister ship, the Tasman Adventurer, from which he had learned two things. First, there was a strong possibility of poor weather as we continued north-west. It looked as if those splendid cumulonimbus clouds that had seemed so magnificent the previous evening, were about to show their nasty side. Second, there might be problems getting us disembarked at Shanghai. Apparently there was a logjam of ships held up in the East China Sea on account of a seemingly static bank of fog that gave no indication of lifting.

Fierce manoeuvring was afoot on the part of dozens of ships' captains for the best position for an early passage into Shanghai. Ships were trying to jump the queue. Tempers were getting frayed. Time, after all, is money.

"We will have to make phone calls," said the Captain. "Perhaps there will be some difficult negotiations."

It was not long before we began to hit turbulent seas; there were two reasons for this. In the first place, we had hit the Equatorial Counter Current. Wind and ocean currents work together to resolve their differences by balance and counter balance. The north-east trade winds, for example, push water over to the west in the form of the North Equatorial Current, and the excess water that builds up in the western Pacific is taken back east by the Equatorial Countercurrent. The Tasman Discoverer had now entered this current and had to counteract its tendency to drag us over to the east. But it wasn't only sea currents that accounted for our turbulence, the main reason was a distinct change in the weather. The ship had begun to pitch and roll, waves slamming into our sides with mighty thuds, making the ship shudder violently. We stood on the bridge and watched as wave after wave thumped into the bow forcing water up the anchor housing and then spewing out over the fo'c'sle like a huge blow-hole. It was as angry a sea as I had ever seen.

"Now we have a normal sea," said the Captain, smiling.

But it did not stay normal for long. It is true that the previous few days had been abnormally calm, with hot and humid air pressing down on us. We had made good use of the ship's little swimming pool, four or five strokes and you were across it, but it sure was refreshing in the stifling humid heat. Now that the sea was getting boisterous, however, the pool had to be emptied.

"It's too dangerous to swim," said the First Officer.

Two days later we watched from the bridge as the winds rose from Beaufort six, to seven and then eight. Out of the Equatorial Countercurrent, we were now being nudged westward by its sister, the North Equatorial Current. The storm hit us in all its fury in the Philippine Sea, wild beyond belief. Force nine, force ten, force eleven. The sea had become the plaything of the gods, it was celestial bath time, a foam bath. The gods screeched in merriment, utterly careless of what they were doing to us. Our boat was a mere toy to be thrown about by them as they vied with each other to see which one of them could make the biggest wave and toss us about the most. The whole world had been turned into a planetary sea of violently heaving white froth, sweeping in long streaks before lifting into the air like a spuming, malevolent spectre. And then, vengeful Vulcan and his noisy father Zeus got to work. They had been at loggerheads since time immemorial and now, their differences as strong as ever, their anger unresolved, thunderbolts were hurled from every point in the sky to the frenzied waters below. Lightning danced, thunder roared. Father and son outbid each other in viciousness, hurling insult upon insult in their contempt for the human race, mocking our pathetic struggles to stay afloat. It was a cosmic son et lumière, a global strobe show, and our frail craft was on a galactic switchback.

The Captain ordered a change of course to the north by ten degrees to try to reduce the cork-screwing. Joan was sick. The Third Officer vomited. Concerned for our welfare, the Captain arranged for us to have an alternative cabin, one lower down on the Poop Deck, where the movement of the ship would not be so severe. It worked for Joan but I loved it where we were, higher up. I needed the light, to look out onto the sea, whatever its mood. I found it all exhilarating.

And then it eased. Beaufort three or four. We were able to walk to the prow once more. The Main Deck was covered with a thin film of salt.

"Was that the north-east trades?" I asked the Captain over lunch.

"No," he said, "it was more than that. That was typhoon."

The name comes from the Chinese *tai fun* (great wind)[6] and they are characteristic of this part of the north-west Pacific. This, being the largest of our oceans, has enormous stretches of open water, and the fetch (the distance over which winds can blow before they encounter land) is therefore vast.

Winds, uninterrupted by land, can build up to colossal speeds. These powerful winds, combined with low pressure, create typhoons which are often more intense than the cyclones that occur elsewhere in the tropical world.

The rain returned in the afternoon and early evening but the sea was calmer. At dinner the ship's hooter sounded. It was something very close to the alarm for emergency drill, but not quite. We were puzzled and waited for a lead from the Captain or Chief Engineer. Should we return to our cabins and get our emergency equipment? The Captain got up and looked out of the window.

"It's just the mail boat. There must be an important message," he said as he calmly sat down and continued to eat.

"Really?" Joan and I said together. "You still use mail boats?"

"Oh, every so often the mail boat brings our urgent mail."

What on earth could be so urgent that it had to be sent in this bizarre manner? A thumping on the stairs suggested someone in a very great hurry. The door banged and a voice called out.

"Mail for the Captain. Mail for the Captain."

In burst a stumbling figure dressed from head to toe in yellow oilskins and sea boots. He looked at the end of his endurance and I wondered what kind of hell was being experienced out there that a man could risk his life to bring us mail in this extraordinary way. He delivered to the Captain a large buff coloured envelope with what looked like a red seal on it. I was all for going out and getting my camera. This was something I had to record.

"No," said the Captain, "I will take some pictures for you later. Stay here. This could be important."

Using his dessert knife to open the envelope, he took out its contents and studied them seriously for a minute or two, whilst we sat with bated breath wondering what on earth could be so important that mail had to be delivered in this way in an age of sophisticated electronic communications.

Then he began to smile.

"It's all right. It's from King Neptune himself. He has granted you safe passage through his kingdom."

He opened the important looking envelope and took out two laminated and beautifully illustrated passports to Neptune's kingdom, duly signed by the King himself, and ceremoniously handed them to us. Laughter, lots of it, and the meal continued with the Captain opening a bottle of wine for us to thank us for our company and to say what a good time we had had together. He told us we would be the last passengers to be carried by Oldendorff, the owners. We had heard of passengers expecting too much and complaining that the beds were not comfortable or the food not up to cruise liner standards. It was beginning to be troublesome. It is sad that such unreasonable expectations should jeopardise the future of such a fantastic way of travelling.

As the typhoon was raging we were passing through the Caroline Islands, in the Federated States of Micronesia, with the miniscule Republic of Palau over to our west. Consisting of about three hundred and fifty islands, it has a total land area of just under five hundred square kilometres and a population of twenty thousand, about the size of a small market town in the UK. Being surrounded by waters of the Pacific Ocean, the inhabitants enjoy a close relationship with the sea. Their theology reflects their geography. The creation myths of these people are woven around images of land, sea and creatures that inhabit the sea. Before there was land or people, there were only gods and the sea. The supreme God, Uchelianged, however, was tired of the emptiness, so he created land to fill all that space. On his command a huge volcano erupted under the ocean, rose through the surface and eventually formed a volcanic mountain island, on top of which sat a giant mother clam, Latmikaik. She remained on top of the mountain and spent her time growing, her soft insides getting bigger and bigger, filling with life. Huge waves battered the mountain, and the island shook as winds screamed and thunder roared. Eventually Latmikaik could no longer resist the power of the ocean, which tore through her body and ripped her open. She then spewed out all kinds of life, beginning with terns and swifts, which called out to the others to come out and be born. And as they did so the ocean laughed with life. The animal to be born was a human child, who was so greedy that it ate everything there was to eat, so much so that it devoured all the food on the land and in the sea and grew into a giant. That giant's greed destroyed the world's first island, the first piece of land ever to exist, and out of desperation, the few remaining people made mounds of coconut stalks around its sleeping body and set fire to it. Waking up bewildered and in pain, the giant realized, as it entered its death throes, how selfish it had been. As it toppled over its body broke into pieces, each one creating a new island.[7] That, according to the people of Palau, is how their islands were created - geography and divinity in perfect accord.

It took us six days to pass through the Caroline Islands and the Philippine Sea and for the typhoon to finally blow itself out. We were now within a day's sailing of the Ryukyu Islands, an island chain more than a thousand kilometres long and belonging to Japan. It is here, in Okinawa, that one of the bloodiest battles of the Second World War took place in June 1945. At 11:53 on our last day in the Philippine Sea, and as we were approaching the Ryukyu Islands, the ship-to-ship emergency hooter sounded. Mistaking it for the general alarm, we immediately gathered our emergency items, life-belt, hard hat and immersion suit and made for our muster station. However, to our consternation and puzzlement, no one else seemed to be in any kind of hurry to do the same, so we deposited our gear back in our cabin and made for the bridge. The Third Officer was just leaving to have lunch, the Second Officer taking over. They were both in earnest consultation with the Captain. We waited a few moments and then the Captain came over and explained. The siren was to warn a Japanese cargo ship that it was on a collision course with us. We were on a bearing of 325 degrees, he was coming at us on our port side on a course of 55, a clear collision course. We had to take emergency evasive action by making a broad sweep to starboard. Leaving the bridge, we heard the Captain telling the Japanese ship in no uncertain terms that he intended reporting him to the Japanese authorities.

The Ryukyu Islands form the south-eastern boundary to the East China Sea, and we passed through them and into this sea the next day. It was here the fog hit us. Fogs are ground level clouds. Apart from altitude, fogs and clouds are the same. In both cases they are caused by air being cooled so that invisible water vapour condenses and visible water droplets are formed. There are several ways in which this cooling can take place and one of the most common is when warm, stable air is carried over a cold surface. This is called advection fog, and it is particularly likely to occur when a warm ocean current collides with a cold one. In the North-west Pacific this happens on a grand scale. Warm moist air sits over the North Equatorial Current (NEC) and is carried westwards. When the NEC hits the coastal areas of the Asian continental land mass and its islands it is diverted north and north-east and becomes the warm Kuroshio, or Japan Current. Meanwhile the cold Oyashio Current is on its way south from the Arctic regions and when the two collide, massive fog banks develop. A similar phenomenon occurs off the north-east coast of North America when the warm Gulf Stream comes up against the cold waters of the Labrador Current and the East Greenland Current. This area too is infamous for its persistent fog banks.

It was no great surprise, therefore, that we hit fog over the East China Sea, where we were forced to drop anchor and await instructions to proceed to the pilot station. After five hours, a telex informed us that the fog had caused such congestion that our berth had been cancelled and we were to wait for further instructions. Another five hours. I counted seventy-eight ships on the radar screen waiting to enter Shanghai. Visibility was about one hundred metres and the crane on the deck was barely visible from the bridge. Another telex told us that the pilot would come on board at 05:00. But it was wishful thinking.

It was eerily still, deathly silent and miserably cold. Ships surrounded us, but not an engine could be heard. Another day went by and as the sun set it left a long tired streak of yellow and gold light shimmering on the gently rippling sea. It was as if a motorway with sodium lights still blazing had suddenly been submerged but was carrying on business as usual, its shivering light stretching away to the far horizon. This was the first sign we had seen of the sun all day. Nowhere in the sky had it been visible. An occasional hulk, looking for all the world as if it had been abandoned or had given up all hope of rescue, drifted in and out of visibility. Elsewhere, shadowy ships appeared and disappeared when the fog thinned, and then closed in again. The silence was unnerving, broken only by the occasional metallic clang as a spanner was dropped or a door slammed.

"I was once at anchor off the coast of Morocco for two weeks in similar circumstances," Third Officer Emilio announced.

This was bad news for us as we had a hotel booking in Shanghai and onward rail reservations to Xian and Beijing and then the Trans-Siberian to Moscow and St Petersburg. Having built six days' slack into our itinerary to allow for slippages of this kind, we had already lost two of them. Our nerves were taut. We sent an email to the Peace Hotel telling them that we had been delayed and asking them to keep our reservation open. Of course, we would have to pay for the days we lost. Our spirits were low as we woke to the prospect of yet another day of sitting at anchor beneath this cold, clammy, dispiriting shroud, but that evening however, it began to lift, as did our spirits,. The dog watch was just beginning, the First Officer taking over from Number Two.

"It's not yet certain we can rendezvous with the pilot," the Second Officer was saying.

Just then the Captain came in and Number Two repeated this.

"I am the one who gives orders," he said, "not the pilot."

Turning to me he said, with a twinkle in his eye, "I have managed to jump the queue. We're on the move."

Within a few minutes Able Seaman Faroog Adam was at the helm, the anchor was lifted, and we were slowly making our way over the next two and a quarter hours to the pilot station. At 17:30 the Captain contacted the pilot.

"Shanghai Pilot, Shanghai Pilot, Shanghai Pilot. This is Tasman Discoverer. Do you read?"

"Yes, this is Shanghai Pilot."

"We are already under way. I'm going to be at Pilot Station at about 18:15. Can you please say which side and how much above water?"

"Yes, that's fine. Port side and half a metre above water." This referred to the height of the rope ladder above the water.

For five hours pilot, trainee and Captain worked in perfect unison to take us slowly up the Changjiang (Yangtze) River and through the heart of the industrial revolution that has been transforming China into a major world power. A hundred and fifty years earlier we had been the workshop of the world; now it was China's turn. At three o'clock in the morning, for mile after mile, the banks on both sides of this enormous river were lit up with yellow sodium lights with what looked like the whole of China at work, creating the wealth that is now buying up real estate and debt in Europe and the United States of America. As our sun was setting, theirs was rising.

By this time, Joan had had enough of freighter travel. I wanted more.

CHAPTER 3: Your Risk

That was almost a year ago. Now I'm doing it solo, a major voyage by two container ships, a complete circumnavigation via Suez and Panama. My ship sails from Tilbury tomorrow morning, but tonight I lodge at Stifford Clays, Thurrock, where I've booked bed and breakfast accommodation at what looked like a delightful farmhouse on the web, but which now, as I step through the front door into a tired and fusty hallway, looks thoroughly dejected. Just as I change my mind about the place, I hear my taxi turning round in the drive and departing, but it's been a long day, I'm tired and I decide I can't be bothered to look for somewhere else at this time of night. A scruffily-clad and unshaven young man comes out from behind what passes for a reception desk and carries my case to a sad-looking room on the third floor.

To lift my spirits, I walk back along the lane to the village of Stifford Clays and there linger for two hours over grilled trout and French fries, followed by apple crumble and custard, at the Dog and Partridge. This puts me in sufficient good cheer to get me through an uncomfortable night in the worst B&B it has been my misfortune to experience.

My taxi arrives at seven-thirty next morning.

"Big mistake, that place," I say to the taxi driver as we set off.

"It's mainly for long-stay people on benefit," he tells me. "I did wonder why you chose to go there. I could have taken you to a decent hotel not far away."

We stop at Asda to allow me to get some cash and a good stock of newspapers and magazines to see me through the next five weeks. Five minutes later we arrive at the Port of Tilbury.

Through the gatehouse I enter a strange new machine-dominated world, one of continuous movement, urgent activity, reminiscent of science fiction films which depict some far flung planet on which human life is only possible if conducted from within tough, giant, atmospherically sealed machines. Once inside those heavily secured gates people disappear. This is a world of automata, but if you look carefully you might just be able to detect a miniscule human being in the driving cab of a monstrous straddle crane high above you. This is a 24/7 world in which the sole purpose of life is moving massive boxes around as if in some urgent game of three-dimensional chess. A constant stream of lorries deliver and collect these boxes, pausing only at the gates, on the way out and on the way in, to undergo rigorous security screening, for these boxes contain the elixir of life for us on planet earth in the 21st century. Without them and their contents, our way of life would be impossible. These boxes are, therefore, treated with the utmost respect. They are picked up and swung into the air by the straddle cranes, whose job is to move them from lorry to ship, ship to lorry, or to place them in neat blocks where they wait until a vessel comes to claim them.

You attempt to walk among these straddle cranes only at huge risk to yourself, for you are all but invisible to them, their drivers are anything up to forty metres (130 ft.) above you, certainly taller than the ships they serve. They are the key players in this deadly serious game of loading and off-loading, arranging and re-arranging giant steel containers. They move with surprising speed and agility and their huge, springy tyres make them almost silent as they creep up on you imperceptibly. Alongside them, the minibus seems miniscule and insignificant as the driver weaves his way through the hazardous complexities of this hive of activity to bring me to the foot of the gangway of the Alexandra Rickmers.

I can never quite understand how these gigantic vessels actually stay afloat. I feel the adrenalin surge within me as I step out of the minibus, a mixture of excitement and apprehension. My luggage is hauled aloft by the ship's crane in a red, metal crate to the Main Deck about ten metres above me. The black hull of the ship that is to be my home for thirty-two days looms over me, and on the Main Deck above, row upon row of red, brown, blue and green containers rise into the grey sky. For this journey I am on my own. I've not done a solo cargo ship voyage before, and my heart is thumping with anticipation and anxiety as I step onto the rickety gangway. It sways with each step and I grasp the rope in my left hand. It is a hard rope, hard as steel, three inches thick and slightly greasy to touch, its surface polished by the friction of thousands of hands. At the top I step onto the bright red floor of the Main Deck. To my right a wall of containers, three storeys high and bearing the name Hapag-Lloyd, rises seven metres above me. There will be yet more on top of these. A neatly dressed young Filipino man, white jacket, black trousers, glistening black shoes, greets me. He is Francis Lagip, assistant cook and passenger steward. Beside him is my luggage. He directs me to an open door just behind him.

Third Officer Dakila Padamada is also a Filipino. Dressed in a uniform he will not wear again until our next port, he comes out from behind a busy desk, shakes my hand and gives me a broad grin.

"You're very welcome," he says. "It'll be good to have passengers on board. Nice to see a new face."

Once again my documents are checked and I am officially signed on. Then, with Francis leading the way, I climb more stairs, eight flights of seven steps, but this time solid, substantial. The brass banisters on both sides are highly polished, and the racing green floors are shiny clean. At the top of the stairs on Deck D, we turn right and walk to the end of the corridor. The soft soles of our shoes squeak as we walk towards my cabin, which is on the left. Immediately in front of me is an open door leading onto a small viewing deck, beyond which I look out onto acres of containers and cranes.

On cruise ships passengers are king. Everything on those five-star floating hotels is geared to the needs and comfort of passengers. They put into port at convenient times to allow tourists to go ashore and explore the nearest shopping mall, and they contrive to sail away just at sundown so that romantic music can play on the ship's loud speakers to accompany magnificent sunsets. You almost wonder whether this too has been organised by some franchise arrangement with the Almighty, so predictable is it. The spectacle over, you just have sufficient time to take a shower before dinner, and if there is any possibility of fragile tummies being upset by a storm, there will be a change of course no matter what the expense, so that the business of eating and partying can proceed without interruption, and the disconcerting sensation of being at sea, and possibly vulnerable, is minimised.

On freighters, cargo is king. What matters here is getting goods shifted round the world as efficiently, speedily and cheaply as possible. On board these ships you will find yourself totally immersed in a working environment and, no matter what, you will have to fit yourself into its routine. Be quite clear that it will not accommodate itself to yours. Times of arrival and departure cannot always be predicted accurately and you, the passenger, have to be prepared to be utterly flexible. These vast floating warehouses obey the economic imperatives of cargo rather than the sensitivities and convenience of passengers. Unlike passenger liners, if you are not there when a freighter needs to leave, there will be no call for missing passengers before departure. It will depart without you. Be there.

I am beginning a round-the-world voyage by cargo ship, stopping off in Australia to meet up with family for Christmas. Joan is travelling by air with the Swiss grandchildren. I like travelling slowly and I like doing it by cargo ship. For this to work properly you have to plan a long way ahead, a year or eighteen months. But this had all been decided very quickly and I had only had eight months to book my passage on the Alexandra Rickmers. It was not early enough to get a good choice of berth, but at least I had secured a passage and was content. I would have preferred a higher cabin, on Deck E or F, away from any possibility of containers blocking my view. But even so, this cabin exceeds my expectations and I relax. It has a good-sized bed with reading lamp within easy reach, a long three-seater settee with blue upholstery, two matching chairs, and a low coffee table, securely fixed to the floor. A porthole gives me, for the moment at least, a good forward view of the full length of the ship. An ample desk, complete with brass reading lamp, bookshelves, and a hi-fi system, fills the far corner. The large fitted wardrobe easily accommodates all my clothes. A door to the side opens to a well-appointed en suite. There are pictures of colourful rural scenes on the walls and a plum coloured carpet under my feet. A liberal supply of power sockets, a small cupboard containing crockery and an electric kettle complete the domestic feel of the cabin. Even if, as I suspect, the worst happens and containers are piled high to block my forward view, I still have immediate access to unlimited vistas just outside my cabin, half a dozen paces away. Perfect. I scatter my belongings and make myself feel at home.

Francis reappears and shows me to the Officers' Mess, three decks and forty-two stairs below, for coffee and biscuits. His round, chubby face has a welcoming if somewhat wistful smile and he appears eager to please. His parade-black hair is brushed tightly back to give him a high forehead and an air of openness. On a sideboard to my right as I enter, there's a giant flask of coffee and a plate of assorted biscuits. Francis unobtrusively departs and after my solitary refreshments I spend an hour on deck before returning to the Mess for lunch. Here I am introduced to Captain Marek Sawicki.

"Welcome on board," he says. "This is the end of my term. I'm leaving the ship at Hamburg. Going home, to Gdansk. It's been a long time."

There are three passengers so far – myself, Gary and Janine, both from Adelaide, Australia. As there are eventually to be four of us, we are to be seated at a separate table from the officers. Gary and Janine have a cabin on F Deck, which I know will give them an excellent forward view, well above any possibility of it being blocked by containers. I fight back a momentary feeling of envy. Damn it. I wish I'd booked earlier.

"Another passenger will be joining you at Hamburg," Captain Sawicki tells us, as he seats himself at the head of the table set aside for officers.

They are both retired, Gary and Janine. He owns a small building company. Set it up in Sydney but then moved to Adelaide. She looks after the accounts. Janine is thin, painfully so, emaciated almost, and the prominent contours of her face are accentuated by black rimmed glasses, kept secure by a matching cord that hangs in great loops, making her look prematurely fragile. Her rasping voice and frizzled grey hair suggest a lifetime of dedicated smoking. There is a tense, scrunched up look about her, almost as if she is clinging on to some precious object she is fearful of losing. She speaks quietly, almost timidly.

Gary, whom I judge to be well into his sixties, has the look of a man who might have been something of an athlete in his youth. Broad shouldered and muscular, with an open smiling face, he seems at ease with himself, a man's man, jovial, articulate, extrovert, contrasting oddly with his withdrawn, nervous wife. His short greying hair handsomely frames his tanned face.

We settle down to our meal. It's bean soup followed by chicken schnitzel, Mexican fried rice and vegetables, with fresh fruit for dessert. Gary and Janine drink a bottle of red wine.

Shortly after 14:00 hours a gentle roll tells us we are on our way, edging slowly down Gravesend Reach. I climb the four flights of stairs to F Deck to watch our progress down the Thames Estuary. There's something about leaving the shores of one's homeland in this lethargic manner that leaves one with a feeling of nostalgia tinged with sadness, as if it is a long drawn out goodbye to a very dear friend. In a plane, the take-off is tense, angst-ridden, noisy and fast, and the experience is so intense it allows little time for reflection.

Gliding out of the Thames estuary like this is a quiet, gentle experience. No adrenalin rush, no surge of anxiety, no need to hold tight. Mud flats, jetties, oil storage depots, tanker terminals, and all the paraphernalia of a major shipping terminal lie on either side, Gravesend on the south bank, Tilbury on the north. We swing north and enter Lower Hope Reach which, upon turning east again, opens up into Sea Reach. On the north bank, just before Canvey Island, is the site of the new London Gateway Port, which will be capable of taking very much larger vessels than the one I am on.

It's a bleak landscape, sands to the south and the narrow Yantlet Channel to the north. Oil storage facilities fill Canvey Island. As we head east the grey of the sky merges with that of land and sea, the horizon disappears and the land slides unobtrusively away. To the south, it is just possible to see the ghostly outline of the Kentish Flats Wind Farm off the north coast of Kent, the turbines looking like pale spectres, desultorily waving their flimsy arms before being lost to the sea. As we move out into the open sea we are enveloped by the dull, grey monotony of a late autumnal day.

Officer Padamada joins me. Gary and Janine are with him.

"We're doing a familiarisation exercise," he says. "Care to join us?"

He leads us up a couple of flights of outside steps to the port bridge wing. These wings are outward extensions of the navigation deck and enable officers to see over the side of the ship when undertaking the delicate manoeuvres necessary for docking. There's normally a control console there, linked to the engines and rudder to allow the ship's movements to be very precisely managed directly without orders having to be relayed to the main console inside. These wings are open to the elements on three sides with access via a door at each end of the wheel house. It is pretty good standing there in warm, tropical weather with a gentle breeze wafting over you, but it can be unnerving in gale force winds, driving rain or bitter cold. Then, no one ventures there except out of necessity. More modern ships, and those whose business lies mainly in high latitudes where the weather is less favourable, have closed bridge wings, where the delicate art of docking can be undertaken in air conditioned comfort. A glass floor gives a perfect view of what is going on below. In tropical waters, however, nothing can beat the open bridge wings.

"At busy times, please avoid the bridge," says Padamada, "especially when the pilot is in control and when we are under manual steering. Apart from that, you can go up to the bridge wings at any time, except when entering or leaving port".

There is a narrow passage way round the back of the bridge that connects the bridge wings. In due course we are to make good use of this. Above the Bridge Deck is the Compass Deck, also known as the Monkey Island or the Monkey Deck – a large deck area housing the global positioning system, radio antennae, and other transmission and reception paraphernalia. This too can be reached from the outside, and from it there is an all-round panoramic view. We always referred to it as the Monkey Deck, as did most of the officers and men.

"You can use this deck anytime," he says as he leaves us, "and when it gets warmer, sun loungers will be put out for you. As for the rest of the ship, you are free to explore it on your own, but please do not disturb men who are working."

Half way through breakfast, First Officer Damian Koziol joins us. It's 08:00 and he has just come off the morning watch. Like the Captain, he is Polish. He is a tall, agile man, with a finely chiselled face and intelligent, probing eyes, probably in his early to mid-thirties. He's confident and friendly and greets us all in turn with a good firm handshake.

"Any questions you may have," he says, "don't hesitate to ask. I'm on the four to eight watch, morning and afternoon. You'll find me on the bridge then. You're welcome to come up and talk to me if I am not too busy."

Up on the bridge, Padamada has just taken over the watch. We are in the sea area German Bight, heading for Hamburg through the Bight of Heligoland, in the south-east corner of the North Sea. The north coast of Germany will soon be visible. It's raw and grey outside, sky and sea both flat and listless. I need some activity so go down to what is grandiosely referred to as the gym and do half an hour on the exercise bike, have a shower, then a coffee and sit down to read John Kampfner's *Blair's Wars*. I want to find out what drives this man, what it is about him that disturbs me. At lunch Gary and Janine talk about cards as a way of passing the time, and I declare my love of canasta. Would I remind them of the rules? asks Janine. We agree to meet in their cabin that evening.

Over a hundred kilometres away from Hamburg and before land is visible, we take the pilot on board. He guides us through the long approach to Hamburg. First Cuxhaven, 90 km from our port of call, and then Brunsbüttel, Glückstadt, Stade slide slowly past us. Although only a modest river by world standards, the Elbe, with a length of over a thousand kilometres, is three times longer than the Thames, and over eight hundred kilometres of it is navigable. As we approach Hamburg, huge stacks of containers stretch away into the distance as far as the eye can see. On the far horizon, building cranes etch thin grey lines against the darkening skyline and immediately below, as we edge closer to the quayside, straddle cranes prepare to swing into action.

Hamburg is the third largest port in Europe in terms of its throughput, handling over one hundred and thirty million tonnes of gross weight per annum. It is also the largest railway port in Europe. More than 150,000 jobs in the metropolitan region of Hamburg are directly or indirectly dependent on the activities of this port. Ten thousand ships a year visit it and each day two hundred freight trains and five thousand trucks deliver and collect cargo[8]. I feel again a tinge of regret that I was not able to book my passage earlier, for we are going to pick up a lot of containers here and some of them will almost certainly be placed in front of my porthole.

There's talk over dinner of going ashore for a quick visit. It's night and we are in the middle of a container port, and there will not be enough time to go in to town. There is, however, a bar that Gary knows, and where there may be computer terminals. It's the bar he is interested in and he wants to know if I will accompany him. He thinks it might be the Mission to Seamen, the International Seamen's Club, but he's not sure. I'm up for it, especially if I can get access to e-mail. Gary seems highly motivated to get there, with a strong sense of purpose.

The gangway is not down yet and we have an hour or so to spare before we can leave the ship, so we retire to the Officers' Recreation Lounge for a game of canasta. This is our first social gathering. I begin to explain the rules, but five minutes into it Janine lights up and a huge cloud of acrid smoke begins to drift towards me. I watch her across the table smiling contentedly, visibly calmed, unaware of the havoc she is doing to my enthusiasm for the game. Gary too lights up. This is not good. Thirty minutes and three cigarettes later I need to speak.

"I think I am going to find this difficult," I murmur.

"Right," says Janine, her face set grimly as she slaps her cards on the table, "so we'll have to take it in turns to leave the room."

The game ends abruptly there. This does not bode well for a convivial social life. Gary and I look at our watches and agree it's time to go ashore. We meet on the Main Deck and make our way down the gangway. Gary has done his homework and assures me that a brisk ten minute walk along a clear quayside free of all traffic will do it. We open the door into a crowded bar and onto a subdued hum of activity. There's a relaxed and quiet atmosphere about the place. Everywhere men, mostly, but a few women, are sitting quietly drinking, talking, writing letters, reading letters, entering and leaving. A sense of purpose permeates the place. It's as if these men are determined to use well and purposefully the short time they have here. There's an air here of deep trust, safety, something about it that makes me feel at ease. We have a couple of Beck's each, but Gary buys a dozen more to take back to the ship, plus four bottles of red wine. I try to do some e-mailing, but it's crowded with men contacting home and there's a long queue for the computers. So we wait for an hour or so until a couple of terminals become free, but it's a membership only scheme and it proves impossible to log on.

Next morning we are still in port. I draw the curtain and look through my window. Overnight a substantial part of my view has been obscured by a growing stack of containers. I spend the morning reading Kampfner and writing up my journal, with occasional visits to the Monkey Deck to check further progress. As we are finishing lunch Gary asks me if I am up for another visit ashore to the Seamen's Mission. At that moment our new Captain, Feliks Grabowski, enters and introduces himself.

We ask him what time we were leaving.

"About five," he says, "though it could be later."

Janine asks, with a touch of anxiety, "Might we leave before then?"

"That's also possible."

"Will we have time to go ashore?" asks Gary.

The Captain gives a shrug. His body language speaks more eloquently than any words. "It's your risk."

We know the score. Time is money, and the ship will not wait. But Gary and Janine have other more pressing concerns. They are worried about the prospect of a week without sufficient supplies of cigarettes and alcohol. Such is their horror of this state of affairs that they are prepared to take the risk. I try to make a joke of it.

"Well, if you miss the ship you can always get a plane to La Spezia and join the ship there".

A look of puzzlement passes over Gary's face and I realise he is about to take me seriously, carefully considering his options, before he catches my smile and returns it. But I'm not going with him. It's not worth the risk. I wish him luck and climb to the Compass Deck to watch the loading and unloading going on below.

The guys who work these straddle cranes do so at what must be a physiotherapist's nightmare. The driver's head juts out at a ninety degree angle as he peers directly down to pick up the container, lifts his head up again as he swings his load over to the ship and then clicks his head down once more to place the load exactly in position to ensure it engages the locking mechanism on each corner. On the deck, an officer makes sure the lashing rods at the end of each stack are properly fixed. Failure to get this right could set off a domino effect in rough seas and bring the whole stack down. Officers have been dismissed for failing to get this right.

We have come a long way in half a century. Even as recently as the 1960s, handling general cargo was a difficult and time-consuming affair and the whole business had not moved on much since the days when my great-grandfather had set sail for New Zealand. Break bulk cargo was transferred item by item, sack load by sack load, box by box, from lorry to ship, or even lorry to railway wagon to ship, and then back again at the destination end. The whole process was so cumbersome that it created massive bottlenecks at the docks, and had a knock-on effect throughout the whole transportation system – road, rail and sea – at the very time when the system needed to expand and become more efficient as world trade began to increase at breakneck speed in the immediate post-war period. This laborious way of handling general cargo made the ports dangerous, chaotic, inefficient and costly.

The container revolution was waiting to happen, and it was in the 1950s that two Americans, Malcom McLean and Keith Tantlinger, collaborated to produce what we now know as a container. Between them they developed what was to become the standard metal box that would fit easily onto lorries, railway wagons and specially adapted ships. With the cargo neatly stored in these containers, which were built to be the size of a lorry's trailer, the whole thing, container and cargo, could be transferred easily from one mode of transport to another in minutes, rather than days.

Two standard sizes emerged that are still in use today – the 20-foot and 40-foot containers. It is the 20-foot container that gives us the standard unit of measure for the carrying capacity of container ships, the TEU, or the Twenty-foot Equivalent Unit. Its full dimensions are twenty feet (5.9 m) long, by eight feet (2.4 m) wide by eight feet tall. One TEU contains thirty-three cubic metres of storage space. The forty-foot container is equal to two TEUs. It soon became common practice for ships, trains and trucks to be designed in such a way that these containers could be carried easily and for the whole unit to be transferred from one mode of transport to another, with the cargo securely stored within it. The age of inter-modalism had arrived and with it the beginnings of a global transport revolution.[9]

Whilst every effort has been made to standardize containers, some anomalies remain. For example, the height can vary, so that some containers are nine feet six inches tall, making it very frustrating for ships' captains trying to ensure that all containers are neatly stacked in regular heights. Perhaps the biggest anomaly is in the unit of measurement. In this day of metrification, it is rather bizarre that the imperial system of measurement is used throughout the world for the size of containers, whilst every other measurement on board ships is in metric units. This is explained by the fact that containers originated in the USA, which still uses the old feet and inches system.

The container idea caught on like wildfire. There is an interesting photograph in the sixth edition of Stamp and Beaver's monumental study of the Geography of the British Isles, published in the early seventies, showing a container being lifted onto a ship at Felixstowe, the country's first container port. As recently as 1967, Felixstowe was not even in the list of the fifteen leading ports of Great Britain; it was mentioned only in a footnote as one of the 'other ports'[10]. In 2011, however, it was the sixth busiest port in terms of the tonnage passing through it each year and the UK's busiest container port. When I was studying geography in the early 1970s, text books were having to be re-written to keep up with the rapidly changing character and spatial distribution of British ports, so fundamental an impact did the container revolution have on the world of shipping.

The revolution that was about to explode on the world of shipping had huge political implications too. In the UK, the unions could see which way the wind was blowing and they resisted it, often violently. The problem had its roots in the collective struggle for a decent living wage and stable employment. It was not until the introduction of the National Dock Labour Scheme (NDLS) in the 1940s that dock workers were given the legal right to a minimum level of work and pay, as well as holiday and sick pay and pensions. The unlucky ones who didn't get work on a particular day would, under this scheme, be paid a back-up wage, provided they reported for work twice a day to prove their availability. For the first time in history, dock workers had some semblance of job security.

But the container revolution threatened all of this. At a blow, traditional methods of handling general cargo would be eliminated and, at the same time, thousands of jobs would be at risk. The 1960s and 70s were bedevilled by a series of dock strikes that posed a threat to the economic stability of the country. Many of Britain's older ports were already under threat when larger vessels, requiring deep-water harbours, became more common. Now, as the new generation of container ships came on stream, they heralded the end, not only of Britain's ports but also of the old traditional labour-intensive ways of working that had caused such costly bottlenecks in the global shipping industry. The effect on dock labour was massive. In 1947 eighty thousand men had been employed in the docking industry, by 1990 this had fallen to fewer than nine thousand. In the Port of London alone, the 20,000 dockers employed in 1970 had fallen to fewer than 500 by 1992.

So intense was the resistance to the container revolution that the government twice declared a state of emergency in the early 1970s. But the national mood was against the dockers who, in the eyes of the government and the general public, were abusing the system and holding the country to ransom. Public exasperation with what was seen as gratuitous militancy culminated in 1989 with the abolition of the NDLS. The old way of doing things had finally come to an end, and a new era had been ushered in, one in which it was now cheaper to carry general cargo halfway round the world than to move it along a motorway from the Port of London to a destination in the north of England.

Maersk led the way by becoming the first major shipping company to invest heavily in the container idea, and in so doing it forced the pace of change. The age of the Lego ship was about to dawn, ships made to carry boxes and themselves looking like boxes. Not only did containerization sound the death knell of the old familiar silhouette of cargo ships, but it also changed the economic geography of shipping, replacing the older, shallower ports with deeper ones. Although new port facilities opened in Tilbury in 1970, even this proved incapable of handling the increasing size of container ships. Felixstowe and Southampton were later developed to absorb the increasing volumes of trade, and today Felixstowe is Britain's largest container port, handling more than 40% of the country's container traffic, or just under 3.5 million TEUs a year. It is, however, currently under threat of losing this position by the new port of London Gateway, which should be capable of handling the new generation of Ultra Large Container ships (ULCs). London Gateway, situated on the north bank of the River Thames, a few miles downstream from Tilbury, will be the first major deep-sea port to be built this century. The size of container ships has grown exponentially since the early days of merely adapting ships to carry the early containers. Whereas the first two container ships that I travelled on almost a decade ago, the CP Jabiru and the Tasman Discoverer, both had carrying capacities of 1,200 TEUs, at that time Rickmers were already celebrating the imminent arrival of their 13,100 TEU container ship, to be built by Hyundai. The even newer giant Maersk Triple-E Class can carry 18,000 TEUs and is four hundred metres (1,312 feet) long, or about a quarter of a mile.

So whereas just over half a century ago, the men who handled general cargo carried it laboriously on their shoulders, now they sit in straddle cranes all day. But there was a benefit for sailors in the old way of doing things, for the inefficiencies of the old system meant that ships were tied up in dock for days, weeks even, giving mariners an opportunity to go ashore, to relax and take a break from the tedium of life on board. It was also, of course, labour intensive and gave much needed employment to work-hungry men. Today, ships turn round in a few hours and neither officers nor men have much time for a break. It is rare for them to have time off, and almost impossible for them to go ashore, and when they do it is only for an hour or so. At least the dockers and stevedores of old kept themselves fit as they carried their heavy loads. Their lofty counterparts today sit above it all, necks tortuously bent, as they peer endlessly below them and manipulate levers. And, of course, there are fewer of them.

We've been delayed a couple of hours and are now due to leave at 19:00. At a quarter to, I go up to the Main Deck. All is not well. A huddle of men peer over the edge and look into the distance, talking animatedly, a look of consternation on their faces. Gary has not been signed back on.

"If he's not back in a minute, we'll have to go without him," Able Seaman Rafael says.

They move towards the head of the gangway and prepare to pull it in. Janine is half demented with anxiety, whether for the imminent loss of her husband or of her red wine I cannot say. But these things cannot be delayed. In our case, the tide is not an issue; the Elbe is deep here. Our draught is eleven metres and any vessel whose draught does not exceed 12.8 metres can enter or leave whatever the state of the tide. But nevertheless, the arrival and departure of international ships is done according to a very precise timetable. An essential element of this is the ordering of the pilot to steer the ship back to open waters. Each port has its own very specific regulations, and in the case of Hamburg, the pilot must be ordered a minimum of two hours in advance of expected time of departure. Pilots are expensive and their time cannot be wasted. When the pilot says go, we go.

We hang over the ship's railings to see if we can catch sight of him. Just as the men are about to haul up the gangway, a stumbling figure rounds the corner, running like mad and clearly struggling with a heavy and cumbersome load, a look of desperation on his face, like a man at the end of a marathon. The gangway pauses as Gary jumps onto the lower step and clutches the rope. We hear him labouring for breath as he struggles to the top. Janine grabs the boxes and checks their contents. Gary collapses onto a bench, grey and wheezing. A contented smile wraps itself round Janine's face as she turns to see how her husband is.

Our journey back down the Elbe begins at just a few minutes past 19:00 hours. A modicum of mercy had been shown. I turn in at about 22:00, but sleep eludes me and at 01:00 I'm hungry. Time to explore the pantry for a midnight snack. Here I find an enticing store of cheeses, pâtés, jams, fish and cold meats. These, plus an ample supply of bread and a good choice of teas and drinking chocolate, are enough to see me through any insomniac night. I take my fill, return to my cabin and sleep well.

We arrive in Rotterdam late the following afternoon. It is the biggest port in Europe and ranks as the fifth largest in the world, handling a throughput of more than four hundred million tonnes of goods per annum. If I had thought Hamburg was big, the Port of Rotterdam is colossal. Located on the Nieuwe Waterweg Canal and at the gateway to the European inland waterway system, it is a densely packed industrial city of ceaseless activity, spilling itself over more than ten thousand hectares. Shipping traffic is impressive, with thirty-five thousand seagoing ships and one hundred and thirty thousand inland vessels visiting the port annually. The length of the port area is forty kilometres and the port alone employs more than seventy thousand people. More than sixty million metric tonnes of container traffic enter and leave the port each year. But the biggest import is liquid bulk, consisting mainly of crude oil and mineral oil products. Strategically located on the delta formed by three major river estuaries, the Rhine, Meuse and Scheldt, Rotterdam is the shipping capital of north-western Europe[11].

It is here that Adriaan Joossens, our fourth passenger, joins us for lunch. He's Dutch, lives in Belgium, and is bound for New Zealand for a brief visit before flying to Noumea, New Caledonia (Kanaky), where his girlfriend works for a French travel agency. I judge him to be older than me, perhaps just over seventy. There is a wide-eyed, intense, skeletal look about him that is intensified by thick, rimless glasses, and it is clear from the aroma that surrounds him and the yellow blotches on the index and middle fingers of his right hand, that he too is a smoker. His thinning grey hair has almost developed into a tonsure, though he has recompensed this by growing thick sideburns to the bottom of his ears. Smile lines gently enfold his thin, sensitive lips and watery, pale blue eyes have a far-away, questioning look about them. While Gary invariably wears a short-sleeved open-necked colourful T-shirt, Adriaan always needs an extra layer, a thick jumper or a jacket. I will find the smoking difficult, but there will be a way of working round this. Five weeks at sea is a long time to spend together. We will need friendship.

Together Adriaan and I go up to the Monkey Deck as we depart. He has a rather brusque way of talking, aggressive almost, precise, very firm. He is an engineer by profession and behind the apparent gruffness, and beneath the cloud of smoke that is his more or less permanent companion, I soon discover an interesting and likeable man. We look below to the tug that is already holding our stern steady, while the bow thrusters push us gently away from the quayside. A burst of soot from the smoke stack behind us spatters the deck floor. It pock-marks the floor of the Monkey Deck like huge scattered flakes of black. As we pick up speed the breeze delivers a welcome breath of fresh air which clears the offending substance. To add to the pollution, my companion decides to light up, and I quickly move upwind.

It is some thirty kilometres along the New Waterway Canal that links Rotterdam with the North Sea and, at its northern end, lies Europoort on our port side, opposite the Hook of Holland. Passing through the mouth of this huge channel, we watch individuals and family groups enjoying a Sunday afternoon stroll on the long, wide stretches of sandy beach and on the concrete walkways. Many of them stop and watch us, pointing us out to small children. I wave and one or two wave back. It's good to see so many wind farms lining the coast of this part of Europe. Aesthetically, they are a pleasing contrast to the noxious industries behind them. A lone hang glider hovers over the wind farm. In and out he (or maybe she) weaves, even gliding round one of the turbines as if playing an aerobatic version of Russian roulette. Eventually, as if bored with this, he drifts off for greater challenges towards what looks like a chemical complex where tall chimneys are burning off surplus gases. Ever on the lookout for yet more excitement, he moves over to the right to test his skill at dodging electricity pylons and power cables. We lose sight of this lone gamester's death-defying feats as we feel the sea swell below us and we realise that we are finally on our way. We have done with grey skies and north European ports and ahead of us lie six days on the open sea before arriving at our next port of call, La Spezia.

CHAPTER 4: Slop Chest

The slop chest takes its name from the loose smock, or sloppy trousers, that used to be sold to sailors in days of old. Nowadays, as well as clothing, a variety of other items are also sold. For the most part, however, the slop chest is for the convenience of the men who live and work on these ships for months at a time so that they can purchase the necessary items that make life a little more personal and congenial, as well as to relieve the tedium of living in the same, closely confined environment without family or friend. Such items as drink, chocolates, soap and shampoo, tobacco, shaving materials, pens, pencils and writing paper, and so on can be bought. It is there so that the men can have some kind of personal life in what is their 24/7 working and living environment.

For Gary and Janine life seems to revolve around the slop chest. They are preoccupied with it; it is the focal point of their entire existence. Although Gary had managed, just, to scramble on board the ship laden with a good supply of alcohol and tobacco, both he and Janine still show considerable anxiety about whether their supplies will last them until we get to Australia. Never content to let each day bring what it may, these two engage in serious long term strategic thinking about the slop chest. In this connection, one particular habit of Janine's has me intrigued. Half-way through every meal she leaves the table for what she calls her 'between break'.

"Excuse me while I go for my between break".

I can contain my curiosity no longer. "What's this between break of yours then, Janine? Do you take a small constitutional to aid your digestion?"

"Oh no, I have to have my smoke."

And off she goes to a small deck area just outside the Mess, to do the necessary thing. A few minutes later, back she comes, smiling and relaxed.

11:15 and my cabin telephone rings. It's Officer Koziol to remind me that the passengers, all four of us, have an appointment with the Captain and Officers at 11:30 in the Officers' Lounge, which doubles as a conference room, on Deck E. Brown, imitation-leather easy chairs and a couple of sofas are scattered about the room and in one corner is a round, wooden pedestal table. On a sideboard close to the door light refreshments have been laid on for us – cheese and grapes, a plentiful supply of crisps, whisky and red wine. We are joined by the First and Second Officers and the Chief Engineer. Third Officer Padamada is taking the watch. The atmosphere is relaxed and friendly. I feel at ease and appreciative of the kind welcome and hospitality. The Chief Engineer, however, is lost in a world of his own, remote, enveloped in a cloud of smoke, which screens him from the rest of us.

We eat, drink, make small talk and introduce ourselves. And then the Captain speaks. He tells us that we are welcome on the bridge at any time during the day, but if we wish to go there during the Third Officer's watch (08:00 –12:00), would we kindly not bother him with questions as he is newly promoted to the post and needs to focus on what he is doing. He is still on a steep learning curve. That is why his watch is arranged at a time when the First Officer is awake and available, to offer help if needed.

At this point Adriaan interjects. He is very keen to take recordings of our position on a regular twenty-four hour basis, but as the ship's clocks will have to be constantly adjusted forwards as we travel east, he thinks it might be necessary for him to have access to the bridge at night as well as during the day. Could he, therefore, go to the bridge at night?

"No," says the Captain, "only during the day."

At this point, Officer Koziol says that the ship's position is recorded every hour and Adriaan would be free to have access to all these records.

"So the problem is solved," he says with a grin.

He invites us to the bridge at any time on his watch from 16:00 to 20:00 hours, and we can ask as many questions as we wish!

"Now," says the Captain, "I will arrange for a guided tour of the Engine Room. There will only be this one visit as we cannot allow the work of the engineers to be disrupted unduly."

Adriaan speaks again. He explains that many years previously he had been fourth engineer on freighter ships and he has kept up his interest in engines.

"It is very important for me that I have many visits to the Engine Room."

"No, this is not possible."

"But it is very important for me," he persists. "It is a special interest of mine."

"No. Only this one visit will be permitted."

"If I make a special request, will you permit it?"

"Absolutely not. It is out of the question."

It is an eyeball to eyeball confrontation. Someone has to give way, and it is not going to be the Captain. Silence hangs heavily in the air until, with a sullen shrug, Adriaan backs off and we all breathe easily again. The merest hint of a smile crosses the Captain's face before he continues.

"There is the matter of the slop chest. It is open on a Friday for you to purchase anything for your personal use. We carry all the normal supplies – alcohol, tobacco, soap, shampoo, toothpaste, razor blades, etc. Let your steward know your requirements in advance and by Friday of each week. There's a price list in your cabin. Drinking water will be delivered regularly to your cabin."

Gary speaks. "I see from the supplies inventory that we are quite low on red wine. There are only fifteen bottles on board. Will we be able to put in a special order, over and above what you will normally be ordering at La Spezia?"

"You see," pleads Janine, "we only drink red wine."

It is not clear from this if she means this is the only thing they drink, or that this is the only kind of wine they drink.

"Sure," says the Captain, "if I can find the chandler when we get there, you let me know how much extra you want and I'll add it to the ship's order. But we must have your order before Friday."

Adriaan speaks. "I would like to send regular e-mails. Can this be arranged?"

"Yes. You will need to give us your floppy disc or memory stick and then it will be easy to attach your file to an e-mail. Do you have a laptop?"

"No. May I use the ship's computer?"

"In that case, we have a problem," replies the Captain. "I cannot allow you to use the computer for any length of time as we need it always to be available for ship's business."

"I have a laptop," I say to Adriaan. "You can use it if you wish."

"Yes please," he replies. "Every Sunday. I wish to send e-mails every Sunday."

"I will look at my diary," I tell him.

Laughter breaks the tenseness of the moment.

At lunch, when Janine excuses herself for her between break, Adriaan joins her. In the pause in the table chatter that this ritual always creates, Gary voices his anxieties about supplies. The reason for his concern is that after La Spezia, the only port where we can be reasonably certain of being able to go ashore is Fremantle, some four weeks away. After that, there's only Melbourne and then Sydney. He's worried that there might not be sufficient wine and tobacco to see them through to Sydney. When Francis comes into the Mess to remove our plates and bring on the next course, Gary questions him.

"Francis, how long will it take us to get from Fremantle to Melbourne?"

"About four days."

"If I let you know how much we want, would you order some more wine and tobacco for us?"

"What's the problem, Gary?" I ask. "Do you really think you're going to run out?"

"Just planning ahead," he laughs, "just planning ahead."

But it's not a laugh. It's anxiety. I feel sad that these two seem to be so weighed down with angst about what might be, rather than taking pleasure in the present moment. One of the benefits of a voyage like this is to be able to switch off from the routine concerns of everyday life and to live, at least for a few weeks, in the here and now, but their attachment to alcohol and tobacco seems to be in danger of ruining what for most would be the holiday of a lifetime, a time to let go.

Our estimated arrival at La Spezia is for 08:00 on Friday 9th November, four days ahead. We expect to be there for about twelve hours and I am hopeful I might be able to get ashore and see something of the town. The next opportunity for getting onto dry land won't be until Fremantle. The prospect of several days at sea without having to put into port has a calming effect on the ship. Activity on the bridge will become more routine and I will be able to spend more time there. The sea has been very calm all day and I hope this is a good omen for crossing the Bay of Biscay with its notorious reputation for rough seas. I wonder whether this reputation is a bit unfair. Of the four times I have crossed the Bay, two have been rough, two very calm.

Most of the instrument panels are on the starboard side of the bridge, but the wheel for manual steering, which is oblong, has a black leather cover, and is so small you almost come across it by accident, is in the centre. Behind all this is an office and chart room, which can be curtained off at night so that if any work needs to be done there it will not interfere with the night vision of the officer on watch. There is a large desk on the port side of the bridge and a couple of comfortable chairs. Behind this, matching the chart room, is a small office which the Captain uses, this is in addition to his main office and personal suite of rooms on Deck F immediately below.

Some technical books on weather and the sea have been made available to passengers and, knowing my interest in meteorology, Officer Koziol gives me a copy of the Beaufort Scale together with a description of what the sea looks like under any given wind condition. Powerful binoculars have been made available and we have been given access to the ship's charts and weather maps. Sitting at this desk and surrounded by open sea, is a glorious way to spend a couple of hours each day. Mid-morning and Officer Padamada offers me a cup of coffee and shows me how to estimate the speed of the wind from the condition of the seas and the number and intensity of white horses.

The best tip I ever had about travelling by freighter was to always carry a pair of old gardening gloves for walking round the Main Deck. Being a working ship, the handrails tend to be a bit greasy, and you certainly need to use these handrails. Inside the accommodation superstructure everything is spotlessly clean and every effort is made to keep the muck outside; outdoor shoes are always left outside cabin doors. My first walk around the full circuit of the Main Deck of the first container ship I ever travelled on was rather daunting. At sea and under full power, when you step onto this working area of the ship you experience a sense of shock. It is all so strange that you don't know what to do, where to go, or what might come crashing down on your head. You don't know what is safe or what is not safe. High up in the comfort of your cabin, or on the bridge in the company of officers who are going about their duties, studying charts, reading instruments, taking measurements, in an almost surreally quiet environment, you can almost fool yourself into believing that you are aboard some kind of marine Rolls Royce, gliding serenely on its way in tamed opulence. It is only when you climb down those one hundred and twelve stairs to the Main Deck, walk aft and turn the corner onto the Poop Deck, that you suddenly find yourself in an entirely new world in which very little is familiar. The sights and sounds that assault you are unlike anything you meet in normal life and you simply do not know what to expect. Every step you take is a venture into the unknown. Primitive childhood fears overwhelm you, making you afraid and over cautious, wanting to explore but not quite knowing how to, needing someone to show you the way. Stepping out into that for the first time was very scary.

There on that Poop Deck, the first thing to hit you is a wall of sound and you are made aware of the sheer power of this vast machine that is thrusting you forward. I make my way cautiously, steering clear of any piece of machinery that might suck me into its jaws and spew me out like some piece of worthless rag. A few men are working there and I hesitate, wondering if I might be interrupting them, but they simply smile at me and I take it as a cue to proceed. With a determined attempt at nonchalance, I stride with what I hope looks like a purposeful step but which is, I am sure, more like a hesitant shuffle. I make my way to the stern and peer over into the seething maelstrom below that leaves a wake which stretches as far as the eye can see towards the horizon from which we are perpetually fleeing. Here on the Poop Deck is an array of appliances used for mooring, engine housings, immense fans that blast out heated air from the engines below, giant coils of rope, capstans. I pick my way gingerly through these and eventually, after much trial and error, define a route for myself that feels comfortable and safe.

Walking forward brings a different set of unnerving confrontations with the extraordinary. Stretching into the distance for about one hundred and twenty metres is a tunnel comprising a solid wall of containers on one side and a menacing line of iron girders, each about three metres apart, on the other. Between them, an iron railing gives a flimsy sense of security should the ship lurch and you need something to take hold of. And always you are aware of several tiers of containers that form a solid steel ceiling above you and you wonder how on earth those girders can possibly support all that weight. Every so often you hear ominous creaks and groans as the containers to your side and over your head adjust to the roll of the ship. The reflex action is to quicken your pace, convinced they have worked loose and that they are about to collapse and crush you to oblivion. Or your ears are suddenly blasted by the roar of fans from the reefers, the containers carrying refrigerated New Zealand lamb, Canadian salmon or Thai shrimps.

It takes some getting used to this every time I do this walk. I think it is because of the hard metallic nature of the world that surrounds you on these ships. That is your total environment while you are out on that deck. You are enveloped by iron and steel, under your feet, above you and to your side, and it is alive, making all kinds of unfamiliar and threatening noises that make you wonder if it is coming apart. The metallic nature of the ship together with its ugly, utilitarian square shape, makes you wonder how it manages to stay afloat. It all seems so unlikely. A passenger liner looks like a ship, its lines softened by wooden decks and hand rails, the bridge in the centre where it should be, officers in pristine white, and you walk past windows partially covered by homely drapes, which give a sense of domesticity and security. But there are no such concessions to the human need for comfort on container ships, where the only considerations are efficiency and lower costs. On the one, passengers rule; on the other, cargo is all that matters. The supermarket shelves must be filled and we must have food on our table and gadgets to play with.

At the end of this seemingly interminable tunnel, you are confronted by a flight of some fifteen or sixteen steps leading up to the fo'c's'le, at the top of which you find another obstacle course, of capstans, windlasses and ropes. But here on the fo'c's'le, you are free of the noise and the claustrophobia. Here, you cannot hear the engines nor the creaking and groaning of the containers. I am drawn to the short flight of stairs at the very tip of the prow and to the little platform at the top, no more than a metre square and flimsily made secure by a hand rail and a few strips of metal railing that anyone could slip through. And I stand there, letting the air wash over me. There is nothing at all in front of me now except water and air, and nothing to my left or to my right, I am alone on the ocean, a seabird on the wing, a guillemot. I can forget that behind me is a giant machine thrusting its way forward and carrying the world's merchandise, and I enter a place of blissful quiet, where the only thing I can hear is the hushed swish of the bulbous bow slicing its way effortlessly through the ocean. Holding tight onto the scarcely adequate rail, I lean over and look down directly onto the smooth metallic outline of this beast's giant proboscis, pushing its way forward and dragging its massive body behind it. It cannot be particularly safe to do this and I wonder if I were seen, whether I would be cautioned not to do this. But the bridge is hidden from view here and whoever is on the bridge cannot see me, and I cannot see anyone. If I were to lose my balance here and slip through, that would be the end. No one would see an inconsequential head bobbing on the water, and in any case I would get sucked down under the ship. It's a frightening thought, and one that makes me aware of how insignificant we may be.

As I return to my cabin, Francis presents me with a large box of biscuits.

"In case you get hungry in the night," he says.

He had spotted me raiding the pantry.

CHAPTER 5: Fallen Gods

"Wear your hard hat," the Captain tells me. "Keep to the starboard side, inform the Officer of the Watch when you are going and report back immediately on your return."

I had asked if it was all right for me to walk on the Main Deck. Yesterday would have been fine, but today it is different. It had been a calm passage across the Bay of Biscay and the sea was smooth and glassy. A day later and we are heading due south keeping parallel to the coast of Portugal. It's getting warmer and I can discard layers. But the wind is up – force 7, a near gale – and with it come high seas. There are lots of white horses everywhere, with foam streaking across the ocean like terrified beasts.

It's a wild and unnerving experience, and I'm glad of the warning. Being so close to the sea down there on that deck, is both frightening and enticing. Even here on the lee of the vessel, I can feel the immense power of the ocean as the grey, angry, heaving waters rise and fall, slamming and sucking against our side like some wild monster, angry at our intrusion into its domain. And yet as I peer over the edge, I feel strangely drawn towards it, as when on top of a high cliff or tower you get that strange feeling at the back of your knees that warns you to keep away but at the same time beckons you. The wind tears at my face, trying to rip my hat off, and the strap tightens, threatening to throttle me. I can't do this. I daren't venture further. I am too close to the horrors of the deep, teetering on the edge of fear. I turn and climb the hundred stairs back up onto the bridge, holding onto the handrail for balance as the ship lurches and plunges, relieved to be heading for the safety and comfort of the bridge. From there, I look down on the scene I had left, onto the waters pouring over the port side, swilling over the deck, running off in miniature Niagaras.

On the way back to my cabin, I pass neat pairs of footwear outside each door. Slippers means someone is out, shoes that you are in your cabin. The practice prevents oil, soot, and other muck getting onto the carpets. I take my heavy shoes off, leave them outside and put my light house shoes on. Amidst all that turmoil, I'm surprised to see that all the items I had left on the coffee table are still in place, kept securely there by fishnet non-slip mats. It's amazing stuff. However much the ship thrashes about, once you put something on one of those mats it will not budge.

At dinner, Gary and Janine return once more to the vexed question of drink. The burning issue is whether they will have enough to last them the whole five weeks to Sydney. They are spurred into action because Francis has reminded us that the slop chest will be open on Friday and that that is the day we are due in at La Spezia, so fresh supplies will be taken on board. If we need anything, we must fill in our forms and make our requests well before then. Janine explains to Francis that they have already given an order to the Captain.

"When we gave it to him," she explains, "he said 'You must be joking'. You see, we need two bottles a day."

"So how much did you order for the five weeks then?" I ask.

"Five crates," said Gary.

"And how much is a crate?"

"Twelve bottles."

"And what about beer, did you order that too?"

"Oh yes," Janine adds, "We must have that."

"How much?"

At this point, Gary begins to look embarrassed and kicks Janine's foot, but it's too late. Out she comes with it.

"Thirteen cases."

Before retiring for the night, I go up to the Compass Deck for some fresh air. By morning, we are on a course of one hundred and five degrees, heading south-east, and have entered the Gulf of Cadiz. We should be passing through the Strait of Gibraltar sometime in the early afternoon. The wind, almost due east, is running at twenty-seven knots, force six. It's extremely brisk on the Monkey Island and I retreat to the relative shelter of the Main Deck, where I do a few turns. But it's unnerving, so I keep it short and hurry back to the bridge, just in time to share a coffee with the Officer of the Watch.

At 15:00 hours, the rocky coast of Morocco comes into view, with the Atlas Mountains forming a dramatic backdrop. The sea is a metallic blue, the surface agitated and speckled with white horses. The mountains rise swiftly and solidly from the sea, blue and grey and forested, dotted with white houses that scramble up their sides, glistening in the afternoon sun. Beyond, another line of mountains towers over them, paler, merging and disappearing into a sky that is laden with steel grey clouds, pregnant with storm.

It was here that Atlas is reputed to have carried on his shoulders the great pillars that kept earth and heaven apart. Having led the Titans in the great war against the Olympian gods and lost, Zeus had condemned him, the powerful, mighty Atlas, to stand for ever at the western extremity of the world and keep heaven and earth apart so that there would never again be a conflict between the two, never again be war between gods and men. For eternity, he would have to carry the burden of the world on his mighty back. I can't help thinking that his burden has been slipping recently. For once again, the great titans of the world consider that they can take on the mantle of the gods, that they are in possession of absolute knowledge and power and can arrogate to themselves the great mysteries of the universe and impose their will on humanity.

Atlas was later turned into a giant mountain by Perseus, and this was then split into two by Hercules. And so all that is left of them are the Pillars of Hercules, one on the Spanish mainland at Gibraltar and the other at Monte Hacho, in Ceuta on the African coast, a salutary lesson for all those who aspire to be gods. But will it be possible to keep these two mighty continents of Africa and Europe apart? To what extent have their destinies become ineluctably entwined? Will we ever be able to keep Africa out of our reckoning, hold its people at arms' length?

I finish reading *Blair's Wars* and realise even more why I am so angry with this man. He has been so convinced of the rightness of his position and of his powers of persuasion, that he has led this country into disastrous conflicts, even when it was so clearly against the wishes of the public. Furthermore, he has allowed himself to follow George W. Bush so slavishly, that he has even adopted his faith-based attitude to intelligence matters; these two men, these two masters of the Universe, were convinced they knew the answers and were impatient to impose their solution. All the intelligence services had to do was find the evidence to support their convictions. They were convinced they had God on their side. We should rightly fear such evangelical fervour, whether it be in the realm of religion or of politics.

We will be going through the Middle East soon, so this is a good time to start reading Robert Fisk's monumental study of that region's recent history and politics – *The Great War for Civilisation: The Conquest of the Middle East*.

We continue past the vast new Moroccan port of Tanger-Mediterranée on our starboard side and the Rock of Gibraltar to port, both clearly visible from where I stand on the bridge wing. Rising almost vertically from the sea on its eastern side to over four hundred metres before sliding down a preposterous angle of forty-five degrees to its west coast, this mighty limestone rock has stood for three hundred years as a symbol of British power at the southernmost extremity of Europe. At this, the narrowest point in the Strait of Gibraltar, just eight miles separate Africa and Europe. It is a time for reminiscence. As I look at those towering Moroccan mountains to the south, I am acutely aware of the massive continent that stretches away behind them to the south, a continent that has had such a profound impact on my life. Forty years earlier, when I thought I knew about God, I worked in Central Africa as a missionary teacher and went there with the certainty of youth to spread the word and change the world. I immersed myself in the history of that part of the world and I also saw the ugly side of colonialism, the dark side of racial intolerance.

More than any other continent, Africa was colonised by the European powers that lay to the north behind where I am standing. In the great Scramble for Africa that took place in the last two decades of the nineteenth century, a handful of European powers grabbed most of this huge continent for themselves. Up to that point, the continent had been largely ruled by Africans in a variety of ways and with a range of political systems. Some, such as pharaonic Egypt and the Sahelian kingdoms of West Africa, resembled European states with centralised authority to bind the people together. Others, like the pastoral Somalis on the Horn of Africa, were more loosely knit together through consensus rather than by the centralised power of the state. But by the turn of the 19th century, most of these indigenous political structures had been overridden, if not swept away, and in their place some thirty colonies and protectorates had been created by the diktat of European powers.

It was a kind of madness that had possessed Europe, a headlong, frenetic rush to gain political prestige at home by grabbing territory abroad. This is what gave the five great European powers of the day – Britain, Germany, France, Portugal and Italy – kudos and clout. Today, it is the nuclear deterrent that gives the aura of power. Then, it was the possession of an overseas empire. The objective was to carve out areas of influence and establish colonies in order to exploit the riches of this continent to satisfy the insatiable demand for raw materials to feed our industrial revolution. Livingstone had blazed the trail, with his missionary zeal and his powerful rhetoric which stirred the imagination of well-meaning evangelists and philanthropists at home. The great mantra of the day was the call to save Africa through The Three Cs –

Commerce, Christianity and Civilisation. Noble as this may have appeared, there is always the law of unintended consequences to contend with. It was assumed that Westernising and Christianising other cultures would be to their lasting benefit, and to ours of course. The political, military, and religious institutions of Europe were mobilised together to fulfil this objective. But as King Cetewayo of Zululand had observed at the time, "First come missionary, then trader, then soldier. When soldier come, it is all over with black man" (Source unknown).. The Bible soon gave way to the gun as the force to be reckoned with, and it was the ethics of the likes of Rhodes rather than of Livingstone that won out. The Three Cs were inextricably involved in Africa in creating much that was good and much that was bad, and at that time in my life, I had been caught between the two as I had sought to bring education to African boys in what is now the troubled land of Zimbabwe.

And now, as impoverished people from this same continent reverse the human flow and seek to gain entrance to fortress Europe in search of some of its riches, I cannot help but reflect that in the great historical scheme of things what goes round comes round. What, in the long run, will be the developed world's reaction to the people of this continent, whose riches we took mostly without asking and often by cruel force, riches which provided much of the seed corn for the industries that laid the foundation for so much of our current prosperity? At that time, we wanted their wealth. Now the flow is in the opposite direction. The giant rock of Gibraltar was formed by the collision of the African and Eurasian tectonic plates; now Africa and Europe are colliding economically and culturally as the inhabitants of that vast southern continent seek to enter fortress Europe to have some share of what we created using their resources. What, I wonder, will be the judgement of the long reach of history?

It is 08:00 hours and another morning. We are on a north-easterly course that will take us to the east of the Balearic Islands, passing Mallorca in the afternoon. A fresh breeze of seventeen knots from the south-west pushes us along. The engine and the wind join forces to give us a relative wind speed of twenty knots. It is shorts weather and I manage twelve brisk laps round the Main Deck after breakfast. I reckon that's roughly five kilometres.

Over lunch, we decide to meet at 15:00 hours for a game of table tennis. This seems to be something we can do together in a smoke-free environment. It has the promise of becoming routine. It's a good game, but Janine has to beat a hasty retreat for a smoke, so Gary and I decide to play darts. He tells me that he had a misspent youth and used to play a lot. I've never played before. Nevertheless, we seem to be fairly evenly matched and the game ends in a draw in which we both need an unattainable double one.

Adriaan is curious about our ages. He's sixty-three he tells me. How old am I?

"What do you think?"

"Oh, late fifties."

The others agree. Great! It seems I am the eldest, but they think I am the youngest!

Janine and Adriaan take rather a long time over their between break at dinner, so much so that by 18:30 when it is time for Francis to clear away, he does so, on the perfectly reasonable assumption that they have finished and are not coming back. A minute or two later back they come. Adriaan is angry.

"I should be able to come to the table at any time between the designated time of 17:30 to 18:30 and be served a full meal", he proclaims loudly and angrily.

"Well, Francis does have rather a lot to do. He seems under a lot of pressure."

"I don't care." he says. "I expect the same standard of service as I would get in a hotel."

CHAPTER 6: White Wine

It's early morning and the wind is gusting between twenty-five and thirty-five knots, Beaufort six to eight. Waves reach up to seven and a half metres. Excitement surges through me to witness this demonstration of the mightiness of wind and sea and the triumph of human ingenuity that has devised vessels capable of gliding through them both with such consummate ease. The ship is remarkably stable and I experience no discomfort, although Janine and Adriaan mention at breakfast that they have had a bit of a rough night.

Dawn sees us rounding the northern coast of Corsica as we enter the Ligurian Sea. By noon, the north-west coast of Italy is well in view and soon after we pass, on our port side, the tiny islands of Palmaria and Tino. They lie off the southern tip of the promontory of Portovenere which forms the western edge of the Gulf of La Spezia. The pilot's launch draws alongside, black hull and white wheelhouse glistening smartly in the bright sun. Its sleek lines, speed and size are perfectly designed for the rapid manoeuvrability and quick action required of these vessels. With both launch and ship still moving, it's a tricky task getting alongside, especially when, as now, there is a good swell. As the well-cushioned gunwales make contact, a rope ladder is thrown out from our Main Deck on the port side, and as he draws level, the pilot steps nimbly onto the lower rung and begins the climb. Immediately, his boat pulls away, leaving him hanging there between the sea and a wall of iron. He climbs the thirty feet to the Main Deck where an able seaman opens a small gate to let him through and takes him to the wheelhouse above. He's smartly dressed with scarcely creased blue jeans, reflective yellow and blue all-weather coat, highly polished brown shoes, stylish sun glasses, and closely trimmed greying hair.

As Corsica recedes behind us, ahead lies a magnificent amphitheatre. The Etruscan Apennines form the backdrop, rising abruptly from the coast, often to over six hundred metres in the space of about a kilometre, with La Spezia itself nestling on the narrow coastal plane. The whole is three quarters enclosed by the sweeping contours of the bay. On this mid-November day, La Spezia looks quite sublime, glistening between towering snow-capped mountains and the deep blue of the Liguria Sea. It is a dazzling setting for this provincial capital. As well as being a naval port, it is also a ship-building yard, a container and bunkering port and a leisure base, with many marinas and hundreds of yachts right round the coast from end to end as far as the eye can make out. Here too, you can pick out the distinctive white and yellow of the Corsica and Sardinia Ferries, which ply a brisk trade across these waters.

In the distance, I can make out a small town perched right on top of a high peak, dominated by what looks like a church spire rising above the buildings clustered around it. It wraps itself round the summit like a mantle. Between this high altitude town and La Spezia below is almost uninterrupted forest. In many parts of the Mediterranean World hamlets, villages and even small towns, have so arranged themselves spatially as to take full advantage of the glorious three dimensional landscape. Whereas we in the UK seem determined to build our settlements on good agricultural land and even on flood plains, here, it seems, they are not averse to building on high land. In many cases, the original impetus for this was the need for defence, but the problem then was that the land on top of hills is often less fertile than that further down because of soil erosion. For communities that survived by agriculture, this was a problem in more troubled times because, for reasons of security, they did not want to venture too far from home more often than was really necessary. The solution was to work the land closest to home very intensively, growing those crops that needed most attention close up to the settlement itself, and those crops that needed less attention, further away. In time, a concentric pattern of land use developed around these agricultural towns (or 'agro-towns', as they have been called). The less demanding crops were grown further away, lower down the hillside on more fertile land, and the more demanding crops were grown closer to where people lived, even though the land there was higher up and less fertile. Agricultural logic would suggest it should be the other way round – the more demanding crops on the best land, and the least demanding crops on the poorest. But in insecure times, and to save long foot-wearying journeys, distance trumped soil fertility in determining what crops should be sown where. And so in many parts of the Mediterranean world, this has left an interesting and curious geographical legacy, a settlement pattern that is most pleasing to the eye.

It is Friday and cabin cleaning day. Francis wants to know if I am going ashore. He would like to talk. He lives in the Philippines, he tells me, and is working hard to save as much money as possible so that he can go to college and train to be a fully qualified ship's chef.

"Then," he said, "I will earn more money and will be able to provide for my family. I miss them very much."

He earns between $200 and $400 US a month (£100 – £200). He is single and will not think of marriage until he is fully qualified and can earn more.

"I like to have passengers on board," he says, "because life can sometimes be a bit monotonous. It's nice having passengers that I can talk to."

It has taken all day to manoeuvre into position and at 16:30, we are at anchor in the Gulf of La Spezia in a queue waiting for a berth, with the tantalising prospect of a brief shore visit beckoning us. A mood of eager anticipation settles over the passengers. The all-consuming question is, will we get ashore? Francis knows the town and offers to show us round. The condition is that we turn up prompt for our evening meal at 17:30. Excitement is high. Then, at 17:00, the Chief Officer informs us that we will not be moving alongside until 22:30. Our enthusiasm subsides as the warmth goes out of the evening sun. It is expected that we will stay there for twelve hours but, as we have a larger than usual cargo to pick up, it is possible we might stay longer; it all depends on how many cranes are available. No one seems to relish the prospect of wandering through a strange port in the middle of the night, but perhaps there will be time for a shore visit in the morning. We dare to allow ourselves some hope. Cautious excitement begins to mount again.

It's a restless night and at about 01:00 hours I make my way to the Mess for a bite to eat. Just at that moment, the Chief Officer comes in and expresses surprise that I am not ashore.

"We drew alongside an hour ago. I thought you'd want to see something of the town."

I am not quite sure if he is serious or joking. What on earth would I do in the middle of the night in an entirely unknown port? In fact, I don't know what I would do in the middle of the night in a town that I know well!

"I'm hoping to go in the morning for an hour or two."

"Bad news, I'm afraid. It looks as if we may be casting off at about 07:00. So there'll be no time to go ashore".

Early morning, and I draw back my curtain. More containers have been stacked up in front of me and my already limited view has been reduced to a narrow arc of about twenty degrees. This is good news for the ship, however, as we now have about seven eighths of a complete load. I must now rely on stepping outside for unobstructed views.

The bad news is confirmed over breakfast. We are almost ready to depart, there is no possibility of a shore visit and the card I had hoped to be able to post for my niece's birthday will have to wait for some other opportunity. The tugs are already in place. The ropes are cast off. The Captain is on the bridge with the pilot. To add to our woes, there's no chance of our being able to go ashore at Damietta either, so our next and only opportunity of going ashore before Melbourne will now be Fremantle. Damietta is a freighter terminal and there's no way we would be able to get through it to the town centre during the brief time it will take to drop off and pick up a few containers.

Behind us, La Spezia and the Gulf of Genoa slowly recede into the sun-drenched distance. In the lee of a long breakwater lies a huge mussel farm. Several thousand round-topped grey and white buoys arranged in long parallel lines, march off into the distance. From each one of these, long ropes will be hanging, to which mussels will be clinging. Here and there, men in small boats are hauling some of them up, inspecting the load, evaluating their readiness for market.

On the western horizon, Corsica looms over us and shadows us for most of the day. To the east, the Island of Elba and the glistening coast of Tuscany beckon. Sun, a cloudless sky and a tranquil blue sea, form the backdrop to this stunning display of Franco-Italianate splendour. With the temperature never rising much above eleven or twelve degrees it is cool, and in the early afternoon a gentle breeze from the south-west catches us almost imperceptibly on our starboard bow.

At 15:00 seven shorts blasts followed by a long one shatter the tranquillity and signal us to an emergency drill. It does not go well. There are problems. The fire team find the handling of the high pressure hoses difficult, the medical detail have problems with the stretcher, and we all have lessons to learn about how to get into the life boat wearing our immersion suit, life jacket and hard hat, in such a way that we don't stumble over each other and get tangled up in our safety harnesses. It's a mess. We will need more drills.

Meanwhile Gary, Janine and Adriaan declare that they are pissed off. Their misery began when they learned that we would not be going ashore at La Spezia. They had attached great significance to this for they saw it as an opportunity to oversee the acquisition of the only two things that matter, tobacco and alcohol. Exploring the town was of no interest to them whatsoever. The critical question is, what has happened to their order for five cases of red wine and thirteen of beer.

Did the Captain order it correctly from the Chandler? Was the Chandler able to supply what they wanted? They have spent the whole day in a state of acute anxiety. What they want to know is – has their order been delivered safely to the ship?

"That's the most important thing," says Janine over dinner.

Half-way through she leaves the table for her between break; this has now become a regular ritual at every meal. Unless she tops up on nicotine, she becomes ill at ease, unable to eat, unfocused on the conversation, but when she returns, she has something approximating a spring in her step.

"There's another problem," she says as she sits down for dessert. "I can't work out what to do with my handbag during emergency drills. You see, I keep my cigarettes there. How can I be expected to deal with that when I'm struggling with life jacket, immersion suit and hard hat all at the same time? It's impossible. Something's got to go, and it's not going to be my cigarettes."

"Couldn't you, just on this occasion, leave them behind?" I suggest. "The emergency drill isn't all that long, is it?"

"Oh no," she says, visibly shocked at the suggestion. "In a real emergency, the first thing I'd grab are my cigarettes. I'd have to leave my bag behind. I'm going to do that on all emergency drills from now on."

So that's that problem sorted. There now remains the really big one, the more serious matter of the wine. Just as we are finishing dessert, Gary spots Francis through the hatch in the galley. He is doing some washing up.

"Francis," he shouts to him, "when will the supplies we ordered at La Spezia for the slop chest be delivered?"

A cloud crosses Francis's face. He drops what he is doing, dries his hands and comes through.

"Today."

"That's the most important thing," Janine breathes once more.

"May we see it?" asks Gary. With a look of exasperation, Francis goes out and returns a few moments later carrying a large cardboard box. He places it on the sideboard. There is a clink of glass as he does so. He goes out and comes back with a crate of beer, putting it beside the box.

"One box of wine and one crate of beer," he says. "I'll bring the rest through when I've finished washing the dishes."

He seems a little sharp today, peeved by the constant badgering about the slop chest. Unusually for him, he is not smiling. He disappears into the galley and resumes his washing up duties.

Gary approaches the box tentatively. The one and only label on it gives the name of the Chandler: Luigi's, Via delle Pianazze, La Spezia. He opens it cautiously, peers inside and lifts out a bottle. His face turns white with rage. His hands tremble. He stands there visibly quaking as if in some kind of fit. Before he can utter a word, Captain Grabowski comes in.

"I am afraid there has been a mistake with your order," he says. "The Chandler has delivered white wine instead of red."

Gary explodes. "This is incompetence," he yells. "What the hell is the matter with this ship? I've never known such a shambles."

The Captain shrugs and leaves the room. Francis can be heard muttering in the galley. Janine looks as if she is going to break down. Adriaan gestures incomprehension. It so happens that I had ordered two bottles of red wine when I boarded, the first of which we drank together several days ago. I have no great need of the second one.

"I have a bottle. You can have that."

"I have two." Adriaan adds. "You can have those."

They are grateful, of course. But our meagre offerings are nowhere near enough to fill the huge void that has so suddenly appeared in their lives. Something close to panic sets in. Forget about emergency drills. They are but unfortunate, inconvenient and quite unnecessary interruptions to their carefully worked out logistical exercise, built on the need for ingesting regular doses of alcohol and nicotine. This is the very stuff of life. Without this, all sense of meaning breaks down. This is what a real emergency is like. It's all very well playing silly games with survival suits and hard hats and climbing into little boats that we will never be called on to use, but the real emergency is here and now. This is what we should have been training for. There is no plan in place and panic sets in.

"Do you think we'll be able to signal ahead to Damietta to see if there's a Chandler there who can get us what we need?" Janine asks no one in particular.

Gary says that this is but one of a whole sequence of episodes that have marred his holiday. The disappointment of not going ashore at La Spezia is the last straw.

"If we'd been able to go ashore to oversee the order, this catastrophe would have been avoided. This is my last trip by freighter," he announces. "It's been one disaster after another."

I go up to the Monkey Deck where I watch Elba glide majestically past us.

CHAPTER 7: Wind and Fire

I am not sure about God, but I like the idea of gods. Æolus, the Greek god of the wind, gave his name to a small archipelago known today as the Lipari Islands. They lie off the north-east coast of Sicily and at the southern end of the Tyrhhenian Sea. Æolus had four sons, two boisterous ones known as Eurus, or the east wind, and Boreas, the north wind, and two rather more docile ones, Zephyrus, who blew from the west and Notus who blustered from the south. This turbulent family made its abode in the otherwise quiet corner of the Mediterranean through which we are making our way and, from time to time, its unruly members made life extremely difficult for ancient mariners.

But it wasn't only these rumbustious little gods who caused mischief here, for Vulcan, the god of fire and otherwise known as Hephæstus, was a close neighbour. He was smarting at the apparent indifference of his mother, Hera, who had shown no gratitude to him when he had suffered an injury whilst trying to rescue her from the cruel treatment of his father, Zeus. Deeply offended, Vulcan refused to join the council of gods that regularly met on Mount Olympus and instead, set up a solitary home for himself on Mount Etna, on the island known today as Sicily. Here, still fuming with indignation, he built a huge forge in which he manufactured a cunningly devised throne for his uncaring and selfish mother. He knew his mother's weaknesses well and so made it pleasing to the eye on the outside, attractive enough to beguile her. This would appeal to her vanity. Once seated on it however, she was unable to extricate herself from its avenging clutches. She was condemned for ever to sit on her beautifully crafted throne, in magnificent royal captivity. Revenge, as they say, is a dish best served cold. But having punished his mother, he found this was not enough. Still his anger was not quelled. So he now devoted his time to inventing deadly weapons to get his own back on the rest of the world he felt had wronged him, the most lethal of which was the thunderbolt. These he deployed frequently to terrorise all who lived close to him.

It was into this turbulent territory that we had quietly made our way overnight, into the land of wind and fire. We had been heading south through the Tyrrhenian Sea, hugging the Italian coast and passing Vesuvius shortly after midnight.

Immediately after breakfast, Gary, Adriaan and I, keen to see as much as possible of the beautiful Italian coast, scamper up to the Monkey Deck. As usual, this is all too much for Janine, so she stays in her cabin with her crossword puzzles, cigarettes and what red wine she has been able to salvage from the disaster of the day before. On our port side, magnificent Stromboli rises majestically out of the sea, its perfect shape conforming to the classic features I once had to draw in my school geography exercise book, a superb inverted cone. This imposing volcano lies at the northern end of the Lipari Islands, of which a small huddle is clearly visible to us, rising sheer out of the clear blue waters of the southern Tyrrhenian Sea – Lipari, Selina, Vulcano, Panarea. The poetry of their names masks the brutality with which they occasionally spew out fire and brimstone, death and destruction. Vulcan is by no means dead here. His anger lives on.

Although Æolus has a reputation for being particularly active here, the best he can manage this morning is a moderate breeze. We have been lining up to pass through the narrow Strait of Messina where both wind and water can be treacherous and a pilot must be taken on board. Expert guidance is needed here, a modern day Odysseus capable of steering ships safely through these dangerous waters. It is here that ancient sailors were forced to steer a perilous passage between the seething whirlpool of Charybdis and the terrifying rock of Scylla, whilst at the same time resisting the sinister charms of the Sirens. All the gods, it seemed, had conspired to make this narrow sea passage one of the deadliest in the world.

At its narrowest, just three kilometres separate Sicily from Italy's mainland. Never more than about a kilometre from the coast, the whole of the city of Messina on the north-eastern tip of Sicily, is set out in front of us, and we can take in the detail – a church, a bar or coffee shop with a bright blue awning, playing fields and tennis courts, hotels, industrial buildings, high rise apartment blocks, and beautiful sandy, but empty beaches. On the opposite side of the strait lies the little town of Villa San Giovanni, where a lighthouse stands to warn modern day mariners of the treacherous nature of the narrow channel. Such a glorious day and so few people. It is Sunday morning, perhaps everyone is at church. And then as we round a headland, the shimmering outline of yet another volcano, Mt Etna, comes into view, its snow-covered slopes rising to over three thousand three hundred metres and dominating the east coast of Sicily.

It is a costly business getting a pilot to guide you through these troubled waters, but it is a necessary expense, especially if you are a large vessel and have valuable cargo on board. Sometimes smaller vessels make the calculation that they might be able to get away with doing it on their own. The trick is to follow as closely as possible in the wake of a bigger ship you know must have a pilot on board. And that is exactly what appears to be happening now, for we are being closely followed by another, somewhat smaller freighter. Captain Grabowski is certain that it is piggy-backing on us and saving itself a whopping fee.

It's getting warmer. At breakfast, the temperature was just over twelve Celsius; by mid-morning it had risen to twenty, and here it has stayed for the rest of the day. Our pilot having left us an hour or so earlier, we have set a course that is more or less south-east, varying between 114 and 132 degrees. A moderate breeze is coming at us from the south-west, helping us gently on our way. But the tranquillity and charms of the day belie the occasional terror of which this part of the Mediterranean world is capable. As sailors of old had learned to their cost, it is important not to be deluded by the region's charms, for you never know what is going on beneath the surface. Who would believe that something moving slower than a snail could cause a collision resulting in the death of thousands? But that is exactly what this region is capable of doing. Deep in the bowels of the earth, forces are at work that can build mountains and destroy cities, and one of the most notorious areas where those forces meet is here, in a line passing right through the Strait of Messina, underneath exactly where we are sailing now.

Throughout the entire length of the Mediterranean region from west to east, along the coast of North Africa, through southern Italy, on to Greece and as far as Turkey, this region has one of the highest concentrations of seismic activity in the world. South-east Europe in particular – especially Greece and Calabria – is especially prone to earthquakes. The Agadir earthquake of 1960 in Morocco killed twelve thousand people and in 1999, at the other end of the Mediterranean, at Izmit in Turkey, an earthquake measuring 7.4 on the Richter scale, killed over fifteen thousand. Between the two, the region around Calabria and Sicily is a veritable cauldron of volcanic activity as Vulcan still pursues his interminable quest for vengeance. In December 1908, the city of Messina itself was destroyed when an earthquake and the associated forty-foot tsunami killed more than 100,000 people.

All this terrifying subterranean activity is caused by a plate moving at the rate of just over two centimetres a year. For 100 million years, the African tectonic plate has been relentlessly pushing itself up against the Eurasian plate, throwing up mountains and shattering the earth as its fragile crust attempts to readjust itself to these subterranean movements. The boundary where these two gigantic plates crash into each other runs almost exactly through the Strait of Messina. Is it any wonder that this is such an incredibly dangerous part of the world and that men and women of old, in the absence of a science of plate tectonics, fabricated myths and legends to help them understand and explain its terrors? It is out of such catastrophic events that great myths and great religions are born.

It is Sunday and Adriaan has his first session on my computer. I put his document on one of my memory sticks to give to the Captain to send as an e-mail attachment, but he tells me that he has not been able to send e-mails, so Adriaan's will have to wait for another occasion. I mention this to Adriaan over dinner and he looks agitated, about to demand that something be done about it. Gary, however, calms him. He was on the bridge earlier and noticed a slight kink in the ship's wake, suggesting a deviation from our course, by about as much as thirty degrees, before straightening up again. He asked Second Officer Ilao about this.

"Oh," he had said, "the Captain asked me to make a slight detour to see if we could get a signal to send e-mails."

Over coffee in the officers' lounge, Adriaan starts telling me about the ship's engine. It has seven cylinders rather than the more usual four, six or eight to be found in most internal combustion engines. He likes the tidiness of these numbers. They have the advantage of dividing neatly into 360^0, unlike the mathematically more cumbersome seven. Engineering is all about trying to control the unruly laws of nature. We are profoundly grateful for this. Throughout this journey, we need the predictability of engineering. But, whereas engineering seeks to produce order and certainty, chaos theory highlights the apparent randomness and unpredictability of the natural world and shows how almost imperceptible differences in the initial conditions of a complicated process, can produce alarmingly different outcomes. Hence the simplistic assertion that a butterfly flaps its wings in Mongolia and a tornado results on the other side of the world. Although we strive to be in control, there is a law of unintended consequences, whether in the natural world or in the realm of human relations. On this voyage, Adriaan and Gary both seem to need predictability and I wonder if this is related to the fact that the one is an engineer and the other a builder, where exactness and predictability are needed. Whereas I love the randomness and unpredictability of life on board this ship, they both seem to be discombobulated by it.

CHAPTER 8: Cockpit of the World

We are entering the Middle East, crossroads of the old world, flashpoint of the new. It stands at the junction of three continents, contains the spiritual homes of half the people of the world, has massive reserves of petroleum and is a vitally important sea link between two hemispheres.

We have set a course of one twenty one, a straight line for Egypt, with a continuing fresh breeze from the south-west gently assisting us. Throughout the whole day, the only sight we have of land is a brief glimpse at morning coffee of the island of Gavdhos, just off the southern coast of Crete. I watch it from the bridge until it disappears over the horizon.

It was at Gavdhos that, two thousand years earlier, St. Paul, the man who probably has had more influence on the development of Christianity and therefore of western civilisation than any other man, sought shelter from one of the treacherous winds of this part of the world. Embarking on a ship at a port then known as Caesarea, he was on his final journey, the one that was to take him to Italy and ultimately Rome where, it is believed, he was martyred. It was one of the troublesome sons of Æolus, Eurus, the east wind, who was the cause of the problem. Luke describes the incident off Gavdhos (also known as Cauda) in the following terms.

> ... they weighed anchor and began to sail past Crete, close to the shore. But soon a violent wind, called the northeaster[12], rushed down from Crete. Since the ship was caught and could not be turned with its head to the wind, we gave way to it and were

driven. By running under the lee of a small island called Cauda, we were scarcely able to get the ship's boat under control. After hoisting it up they took measures to undergird the ship; then, fearing that they would run on the Syrtis[13], they lowered the sea-anchor and so were driven. We were being pounded by the storm so violently that on the next day they began to throw the cargo overboard, and on the third day with their own hands they threw the ship's tackle overboard. When neither sun nor stars appeared for many days, and no small tempest raged, all hope of our being saved was at last abandoned.[14]

For fourteen days, they continued in this fashion until eventually the ship was smashed to pieces off the coast of Malta, where all managed to get ashore safely. It is difficult to imagine the island of Gavdhos other than it is today, a peaceful island with a mere handful of inhabitants, set in a tranquil sea. Yet here, momentous events had taken place and the man who survived wrote letters that were to help shape the world as we know it today. Without St. Paul's interpretation of the teachings of Jesus Christ, it is doubtful if Christianity would have become the accepted religion of the Roman Empire and the established religion of the UK.

The Middle East was the birthplace of three of the great religions of the world, Judaism, Christianity and Islam. They are known as the religions of the book, because their core teachings are set out in the three most powerful books in the world – the Torah (the Old Testament), the Christian Bible and the Koran – and these have arguably had more influence on the course of human history than any other literature. We owe some of that literature to the letters of our thrice ship-wrecked hero, St Paul, which eventually found their way into the New Testament, which became part of the foundation document for the Christian religion.

Although born in this part of the world and therefore having many features in common, each of these religions has been at the centre of conflict ever since they came into being, such is the powerful hold that ideas about matters that are essentially unknowable can have on us. Christianity grew out of Judaism, and Islam honours both the Old Testament prophets and Jesus Christ. All three of them are agreed about the existence of one all powerful, all knowing God, but they have always disagreed about who that God is and what his wishes are for mankind. What they have in common is forgotten; the differences continue to separate.

Morning and we are waiting just off the coast of Egypt to enter the port of Damietta to off-load some containers and pick up others. I give my niece's birthday card to Captain Grabowski for him to give to the port agent, who will post it along with all the other ship's mail. About fifty kilometres north-west of Port Said on the Nile Delta, Damietta is being developed as a port capable of accommodating larger vessels than Port Said can handle. It is situated on one of the Nile's many distributaries, also called the Damietta. To encourage use of the port while it is being developed, ships that use it pay a reduced fee when they subsequently pass through the Suez Canal. To take advantage of that concession, ships sometimes act in tandem, one off-loading a few containers at Damietta and the other picking them up. That way both ships get to use Damietta and both qualify for the reduced transit fee through Suez.

It's a landscape of metal boxes dominated by the whine of straddle cranes and the clang and thump of metal on metal. The sky is blue, the water more intensely so, the air warm. While the Captain and pilot work in silent concentration on the port bridge wing, a tug comes up on our starboard side and nudges our bow gently into position. On A Deck, a crew man loosens the chain that has held the ship's crane in position, releasing it for on-board work, sorting the containers we have exchanged.

Our business in Damietta over, we once again head east and by 20:45 have joined the southbound convoy for Suez. We are scheduled to commence our passage at 01:00. Gary, Adriaan and I plan to be up by 06:00 to watch the proceedings from the Monkey Deck, where comfortable chairs have been placed for us.

The next morning we're on deck by 06:45. We have developed an agreeable camaraderie, the three of us, flitting from one side of the ship to the other to get the best possible vantage. Janine we only see at meal times, or at the emergency drill. The wind is surprisingly chill. It's Egypt; it should be warm. Adriaan and Gary join me. From our position high up on the Monkey Deck, we have a clear view of this bustling city port. All kinds of small craft are tethered to the canal-side at right angles, part of the brisk commuter traffic that darts to and fro across the canal. It's rush hour. Streets terminate abruptly at the water's edge, where cars are lined up for the next ferry to take them across the water to whatever business lies on the east bank. One such fully loaded ferry waits impatiently for us to pass, so that it can get on its purposeful way. Tightly packed on its wide deck are four lanes of cars and commercial vans. Crammed into every conceivable space, between the rows of vehicles, pushed up against the gunwales, seated on car bonnets, are some eighty to a hundred pedestrians and drivers, all men, and all in light shirts or jackets. A couple of metres above them and on the port side, two men stand in the wheelhouse, their backs to us and deep in conversation. These dark green ferries, long, sleek, nimble, lying low in the water, and always fully laden, cut across us fore and aft at an unnerving speed, sometimes two abreast as if racing each other, and with startling frequency. From our vantage point high above, these diminutive looking craft seem to be playing chicken with an unwelcome intruder that insists on slicing its way through their daily lives, while we in turn make our determined way as if oblivious of them.

Two uniformed policemen lounge outside the police station, one standing, the other sitting, on a grey stone wall. On the other side of the road, an untidy cluster of blue and white police cars wait for business, while two more approach from either side, adding to the confusion. Fishermen in sleek feluccas, lateens neatly furled, put away their nets after their early morning fish, patiently and methodically folding them, making sure they are ready to deploy for the next catch. They undertake their task with sublime indifference to this leviathan sliding past them, as if totally unaware of our presence. We could smash into their small craft and break them up like matchsticks, but they go about their business with impressive nonchalance, even occasionally looking up and waving at us, sometimes calling out as we wave back.

A young boy in smart uniform is on his way to school. A canal cruise operator waits expectantly for the first tourists of the day. High rise blocks of flats line the waterfront and march in straight lines into the distance. Above them, satellite dishes direct their gaze obediently on the same celestial spot, eagerly awaiting the day's instructions. The early risers have drawn their awnings down to protect them from the intensity of the already strong sun. Some balconies are festooned with colourful shrubs. Palm trees line the waterfront. The occasional minaret reaches gracefully into the pale blue sky.

Four hours and fifty kilometres later and with the temperature in the low twenties, we are passing El Qantara, a large town north of Ismailiya that sprawls into the distance on either side of the canal and once again, we have an excellent view of the town and its palm-fringed streets. Here, the buildings are, on the whole, lower and less dense than Port Said's, making the soaring minarets more visible. From our vantage point on the Monkey Deck, we can see clearly where the town ends and the desert begins. The desert is never far away. It creeps up to the very fringes of the city, to the edges of the roads and into people's gardens. Visible too are the other two great lines of transport that bind this elongated country together – road and railway, forced into close proximity and parallel strips, by river and desert. A smart blue, grey and cream commuter train, pulled by a single diesel engine, speeds past a line of commercial vehicles, some of which are carrying containers bound for Port Said or Damietta, queuing at a petrol station to fill their hungry motors.

Ahead, we can make out the huge concrete piers of the new El Qantara road bridge, completed eight years earlier. Suspended seventy metres above the canal by cables held in place by two giant piers over one hundred and fifty metres high, it dominates the skyline. On either side, pairs of columns of steadily diminishing height, march in a long line into the desert, easing the road down to ground level and giving the bridge a total length of almost four kilometres.[15] Most of the irrigated land is on the west bank, although there are indications of irrigation works being developed on the east side too. Unbelievably, we cross over an irrigation channel that passes under the Suez Canal using a system of locks to take this precious liquid to where it is so desperately needed.

Egypt is defined by The Nile and the desert. Ninety-five per cent of the country is desert and virtually uninhabited, whilst ninety-nine per cent of its entire population is squeezed into the remaining five per cent of land, along the banks of the narrow artery that carries the country's life blood. It is the Nile that gave rise several millennia ago to one of the earliest riverine civilisations known to humanity, long before the books of the Old Testament were written and long before the events which are recorded in those books took place. The whole history of Egypt can be seen as the story of the taming of the Nile, the struggle to develop a sustainable way of life in response to the physical geography of the place. It may even be that this is where agriculture had its origins, as hunters from the arid lands of the Sahara moved into the fertile, moisture-laden Nile Valley and began to develop creative ways of using the life-sustaining waters of this massive river.

This was the time of the Neolithic Revolution, which marked the transition from hunting, gathering and pastoral nomadism to settled communities of agriculture and domesticated animals. Developing a civilization based on irrigation and control of the Nile, required a strong, centralized authority to run the country, and that is exactly what happened under the pharaohs. Whilst this was happening in the Nile Valley, a similar process was at work in the Fertile Crescent centred on the Tigris-Euphrates river system in modern day Iraq, in the Yellow River valley of China and in the Indus catchment of what is now largely Pakistan. In all these areas, hierarchical systems of government arose that were capable of exerting the necessary control over complex irrigation systems and the collection and distribution of the raw materials necessary for building the earliest towns and cities.

Some of these Neolithic communities were to be found here in the Middle East round about 9000 BCE, and Egypt found itself at the heart of this revolutionary movement. It was a major transformation in the way human beings won a living from the land and organised themselves, politically and socially. As with all revolutions, however, not everyone was happy with it. Many looked on it with suspicion and a sense of foreboding. And as all revolutions always do, this one too brought with it a deep-rooted conflict between those who wanted to cling to the old way of life and those who embraced the new.

The story is eloquently told in the book of Genesis. It is a classic story of the turmoil caused when two powerful traditions find themselves on a collision course. Much of the early part of the Old Testament can be read as the story of the tension between wandering pastoralists and settled farmers. It is epitomized in the story of the brothers Cain and Abel and it shows how long-held traditional ideas about how to organise society, soon take on a religious significance, telling us the correct, God-ordained way of doing things and the wrong, sinful way of doing things. It shows how geography and religion become intertwined. So closely was the God of the Old Testament identified with nomadism, that the people carried him around with them in the form of their Ark, sometimes known as the Ark of the Covenant. It was not until much later, when these nomads too had adopted a more settled way of life, that the Ark was given a permanent location in the temple in Jerusalem.

Abel was a nomadic herdsman, a wandering pastoralist, an adherent of the traditional way of doing things; his brother Cain wanted to embrace the new and became a 'tiller of the ground', a settled farmer. According to the Old Testament, Abel's way of life as a herdsman was approved of by God; the word used in the Authorized Version of the Bible is respect.

God showed his respect for Abel's nomadic way of life by accepting his sacrificial offering of a firstling sheep. Cain's offering of corn, however, was not accepted because it symbolised the settled agricultural way of life; his offering was repulsive to the God of the nomads. The bitter rivalry that developed between the two brothers, culminated in Cain murdering Abel and as a punishment, Cain was forced to live his life as "a fugitive and a wanderer on the earth", the exact opposite of the settled, agricultural way of life he had loved so much. "Today," he cried to God in desperation, "you have driven me away from the soil."[16]

This story of the rise of civilization and the clash of the new over the old, is given a religious interpretation in the Bible, an epic drama of a fundamental conflict over who had the correct understanding of God. To practise agriculture you need to live in one place, in villages, towns and cities, so that you can go to the fields and cultivate your crops. This was abhorrent to people who had always been nomads. So when a natural catastrophe (probably a volcano) reduced the towns of Sodom and Gomorrah to rubble, it was seen as God's judgement for their wicked ways and the nomads saw it as a vindication of their point of view.

Geography and religion dominated life in this cradle of civilization through which we are passing. Home of the two most explosive forces in human history – politics and religion – this cradle of civilization, birthplace of three powerful world religions, has aptly been described as the cockpit of the world. It is also noteworthy that it was the monotheistic religions that were born here. These people were used to wide spaces, lived under enormous skies, pitched their tents under the heavens that seemed to govern their lives, wandered over vast deserts with almost limitless horizons. They needed an all-powerful God to be in control of all this lot, this fearfully majestic and awesomely unpredictable universe. They needed one mighty deity in overall command. The minor gods of wind or fire, sun, harvest, abundance and thunder, were not enough for them. They needed a god who was with them all the time, wherever their wanderings took them. And so strongly did they believe in this God, that they were determined to impose their belief on the inhabitants of the land into which they were moving.

A lot of the Old Testament is concerned with this great war for religious supremacy. It is epitomised in the struggle between Baal and Yahweh as recorded in the first book of Kings. The cult of Baal, the Canaanite god of storm and fertility, and of his consort Asherah, was widespread in the land which has come to be known as the Promised Land, and the lethal struggle between these nature gods and the new god, Yahweh Sabaoth, the God of Armies, is a persistent theme of the early books of the Old Testament.

It came to a head one day on Mount Carmel, a place sacred to worshippers of Baal. Here Elijah issued his challenge to the people of Israel: "How long will you go limping with two different opinions? If the LORD is God, follow him; but if Baal, then follow him."[17] The test for the two gods was to see which one would send a lightning bolt and set fire to an altar on which lay the flesh of a newly slain bull. Yahweh's victory was the signal for the prophets of Baal to be slaughtered, a task which was carried out enthusiastically. I cannot but help ponder on the fact that both sides of this dispute were in essence about who was in control of nature. One side thought it was Baal, the other claimed it was Yahweh. In both cases, it was about which divine being was capable of sending a bolt of lightning. Is it our god or your god who is in control? That was the argument. But in this case, there were wider implications, for the gods of fertility and abundance were finally dethroned in this rampage of theocratic cleansing and much of the world became monotheistic.

Just how powerful the relationship between religion and geography is, may be demonstrated by the Egyptian god, Osiris and his wife, the goddess Isis. In popular thought, they were the god and goddess of nature and fertility. They were responsible for the annual flooding of the Nile which brought with it fertile soils, renewing and replenishing the land ready for the sowing of next year's corn. Without this gift from the gods, settled agriculture in Egypt would have been impossible. "Corn in Egypt" has become a byword in English for abundance. It was all down to Osiris and Isis, who between them took wild barley and corn and showed their people how to cultivate them. They were the god and goddess of the Neolithic Revolution, and, according to ancient mythology, Osiris travelled the world spreading the "blessings of civilization and agriculture"[18]. Osiris was celebrated in festivals of death and resurrection. When the seed was sown, it was said to die there and then come to life again in the form of new crops. Death and resurrection of the gods, reflected in the coming and going of the seasons, seems to be a recurring theme throughout the great religions of the world.

Just south of El Qantara, the canal bifurcates into the West and East Branches of the El Ballah By-Pass. We wait here in the West Branch for the north-bound convoy to pass on the East Branch. After two hours, the first ship appears, a pale blue Maersk ship glides over the sand. And so for five hours, in the blazing sun and sticky heat, we watch a succession of ships moving interminably slowly through the desert, without any visible waterway.

On the western horizon, a magnificent ball of yellow and orange fire gradually sinks towards an ink-black sea, and over our heads, the purple sky merges to red and then pink before the blackness overtakes the sky as well. As the ball of fire touches the horizon, the smoking trio invite me to join them on F Deck for what they have begun to call their happy hour, timed to precede the evening meal. This has become a daily ritual and it takes place in an L-shaped corner of Deck F, just outside the Captain's quarters, giving shelter from the wind and grandstanding the setting sun.

Four sun-loungers are arranged around a low table facing the sea. The happy hour is in full swing when I arrive and the red wine is a perfect reflection of the setting sun. Not a breath of air can be felt in this neatly tucked away corner, but my chair is positioned in such a way that I can move it ever so surreptitiously backwards, to allow me to capture as much as possible of a gentle stream of fresh air flowing just behind my back. This conveniently whisks away the fumes that drift in my direction. In the half hour I am there, many cigarettes are smoked and the red wine flows liberally and congenially. It's a convivial occasion and for them, the drinking continues over dinner, half way through which Janine and Adriaan take their habitual 'between break'.

We start to move again shortly after dinner, finally coming out of the southern end of the Suez Canal just after midnight. Out on deck and before breakfast the next morning, I find the sun on the wrong side of the ship. As we should be heading south, the sun ought to be on the port side, but it's to starboard. On the bridge, Officer Koziol tells me that we have been anchored in the north end of the Gulf of Suez since just after 03:00. The wind has swung us round so that we are facing north, together with half a dozen other ships that are queuing up waiting to go northwards through the Canal. Apparently, some emergency maintenance work has to be undertaken, so an engineer from the manufacturer, Burmeister and Wein, has been brought on board. He arrived during the night from Port Said by helicopter and then by lighter. He commenced work during the night and continues throughout the day, replacing one of the crossheads. This, Adriaan explains to me, is the connection between the crank shaft and the piston rod. The engineer finally leaves the same way he came, by lighter and helicopter.

The Sinai Peninsula and the continent of Africa are both tantalisingly close. While Africa holds a certain nostalgia for me, it is Sinai on our port side, that compels most of my attention today. This is the peninsular that was captured by Israel during the six-day war in 1967, a conflict that had, and continues to have, its roots in religious strife. We are close enough to make out some of the settlements, the Power Station and Pilot Station at Ra's Sudr and the town of Bi'r Abu Suwayrah.

To the west, a huge wind farm near Râs Abu el Durag desultorily waves innumerable arms and opposite, to the east of us, is the town of Râs Abu Suweira, a white nucleus of human activity huddled on the narrow interface between desert and sea. With an air temperature of twenty-seven and a gentle following wind, we have a relative wind speed of zero, making the air uncannily still and giving us perfect conditions for being out on the Monkey Deck, where the warm air wraps itself seductively round me. The mountainous hinterland forms a brown, arid, treeless backcloth, and I wonder about those fleeing slaves several thousand years ago, lost, bewildered, terrified, wandering about in a land they did not understand, and whose story has left such a profound imprint on all of our lives.

Tradition has it that this peninsula was where the freed Hebrew people wandered for forty years in the wilderness after being liberated from slavery under one of the pharaohs. Their experience of slavery and liberation embedded itself deeply in the religious thinking of both Jew and Christian and so helped to mould the belief systems that have become part of the cultural heritage of our world. The Bible suggests that their wanderings before they entered the Promised Land, took place here in the Sinai Peninsula, but the evidence in it is ambiguous and it may well be that they meandered over a far wider area.

Clearing the Gulf of Suez, we enter the Red Sea proper. Rather alarmingly, the charts have frequent pencilled notes warning of "Terrorism Risk" at the southern end. It will take us three days to get through. A day later, we cross the Tropic of Cancer, passing Jeddah in Saudi Arabia. On the western shore, Egypt has given way to Sudan. This elongated sea occupies a great rift valley which has been created by the pulling apart of the Arabian and African tectonic plates, thus allowing the Indian Ocean to flood in and fill it. And it is getting wider, for these two plates are still moving apart. In fact, it is part of a much larger geographical phenomenon starting further north in the Jordan Valley in Syria, running between Jordan and Israel, through the Red Sea and into the great East African Rift Valley. It is known as the Syrian – African Rift and it is 6,500 kilometres long.[19]

My daughter sends me a text to ask me to take a photograph of the Red Sea for my grandson. Ben wants to know if it really is red, so I take the picture at sunset, when the sun is a flaming circle of yellow hovering just above the horizon, turning the sky red and the sea a deep purple. I send it and it seems to convince him.

For the third time since leaving the UK, clocks are advanced by one hour, so we now have just six more hours to gain by the time we reach Australia. I prefer the twenty-five hour days you get when travelling slowly west, but even these twenty-three hour days going east are hardly noticeable and are infinitely better than jet lag.

CHAPTER 9: Geography is Better than

Divinity

Seven short blasts followed by one long one. Another emergency drill. The previous one had not gone well and the Captain is determined to get it right.

I grab my hard hat, neoprene immersion suit and life jacket and make my way to the muster station on the Poop Deck. Here, we are directed to a newly-painted rectangle on the starboard side surrounded by 27 coded spots. Our instructions are precise. We are each allocated a numbered spot on which to stand with our equipment. From now on for all emergency drills, we must report to this exact spot, clamber into our bright orange life jackets and hard hats and place our immersion suits, also in reflective orange bags, beside us ready to put on should the need arise. The First Officer takes charge. Then, with the exception of the Captain and Chief Engineer who remain at their stations, each of us in turn call out our number from 1 to 27. All are present and correctly attired.

Now on to the lifeboat muster station to which I have been assigned, two decks up on the starboard side of Deck B for half of us, the others on the port side. Here we wait while a select handful of men swiftly and silently go up to Deck C above to carry out the necessary tasks to prepare the lifeboat, swinging it down and over on its davit to bring it into position before opening the door. Finally, the order is given for us to go up and board the lifeboat. One by one, we make our way up the flight of fourteen stairs to our left, turn right at the top and enter the lifeboat in turn, taking our places alternately on each side, starting at the rear, number one on the starboard side, two on the port side, and so on until we are all in. Once seated on the narrow benches, we fix our safety harnesses. The First Officer requires each of us to call out our duties. Looking at me he says, "Yours are to assist where necessary". The whole thing goes smoothly this time, and when we all gather together for the debriefing, Number One, with evident satisfaction at a job well done, dismisses us while the crew carry out more specialised procedures.

The weather is perfect for a few circuits of the Main Deck. The breeze from the north has now veered to the south-east at seven knots, so we are heading straight into it, giving an effective wind speed of twenty-seven knots, equivalent to force six. Earlier that morning, it had been thirty-two knots, a near gale, making walking round the deck an unnerving experience.

We are now midway between the coasts of Yemen to the east and Eritrea to the west, and over the next few hours, the gap between these two coasts gets smaller as we approach the Strait of Bab El Mandeb, the narrow stretch of water between Yemen and Djibouti, where Africa and Asia almost touch and are just eight miles apart. At times the coast of Eritrea is visible, its pale, brown mountains forming a stark contrast with the deep blue sea and pastel sky.

High above me, two members of the crew are painting the ship's stern crane. They are dressed in khaki fatigues and their heads and faces, except for their eyes, are entirely enclosed by white cotton cloths to protect from the fierce heat of the sun. Around their waists are wide, brown leather belts carrying some of the equipment they need, but whose main purpose is to secure them and their safety harness to a rail running the full length of the crane's jib, giving them security and freedom of movement. On their feet are strong canvas boots.

They sit astride one of the pair of blue beams that constitute the jib and wield wide paint brushes attached to poles about three feet long.

Adriaan has been doing research on the ship's engines and over dinner he tells me what he has discovered. There are, of course, larger ships, but I find the sheer scale of even this ship's engines, mind blowing. Each of the engine's seven cylinders, has a diameter of seventy centimetres. Fuel consumption is one hundred and fifty kilograms per nautical mile. This means we will need over two thousand six hundred tonnes for the thirty-four days we are to be at sea. Each cylinder exerts a total force on top of the piston of three hundred and thirty metric tonnes per combustion, and there are eighty-nine combustions per minute. With seven pistons working away at this speed, that gives a combined force of over two thousand, three hundred metric tonnes per combustion. No wonder the only place where it is not possible to hear the engine is at the prow and on the bridge. The propeller has a diameter of seven metres and each revolution takes us forward at least about seven metres. The sheer scale of the engineering and the fuel consumption makes me wonder about the pollution this must be causing. Should I have gone by plane instead?

Later that evening after our meal, I watch a DVD in the Officers' Recreation Room. Hurried footsteps approach the door and Adriaan bursts in, very excited.

"There's a volcano erupting. You must come and look."

I switch off the screen, tear off my head phones and rush outside to the port side of the ship. On the eastern horizon, is a ball of fire about the size of the sun I witnessed setting a couple of hours earlier. It's Jazira at Ta'ir, a small volcanic island off the coast of Yemen, a mere two hundred and forty-four metres high. I focus the binoculars on it, my first sighting of an erupting volcano. Although the sky is dark, it is not as dark as the huge pillar of jet black smoke that is forced vertically upwards with tremendous power like that of a giant pressure cooker blowing its valve. Pencil straight, it rises into the night sky, and every so often the dark red glow beneath it becomes agitated and turns into a brilliant, pulsing red as further molten lava is spewed out, thrust upward a short distance and then tumbles back on itself and creeps down the mountain side.

"It's all very Biblical", Adriaan says beside me.

Indeed it is. His comment puts me in mind of an ancient, biblical description of what can only have been an erupting volcano, reputed to have taken place in this very region several thousand years ago and a dramatic example of the collision of geography and religion.

When the Children of Israel had been freed from slavery in Egypt, they were to spend the next forty years or so wandering in the wilderness somewhere to the east of the Red Sea. Here their experiences were quite unlike anything they had known before and they were terrified. As I stood there, leaning with Adriaan over the rail of the deck, watching the throbbing red glow of the distant volcano, I understood for the first time how spectacularly easy it would have been for those ancient people, with little understanding of the processes that drove the natural world, to experience such events with a combination of awe, wonder and terror. What else could they do than interpret them as a divine manifestation? The story is told in the book of Exodus:

They set out from Succoth, and camped at Etham, on the edge of the wilderness. The LORD went in front of them in a pillar of cloud by day, to lead them along the way, and in a pillar of fire by night, to give them light, so that they might travel by day and by night. Neither the pillar of cloud by day nor the pillar of fire by night left its place in front of the people.[20]

On the morning of the third day there was thunder and lightning, as well as a thick cloud on the mountain, and a blast of a trumpet so loud that all the people who were in the camp trembled. Moses brought the people out of the camp to meet God. They took their stand at the foot of the mountain. Now Mount Sinai was wrapped in smoke, because the LORD had descended upon it in fire; the smoke went up like the smoke of a kiln, while the whole mountain shook violently. As the blast of the trumpet grew louder and louder, Moses would speak and God would answer him in thunder.[21]

The wilderness was a deeply traumatic place for the Children of Israel, a "great and terrible... arid waste-land with poisonous snakes and scorpions."[22] These wandering people, newly liberated from slavery under pharaonic Egypt, would have been glad of anything to hold onto that might help them to interpret these terrifying experiences as the guidance of a supernatural being. Whilst it might seem obvious to us today that if you walk towards a mountain out of which is spewing smoke and fire, you'll end up at an active volcano, for them this was not a volcano at all but nothing short of a direct manifestation of the awesome power of God. This explains why God is sometimes described in the Old Testament in terms closely resembling an erupting volcano.

The mountains quake before him, and the hills melt; the earth heaves before him, the world and all who live in it. Who can stand before his indignation? Who can endure the heat of his anger? His wrath is poured out like fire, and by him the rocks are broken in pieces.[23]

In these descriptions we have everything – smoke, fire, falling rocks and even the sound of a trumpet. Modern observations record a variety of sounds emitted by an erupting volcano, among them something similar to that of a jet engine. This is hardly surprising when we remind ourselves that hot gases are being forced at tremendous speed and pressure through a narrow vent. It's a gigantic whistle. The only comparable sound this wandering band of freed slaves several thousand years ago had available to them, was that of a trumpet.

For us, reading these Old Testament passages today, it seems pretty clear that their wanderings were taking place in an area of volcanic activity and they simply didn't know how else to interpret what they saw. So impressive was the experience that their first laws, the Ten Commandments, are reputed to have been given to them by a God of Fire and

Thunder from the top of a mountain. We might also ask whether such a volcanic eruption might have triggered off a tsunami, and whether this might explain the way in which the Egyptian military who pursued the fleeing slaves, were all drowned. The sea was driven back, we are told, before sweeping in once more and engulfing the wretched pursuers[24].

The Old Testament account is a vivid description of volcanic activity, and you can interpret this as divine intervention or simply as a natural disaster over which they had no control. Whatever it was, it worked to the advantage of one group and the disadvantage of the other. One group was drowned, the others escaped. We are all more familiar with this type of event now after the great Christmas tsunami that struck Indonesia in 2004 and video recordings show how the deadly waters first drew back before sweeping inland and killing thousands, as appears to have happened when the pursuing Egyptians were drowned in the Red Sea. Vengeful God or indifferent nature? Religion or geography?

In a work called *Cosmographia*, the seventeenth century theologian Dr Peter Heylyn records, that one day when he was on his way from Westminster to Whitehall, a man thrust him rudely aside with the words, "Geography is better than divinity," and then passed on his way[25]. Perhaps this stranger had a point. Geography certainly moulds the way we look at the world. It also, according to Jared Diamond, explains why societies have developed so differently in different parts of the world[26]. Whilst I am not into geographical determinism, which holds that the geographical setting in which we are raised somehow predetermines the pattern of our lives, I do believe that the nature of the physical environment in which we happen to live out our lives, has a deep and profound effect on our thinking, our beliefs, our sense of spirituality and the way we understand the world.

It is late afternoon and to starboard is the hazy coastline of Eritrea. To the east, lies the arid coast of Yemen. Here, I finally win my battle against a troublesome fly. I made the mistake of opening my window during our enforced idleness in the Suez Canal but hadn't reckoned on the flies. I had managed to swat all of them except for this one pesky nuisance that has been bothering me ever since. Now it makes the mistake of landing on the edge of the table, in a perfect position for swatting with my rolled up towel, with nothing else nearby that might be damaged by an extremely energetic and triumphant swipe. Yes!

CHAPTER 10: The Spaces In Between

'Warning: Pirates. High Risk'. The notes on the charts I am studying as we enter the Gulf of Aden, are not encouraging.

Because of pirate activity, Officer Koziol informs us, we are to keep at least one hundred and twenty miles off the Somali coast. This means we have to go north round the Yemeni island of Socotra instead of taking the more usual direct route to the south, which would take us too close to the pirate coast for comfort. Company policy states that if attacked by pirates, the crew and officers should offer no resistance and hand over whatever goods might be demanded. We are told that it is unlikely that pirates will attempt to board a ship of our size and at our speed, but on the other hand it has been known for whole ships to be captured, taken to remote ports and cannibalized. During the night, additional lights have been placed all the way round the main deck so that anyone attempting to board might be easily seen.

It's the middle of the forenoon watch and a touch of concern runs round the bridge as we spot a high speed boat to starboard that appears to be heading for another ship. It then turns away and heads directly for us, but then changes its mind once more and disappears from view. Despite the ship's sophisticated monitoring equipment, we are not able to identify the vessel and nothing more is heard about it. Perversely and to my very great surprise, a slight feeling of disappointment descends, as if some promised excitement, something for me to really write home about, has been offered and then taken away. Three days earlier, a chemical tanker was pirated in the Gulf of Aden.

At noon, we pass Aden, the former British colony and now the second largest city of Yemen and the economic core of the country. We hug the Yemeni coast and, at just over twenty knots, are almost at maximum speed. Throughout all that day and night, we follow the same course, east but with a slightly northern component, to keep us as far away as possible from Somalia. Another warning on the charts emphasises the message: 'high risk of pirates'. Mid-morning next day and we are still at the same speed with Socotra to our south. We have entered the western Arabian Sea now and at 13:40, we turn slightly to the south. The wind, still from the east, has strengthened to a moderate breeze, giving a relative wind on the Monkey Deck of thirty-five knots, which is a gale. We begin our wide turn round the eastern end of Socotra and by the next morning, have set a course of one twenty-eight, bringing us almost directly in line with Fremantle. The wind direction, still a gentle breeze, is from the north-east. For the next few days, we will have these north-east trades hitting us square on our port side as we head south-east across the Indian Ocean.

Why do I undertake this kind of voyage? Mostly, it is because I like to see what I call the spaces in between. I first fell in love with slow travel half a century ago when I set off for Central Africa as a young teacher. I was lucky to catch the tail-end of the era of the grand passenger liner, for the ship I travelled on was the Pendennis Castle, the last of the Union Castle ships to be built by Harland and Wolff. It was for me then, a beautiful and totally satisfying way to travel from Southampton to Cape Town. They were glorious, sun-drenched, languid days and my wife and I were intoxicated with feelings of wellbeing and euphoria as we slowly emerged from the winter gloom of the British Isles into the warm air and bright skies of the sub-tropics. We were lucky, for the sea was not by any means rough, and the worst that could be said of any part of the voyage was that there was a moderate to heavy swell when crossing the Bay of Biscay. After a week, the deep greens and blues of the Atlantic gave way to shimmering silver as we entered the region aptly known as 'the doldrums', or the torrid zone. Here, if it were possible, the sea became even calmer, and one could be forgiven for imagining that we were silently pushing our way through a sea of quicksilver, so small an impression did the ship leave on the ocean. The sky took on the same silvery sheen and it became difficult to distinguish it from the water below as the horizon all but disappeared. Here, dolphins acted as our escorts, playfully weaving in and out of the bow waves, leading us on, inviting us to play.

Those who have never approached South Africa by sea, have missed one of the great wonders of that ancient continent. Almost imperceptibly at first, the huge bulk of Table Mountain asserted itself against the crystal clarity of the early morning sky, its flat surface lifting some three thousand feet above us, pushing the sky and the early morning light ever upwards until it was towering majestically over us as we edged cautiously into Table Bay. A small triangular white banner of cloud flew just above the mountain on the landward side, whilst to the south, the African continent came to an abrupt end at the Cape of Good Hope and emptied itself precipitously into the Southern Ocean.

Then to top it all, there was the three day train journey up-country, to which I abandoned myself with utter delight. As the maroon and cream train pulled effortlessly out of Cape Town Railway Station that afternoon, we were beginning a 1,500 mile journey on one of the great railway routes of the world. Towards evening, we slid through the lush vineyard country of the Hex River Valley before beginning the tortuous climb up the great escarpment of the Little Karroo, over the Swartberg Mountains and onto the undulating plains of the Great Karroo, some four to five thousand feet above sea level. The next day, we crossed two of the great rivers of South Africa, the Orange and the Vaal and, as the by now dust-laden and smoke-begrimed train hauled us northwards, the landscape became more and more harsh, with only sporadic tufts of course grasses and isolated thorn bushes to break the monotony of what otherwise looked like a desert. A day later, we emerged onto the wide open belt of green and gold savanna that sweeps down the east of the African continent and across its southern heart. It was endlessly and gloriously fascinating.

I was hooked. Several years later, I had occasion to revisit that part of the world, but the only option open to me then was to fly. As I looked down from 35,000 feet over the rolling savannas of southern Africa, I felt disappointed, cheated. I wanted to be there taking it all in, the crisp sharpness of the early morning air of the high veldt, the sounds of excited chatter at railway stations, the dust of the dirt roads, the smell of cattle. This was not travel, it was the bulk movement of human cargo.

A close second reason for choosing this kind of travel, is the question of the environment. This is a difficult matter and it is not always clear-cut, but there is fairly strong evidence to show that travelling slowly is more environmentally friendly than going at high speeds.

"Look at it this way," says ex-engineer Adriaan, "this freighter would travel anyhow, with or without us. We make very little difference to the overall weight of the ship. In aeroplanes, the whole cargo is passengers."

"But that's no answer. If everybody travelled this way, the ships would be carrying only passengers, just like cruise ships, and the pollution would be immense."

"But don't forget that the faster you go, the dirtier it is."

Apparently, emissions from an engine increase with the square of the increase of the speed. So if you double the speed, you increase the pollution by two-squared or four times: if you treble the speed, the pollution increases by three-squared, or nine times. We were travelling at about twenty knots, or twenty-three mph; jets fly at about five hundred mph, about twenty-two times faster. This means that the pollution caused by flying is almost five hundred times that of going by freighter. However, there are other considerations to be taken into account, such as the greater resistance of water compared with that of air and, a major point, the filthy fuel that is used by most freighters. Cargo ships use bunker fuel which, while it is one of the dirtiest fractions left after the other higher grade fuels have been distilled off, is cheap but nasty.

I do not know how accurate Adriaan's figures are about the polluting effect of speed, but I do know that a few months ago, Eurostar produced some figures showing that a passenger making a return journey between Paris and London by Eurostar, would generate twenty-two kilograms of carbon dioxide emissions, whereas flying the same journey would generate more than two hundred and forty[27].

"And," continues Adriaan, "the harmful emissions from an aeroplane, go directly into the stratosphere, causing the maximum harm."

But there are other reasons to travel slowly. It is becoming increasingly difficult to escape from the frantic activity of everyday life. In an age of rapid electronic communications and the pressure to be always available, always ready to respond to other people's demands, the need for silence and solitude becomes more urgent. We seem to have developed an aversion to being on our own, afraid of what might happen if friends, acquaintances or family are unable to contact us. We are suffering from information and contact overload. Incessant demands for permanent availability and answerability, divert us from simple enjoyments. On a cargo ship, you are thrown back entirely on your own resources. Here, you can step back, take stock, reflect, enjoy the moment, take pleasure in what is new, listen to the silence.

Few experiences are so stressful and so utterly tedious as air travel. The world is a fantastic place but when we fly, we see very little of it, and almost nothing of the spaces in between. Travelling slowly enables you to take in the detail, to experience how the world works, to see how it all links up. Maybe, there would be some merit therefore, in making travel something we do less often, so that a long journey would become special. What a pity to flit backwards and forwards so often across this glorious world that it becomes ordinary. What a waste of wonder!

Jet travel is killing distance. We measure distance now by hours rather than by miles, by the time it takes to get from A to B, rather than by the distance covered. With slow travel, you get to understand distance, to feel the spaces in between. Spaces define the boundaries of where we live; they give character to home. Some of the most spectacular spaces, are the oceans. Most of the earth's surface (about seventy per cent of it) is water, and we actually know comparatively little about it. Yet, the oceans hold about ninety-six per cent of the world's water and have an abundance of life and beauty all of their own. Travelling this way, you get to see magnificently bejewelled skies, darkness so thick you can touch it, an occasional encounter with fear as mighty seas are thrown into terrifying turmoil by awesomely powerful winds.

It is good to rediscover distance. I know of no better way of recharging batteries than by travelling slowly. Even taking the local bus instead of driving the car, is like a mini retreat. You can look out of the window, read the paper, write a letter. Ordinary things become sensationally beautiful. You get surprises too, erupting volcanoes, flying fish, spectacular sunsets, magnificent cloud formations, moonrises and moonsets. Unlike on cruise ships, you will not have more deliciously tempting food thrust in front of you than you can possibly consume, but you will have a reasonable sufficiency. Furthermore, you will not get jetlagged and for several weeks you will not see a newspaper or watch television. Politicians may dazzle us with their whizzing about the globe attending this and that important meeting, but I have the feeling that if only they travelled more slowly, arrived at their impressive destinations relaxed, refreshed and biologically adjusted, they might be able to make better, slower, more considered decisions and, in the process, make the world a safer place.

The barometric pressure is falling, the wind has increased to twenty-one knots and is backing northwards. We are still on a course of 128, heading almost directly south-east into the

Indian Ocean, a route that will take us between the Laccadive Archipelago, the Maldives, and the Chagos Islands. The conversation round the table is about the tropics and crossing the equator. The First Officer asks us if we would like to be woken during the night when we cross the equator, but no one takes up his offer. The sun is scorchingly hot, all right for walking where there is a mixture of sun and shade, but far too hot to sit in. We're always hankering after the sun in the British Isles, seeking out every opportunity to bask in its warmth; in the tropics, it's an ever abundant reality and people look for shade.

This sun deficit in high latitudes, affects us profoundly; it is why so much importance is attached to the solstices. We yearn for the sun and mourn its passing. This is reflected in much pre-Christian religious thinking among the Celts. Many ancient monuments throughout the Celtic world, the most famous of which is Stonehenge, are believed to have been laid out in such a way as to capture the moment when the sun begins its long journey away from us on the summer solstice and the day, six months later, when it begins its return. From Maeshowe in the Orkneys to Newgrange in Ireland and Bryn Celli Ddu on Anglesey, the story seems to be the same, holy sites aligned to celebrate one or other of the solstices.[28] In the ancient Irish tradition, the god Dagda is thought to have been roused to new life as the sun rose on the morning of the winter solstice. In Wales, the longest day is a holy day dedicated to Rhiannon, the White Mare Goddess.[29] The Celtic festival of fire, Beltane, is held between the spring equinox and the summer solstice and celebrates the longed-for fertility of the coming year, as symbolised by the union of the Goddess and the God.[30]

The worship of Mithras had much in common with Christianity. According to James Frazer, the twenty-fifth of December was the winter solstice in the Julian calendar, and this day was regarded as the Nativity of the Sun. In the annual ritual of the nativity, the celebrants emerged from their shrines at midnight with the cry, 'The Virgin has brought forth! The light is waxing!' This new-born sun was represented by the image of an infant, whose birthday was on the 25th December. The Virgin who bore this child was the oriental goddess, known to the Semites as the Heavenly Virgin or Astarte. The Christian Church it seems, deliberately, chose the 25th December to celebrate the birthday of Jesus so as to turn people away from the worship of the Sun of Heaven to the worship of the Son of God. Whichever way we look at it, there can be no doubt about the heathen origins of the festival of Christmas and its ancient links with the solstice.[31] And there are plenty of sun worshippers around today. The British holiday industry is built on it.

We owe the annual coming and going of the sun to a tilt in the earth's axis. The fact that we lean over by 23.5 degrees gives us our seasons, defines the position of the tropics and provides us with our most important topic of conversation. If it were not for this tilt, a great deal of ancient religious thought and festivals, would not have been developed and Christmas would not be in December. It's this inclination to the ecliptic, the plane of the earth's orbit around the sun, that makes so much of our lives a cause for celebration, and it is also the reason why the closest the sun gets to us in Britain, is when it is overhead at the Tropic of Cancer. But even then, it is never properly overhead for us but well to the south. It is only ever truly overhead in the tropics and then, only on two days of the year and even then, just at noon. At the tropic of Cancer, that one day is our summer solstice (usually about June 21st) and at Capricorn, it is our winter solstice (about December 21st). Between those two dates and between these two tropics, there will be just two days in the year when the sun is directly overhead at noon. At no other point outside of the tropics, is the sun anywhere directly overhead; where we are in the UK, the sun is always to the south of us and south of the Tropic of Capricorn, it is always to the north.

So Janine, in true Australian tradition, seeks out the shade. Actually, Janine doesn't like the sun at all, even when it's cool at the beginning and end of the day. Most Australians, fully aware of how cruel the raw sun can be, erect massive, protective sun shades. We north-west Europeans however, embrace the sun, go on holiday to find it, bathe in it, and even build conservatories to capture as much of its warmth as possible. Janine positively shrinks from it at all times. As she drinks a glass of what remains of her cache of red wine, she squeezes herself into her favourite corner on F Deck next to the Captain's suite, where the last vestiges of shade are to be found and, well away from any hint of breeze.

"Well, make the most of it, Janine. The shade is getting smaller every day."

"Whad'ya mean Clive?"

"We're getting closer to the overhead sun."

"The sun's always overhead."

"No it isn't. I mean directly overhead. Dead true vertical so that a flag pole wouldn't have a shadow. We never see this in the UK, but we will see it soon."

"When?"

"When we catch up with the overhead sun. I'll calculate when that will be and on the day, we'll put something tall and thin out on the Monkey Deck to test it."

"Like a wine bottle?"

The sun's got a hundred and eighty-three days (half a year) to move from 23.5 degrees south to 23.5 degrees north, a total of 47 degrees. A simple calculation, based on the speed of the ship, of where we will be on any particular day and the slow apparent movement of the sun, should allow us to calculate where ship and overhead sun will coincide. On this day, there should be no shadow at midday. I calculate it to be on the 25th November and we all agree to meet on the Monkey Deck on that day and test it out.

I have now finished reading Robert Fisk's book and feel depressed about world politics, particularly those relating to the Middle East. It seems that so many of the problems in that part of the world have been caused by constant outside interference, particularly by Western powers.

The British occupation of what was called Mesopotamia in 1917, was predicated on the need to safeguard British oil interests in Persia. In pursuit of those interests, red lines were drawn on maps over which there would be conflict for generations to come. "How much longer", asked The Times on 7th August 1920, "are valuable lives to be sacrificed in the vain endeavour to impose upon the Arab population an elaborate and expensive administration which they never asked for and do not want?"[32] When Iraq had entertained ideas about independence after the defeat of Turkey in the early twentieth century, France and Britain denied them this option and instead divided up the area between themselves. And so out of Mesopotamia, we created the geographical absurdity which is modern-day Iraq, a hotchpotch of different cultural and ethnic groups that included Shia and Sunni Muslims and Kurds[33]. Iraq is not a nation state; it has not grown up organically into a group of people with a shared culture or a common understanding of themselves as Iraqi. These people are struggling with a false identity imposed on them from without. It's as if Hitler had won the war and compelled the Germans, French and British to live together as one state and we in turn, had been forced to call ourselves German. An army of resistance fighters would have grown up and they would have been regarded by us as heroes, but by the occupying power as 'insurgents' or 'terrorists'. The same can be said of almost the whole of the continent of Africa, which was similarly carved up by a handful of European powers with no respect whatsoever for the linguistic, cultural and geographical realities of that vast continent, of which the colonial powers were largely ignorant. The historical legacy for much of the Middle East and Africa, has been the challenging task of endeavouring to create a sense of nationhood within the confines of illogical and sometimes crumbling boundaries.

The threat of pirates and the noisy turmoil of the Middle East and Africa seem incredibly distant now as we continue our voyage towards the centre of the Indian Ocean, into a zone of absolute stillness and haunting silence.

CHAPTER 11: Doldrums

I, Neptune, Sovereign Ruler of All Oceans, Seas, Lakes, Rivers, Ponds and Puddles, declare that henceforth, the Born from Dirt and Dust, Robert Wilkinson, aboard our well-loved ship Alexandra Rickmers, was this day cleansed from the Dirt and Dust of all those Land Masses, also known as Continents, Islands or Atolls and following our Equatorial Rite, is baptised with the name of Auk and has thus been properly anointed and so well prepared to sail on all Waters stretching North and South of this Equator. Neptune.

It is 11:30 and Captain Grabowski has called us all to our favourite gathering place on F Deck. Here he presents each of us with certificates granting us safe passage through Neptune's kingdom, and then cracks open a bottle of champagne to celebrate our safe crossing of the equator. From now on, I am to be 'Auk', after the pelagic bird that lives out its life on the open sea.

We had crossed the equator at 10:44; we three men had gathered round the ship's GPS system to watch it flip over from north to south. One minute our position was given us $00^0 00.127'N$ and sixty seconds later, it read $00^0 00.108'S$. We are at longitude $71^0 22$ East, almost exactly midway between the Maldive Islands to the north and the Chagos Archipelago to the south. These island groups lie atop the Chagos-Laccadive Ridge (CLR) in the central Indian Ocean, to the south-west of the Indian sub-continent. It is a volcanic ridge, about two thousand kilometres long, on the Indo-Australian Tectonic Plate that is slowly moving northwards towards

Asia, where it collides with the Himalayas. Apparently, the CLR owes its origin to what is known as the Réunion Hotspot, a static part of the earth's mantle that is unusually hot and through which there have been, in the past, huge eruptions of lava. As the Indian Plate has drifted north over this hotspot, periodic eruptions have pierced holes through it, so creating the line of volcanic islands that we now know as the Maldive and Chagos island groups[34]. The Hawaiian Islands are thought to have been formed in the same way[35]. The islands making up the Republic of the Maldives, is what remains of these once active volcanoes and this physically fragile country, is extremely vulnerable to the dangers posed by global warming and rising ocean levels, for there is no place in it that is more than three and a half metres above sea level. It will be one of the first countries to disappear should the ocean levels continue to rise.

For the past two days, the sea has been extraordinarily still, the air hot and clammy. The surface of the water is like a mirror, silvery and eerily flat. The horizon has all but disappeared in the sticky haze that envelops us. It is like slithering through a sauna. We have entered the doldrums, that area of rising air and low pressure between the parallel bands of sub-tropical high pressure to the north and to the south. Here in this equatorial region, lying midway between the two trade wind belts on either side, the default condition is calm. At thirty-two degrees and under a blazing sun, it feels stiflingly hot on deck, with only the ship's motion bringing any relief.

It is not too difficult to imagine what it must have been like in the days of sail when, emerging from the brisk north-east trades, these ships suddenly found themselves becalmed in enervating heat and with very little water. While the trade winds provided very favourable conditions for westward travel, for these heroic ships, entering the doldrums was fraught with hazards. This must be the region where the ill-fated ship of Coleridge's *Ancient Mariner* was so horrendously becalmed until all on board, except for the haunted warrior himself, died a painful and lingering death.

Day after day, day after day,
We stuck, nor breath nor motion;
As idle as a painted ship
Upon a painted ocean.

Water, water, everywhere,
And all the boards did shrink;
Water, water, everywhere,
Nor any drop to drink.

The very deep did rot: O Christ!
That ever this should be!
Yea, slimy things did crawl with legs
Upon the slimy sea.[36]

We, however, are not becalmed and are in party mood. The celebration of Neptune's magnanimity in allowing us safe passage through his kingdom, continues with a second bottle of champagne that takes us up to lunch. Later, I decide to walk round the main deck, but the heat and humidity drain my energy, making me listless. The best I can manage is a gentle stroll. This is suddenly shattered midship by the jarring sound of the reefers. I need to get to the prow to feel some cooling fresh air. It's more of an effort than usual to climb the steps to the fo'c'sle and make my way through the array of windlasses and coiled ropes littering the deck.

At the prow, half a dozen cast iron steps take me to the little platform surrounded on three sides by security railing. It is the spot where Leonardo DiCaprio and Kate Winslet in the film *Titanic* held each other in amorous embrace on the prow of the doomed ship just before it went down. Joan and I tried to recreate this scenario on the Tasman Discoverer on our way to Shanghai, and although it was no doubt equally memorable to us, it probably didn't have the same filmic quality. For now, mine is a far more pedestrian experience, however, and I am content with taking in the emptiness and silence in front of me. At this point, everything is behind me, even the noise of the engine. Before me is water and sky. I lean over the thin railing once more to study the smooth contours of the bulbous bow, sleek and brown, tinged with green slime. You can lie flat on the iron floor here and poke your head through the railing and get a much better view of it, but I wouldn't have dared to do this on my own. I did this a few days earlier with Adriaan, however; we wanted to get photographs. He held my legs to stop me slipping through, and then I did the same for him. If any of the officers had spotted us, they would have put an end to our little escapade, but we were safely screened from their view by the mountain of containers behind us.

The bulbous bow thrusts its silent way through Neptune's domain. The only sound is the soft swoosh of water over its rounded contours. I stand alone and listen. Suddenly, there is a disturbance below me; the water is in turmoil. Myriads of flying fish leap about in what appears to be a desperate flight from this leviathan that they sense is a giant predator. It's like a mass panic attack as these little marine creatures come up against us and, in synchronised reflex action, jump out of the water and literally fly away from us. Shoal after shoal come up against the heavy bow, leap out of the water and speed away, some of them travelling as far as a hundred and fifty or two hundred metres in one long glide over the silvery sea before diving back in again. Some of them swoop down, touch the surface and then speed off again, often in a different direction, only to resume underwater life when they judge they are well clear of the predator they mistake us for. They are moderately sized creatures, about twenty to thirty centimetres long, and they have a sleek, streamlined shape that seems perfectly designed to enable them to build up sufficient speed under water to leap out in this dramatic way. Their unusually large pectoral fins double as wings, but they rarely rise more than maybe a couple of metres above the surface of the water. Because of the strength of the sunlight, it's difficult to tell with these fish what their colour is but they look to be a kind of grey or even dark blue, although their wings appear silvery and almost transparent. It is a remarkable spectacle and I feel rejuvenated and ready for a brisk walk back to my cabin for a refreshing shower before I meet up with the others for table tennis.

Cumulonimbus clouds fascinate me, especially in the tropics, where they can be gargantuan. After our game, which Adriaan and I win, I go out to look at a line of these magnificent clouds that we had spotted through the port hole of the table tennis room. This room did at least have the advantage of an efficient air conditioning system and, as I step onto the Main Deck, I am unprepared for the blast of hot air that hits me. It's if I've opened an oven door into the thirty-five degree heat. But it is the clouds I'm after and I pause for a moment to take in the sight. These specimens are real beauties and they threaten an impressive storm. I love the way they arrange themselves horizontally, all their bases smartly organised as if some celestial sergeant major has ruled a neat line for them to stand on and got them ready for inspection.

Cumulonimbus clouds (Cb in meteorological shorthand), are the result of rising air currents, which can be particularly powerful and reach to tremendous heights in the equatorial area of low pressure through which we are still passing. This is where the trade winds converge and eventually blow themselves out in what is known as the inter-tropical convergence zone (the ITCZ). The trade winds originate in the high pressure belts to the north and south from which air flows down and outwards towards the low pressure system straddling the equator. Here, where the pressure is low, the air begins to rise, and as it does so it cools, at a rate known as the adiabatic lapse rate. This varies according to whether the rising air is dry, when the rate is about 1^0 C per 100 m of ascent, or moist, when it is about 0.6^0 C per 100 m.

The air continues to rise until it reaches an altitude where any water vapour in it condenses into tiny water droplets or, if it is very cold, minute crystals of ice. This will happen at more or less the same height, known as the lifting condensation level, and this explains why these clouds line up with such neat militaristic precision. It is these tiny water droplets or ice crystals that we see as clouds. You can't see the water vapour (which is an invisible gas) but you can see the water droplets to which it condenses, and you see them in the form of clouds. When they are very thick, these clouds will appear grey or even black underneath because this is their shadow side, and it is this black base, and the fact that they accumulate to great heights, that gives these clouds their name. They are black and they accumulate – cumulonimbus.

The more the air goes on rising, the more the process of condensation continues. Eventually, the rising air reaches a point where no more cooling can take place. This is because it is the same temperature as the surrounding air, and this level is called the tropopause, which marks the boundary between the troposphere and the stratosphere. The tropopause limits the height to which cumulonimbus clouds rise. In higher latitudes, such as our northern regions in the UK, the tropopause is about ten kilometres high, so that clouds don't go much above this height. But in equatorial regions, the tropopause can extend up to about eighteen kilometres. It is for this reason, that Cb clouds are much bigger in the tropics than in the British Isles and the rainfall and storms that accompany them here, can be truly stupendous.

When the upward movement ceases, the air has nowhere to go, so it spreads out horizontally, giving the tops of these clouds the appearance of an anvil head. The currents lifting the air upwards can reach astonishing speeds of over a hundred kilometres per hour, and anyone who has been in an aeroplane passing through turbulence, will know how scary that experience can be. When the uplift eventually ceases and the water droplets are released, the downpour can be pretty spectacular, especially if it is in the form of hail stones which, in the tropics, can be big enough to cause considerable damage to any cars left outside. It is because of the height of the tropopause, that tropical and equatorial weather is so much more impressive than in mid-latitude countries because the troposphere, where all weather takes place, is so much thicker there.

An impressive line of Cb clouds is on parade directly ahead of us and I am wondering when we will reach them and if we will manage to slip under them before they unleash their load. I don't have long to wait. We collide with the system very quickly. While I am on my way to the fo'c'sle, a wall of water hits me as if I have walked into a mechanical car wash. I beat a hasty retreat, but in the short time it takes me to get back inside, I am sodden and hasten to my cabin for a quick change before going to the bridge, where the Second Officer makes me a cup of coffee while singing *I Can't Get No Satisfaction* to a Rolling Stones CD. Here, we chat and listen to music, while I peer through the bridge windows as the windscreen wipers do battle with the lashing rain, and the by now turbulent sea, washes over the deck below. The turmoil outside contrasts amiably with the tranquillity inside. What a brilliant way to travel.

The day ends with a gale warning for the Western Area with winds expected to reach gale force eight, but with the usual proviso, the Captain reminds me, that they could be forty per cent greater than this.

"If we are lucky," he says, "we might miss it."

CHAPTER 12: Collision Course

I don't think the Chief Engineer likes us. Whenever any of us see him, we always give a greeting, but he never answers. Today, we meet almost eyeball to eyeball as I am coming out of my room and he is going into the laundry, the door to which is immediately opposite my cabin. It's great having washing machine and tumble drier so close. The machines are very quiet and whatever noise they make is completely inaudible from inside my cabin. I use the laundry maybe twice a week, and it is used by all the other passengers and officers. It's about a three-hour process to do a complete job, and at some time or other I have met every officer and passenger there. You have to be quick to seize a moment when one machine or the other is free, and my proximity gives me a clear advantage. The Chief Engineer and I were bound to meet at some time, and on this occasion, we couldn't miss each other. As I come out with an armful of clothes, he is on his way in, similarly laden. We nearly collide.

"Oh hello," I say, trying to be cheerful.

Nothing. Just a blank stare. He looks through me as if I am not there. I get the feeling he resents our very presence on board his ship. And he certainly does regard it as his ship. He wields enormous power, for the engine room is very much his domain and we are in his hands. On none of the occasions when our paths have crossed, have I been able to exchange one word with him. I have long and agreeable conversations with all the other officers, including the Second Engineer, but have not received a single word from the boss. I ask round, it seems to be a common experience.

His heavily jowled features and dejected look give him a hangdog appearance, which is accentuated by his rounded shoulders and slightly stooped demeanour. But beyond this picture he presents of himself, you will see a remarkably powerful physique, that of an ageing athlete, a champion boxer forever holding himself in check. I would never want to cross him and I suspect he is capable of great violence. It is not possible to evaluate his character from his eyes for I never see him look up, let alone look anyone in the eye. Whenever I catch sight of him walking along the ship's corridors, it's as if he is intently studying the deck floor in some desperate attempt to detect some underlying fault. If he sees me or any other passenger coming towards him, he immediately slinks into the first convenient doorway. Perhaps he is a deeply unhappy man, fighting some desperate inner battle. Maybe he just doesn't like people, a bit of a misanthropist.

Whatever the cause of his unhappiness, it's with a sense of relief that we greet the Captain's announcement that it is to be the Second Engineer who is to show us round the engine room. I imagine that if the Chief were asked to do it, he would simply refuse, and that the Captain, knowing his ways, always delegates this task to his second in command. On every other cargo ship I have been on, it has always been the Chief Engineer who has been proud to show us round his empire.

The sheer size of the engine astonishes me. On each of three decks, it occupies a floor space the size of a respectable school gymnasium. Going down into the ship's belly, is like entering a vast subterranean cathedral whose organ is blasting out rhythms that emanate from the bowels of the earth, with the base turned up to full volume. Monstrous roars of energy fill the air and we are grateful for the ear muffs. But these engines don't simply propel us through water; there are other engines to generate electricity, purify water, deal with waste and sewage, keep our air clean and maintain a comfortable temperature. We can hear little of what is said to us or of what we say to each other and I'm relieved when we are eventually invited into the abrupt silence of the control room to see the computer dials and monitoring systems that control all this energy and make it possible for twenty-seven people to live comfortably on board for several weeks.

As we come out of the engine room and retrace our steps along the main deck to the Poop Deck, I catch sight of the Chief Engineer standing in a doorway that we need to pass. He disappears inside like a frightened rabbit. I dislike the idea of not exercising the normal courtesies of exchanging greetings, but his surly attitude makes me inclined to give up on him and cease the struggle to communicate. Perhaps that is what he wants, to be ignored.

We are three weeks out from Europe and it is time for a party on the Poop Deck. This is the only place on the ship where there is some sort of open area, where all the crew can congregate. Measuring about twelve metres by thirty it is, even so, a rather confined space. For one thing, although open on three sides, there is an uncomfortably low roof consisting of forty-eight forty foot containers, each one weighing almost four tonnes and carrying twenty-five to thirty tonnes of consumer goods of one kind or another.[37] This means that there is somewhere between a thousand and fifteen hundred tonnes of loaded containers creaking and groaning above us. It's a daunting experience when you first walk under this lot, and although you soon get used to it, I can never quite escape the uneasy feeling of what would happen if one of the supporting pillars were to give way. Every conceivable space on these ships has to be given over to the main business of carrying containers, and we have to fit whatever social life we are able to improvise around this.

I'm curious to know what an (almost) all-male party in an all-male environment will be like. It's not the most promising venue for a party. The floor is littered with bollards, windlasses and winches. It's true, that the only movable objects, large coils of heavy rope, have been temporarily moved to the sides for the occasion, but even so, the place looks more like an obstacle course than a party room. And then there is the bulkhead. This houses the ventilation system's enormous exhaust fan from which recycled air is thrust with an almighty roar twenty-four hours a day, right into the middle of the very area where we are going to be partying. A few metres below us, the engines growl and on the other side of the transom stern, churning waters join in the thunderous chorus. A few men are optimistically setting up a karaoke system, but it's hard to imagine it will be heard over this deep-throated cacophony. They've set up a temporary table to hold this, using a pile of old pallets pushed up against the bulkhead.

On the other hand, it's an ideal setting for bunting, with lots of hooks and railings for tying loose ends. Two long trestle tables linked together to form an L-shape, complete the party arrangements; one, for the officers and passengers, is arranged parallel to the starboard railing and the other, for crew, is along the stern. I feel a little uneasy at this separation of officers and men, but it is how the ship works and there seems to be easy repartee between us all.

When the party eventually gets under way at about 18:00 hours, the full extent of the men's creativity is revealed. The bollards have served two purposes: they are superb as small side-tables to hold various salad dishes and the inexhaustible supply of sausages that the chef and his assistant, Francis, keep us supplied with. And they are ideal as impromptu mini-stages for the constant flow of karaoke singers, eager to strut their stuff. They are completely uninhibited, these men. Nothing represses them. As soon as one finishes singing, another jumps up onto any available bollard or table and performs with magnificent brio, pouring out their souls in wistful nostalgia. But they do not just stand there and sing. Dance and music are two sides of the same coin. They cannot help themselves but move their bodies to express the emotion of the words they sing. I am enthralled by the musical talent of these men. If they are representative of the Filipino nation as a whole, it must be a remarkably musical one.

Second Officer Ilao is sitting next to me, so I lean across and speak, hoping I can be heard above the competing sounds of karaoke, ventilation fan, engine and roaring water.

"Filipino men seem to have music in their souls."

"Oh, I can feel music everywhere," he says, "in the wind, in the waves, in people, in birds that sing. Everywhere."

The food is excellent, very meaty of course, but also with some exceptionally tasty salads, savoury rice dishes and sauces. Knowing my preference for fish, the chef has also prepared some succulent, barbecued red snapper. I am not so keen on the squid, which seems to be a favourite with the men but which I find rather like unflavoured chewing gum. Gary and Adriaan tuck into their sausages and steaks with evident delight, Janine with something approaching timidity, disappearing every twenty minutes or so for a smoke. Although I have no idea where she goes for this, I do know she is scrupulously careful to observe the prohibition on discarding cigarette ends over the side of the ship. She eats a painfully small meal and I wonder how she manages to get sufficient sustenance to keep her from withering away completely.

The barbecue fire itself is contained in a forty-five gallon oil drum with a quarter segment cut out. It is placed as far towards the end of the ship as it is possible to be, so that less than a metre separates it from the boiling foam of the ocean. The head chef, Eldefonso, and his assistant, Francis, stand one at each end, barbecue instruments in hand, proudly attired in white, awaiting our requests and enthusiastically turning out a continuous supply of well-barbecued steaks, sausages, baked potatoes and burgers. Behind them, our aquamarine wake, streaked with white, reaches to the horizon, closely followed by a trail of smoke from the barbecue that is sucked out behind them. Here, struggling to be heard above the roaring engine, seething sea and blaring karaoke, we shout our requests for sausage, steak or baked potato.

After a while, Gary and Adriaan leave the table and make for the flimsy-looking rail which is all that separates them from the spume being churned up by the mighty propellers immediately below. Each places a foot on the lower rung and there they lean, looking steadfastly to the far horizon, and lose themselves in conversation, returning to the table only to replenish their supply of beer. As they stand there, lost in a world of their own, the light gradually seeps out of the sky and the music becomes ever more wistful, men longing for their homes, wives, children, girlfriends, lovers. If you really want to understand how I feel, a young man croons, just cut open my heart and there you will see only your picture carved into it.

The lights are lit and the music and the merry-making continue. I sit and watch and listen as one crew member after another, officers and men, take the microphone and pour out their hearts, dispelling momentarily the loneliness of long months at sea. The emotions flow freely, and the expressions of joy, sadness and yearning in their voices and on their faces, speak to me more eloquently than any words possibly could of the real cost to them and to their families of this way of life. My mind recalls the Seamen's Mission in Hamburg and the importance of the service it offers to these men, practical support, the confidentiality of the confessional, a sense of connecting. We passengers have very little opportunity to mingle with these men, who are the real heroes of our global commodity trading system. The Captain is in jovial and expansive mood, but we see nothing of the Chief Engineer. He remains elusive, evasive even, a total enigma, lost in his own world of glum reality, hovering on the edges of this floating community of which he is an essential part but seems to be only a reluctant member.

I leave the table soon after midnight, in the middle of some soulful song about lost love and faithlessness. Past the bulkhead, the sound begins to fade away, and by the time I reach the top of the first flight of stairs, it has disappeared altogether. Here, the growling reverberations of the engine take over as I climb the remaining stairs and walk along the corridor to my cabin. Before retiring for the night, I go out onto my little private deck to lean over the railing for a few moments and let the silken warmth of the air wash over me, interfused with the distant strains of music.

I finish breakfast early the next morning and go immediately to the bridge just as Officer Koziol is coming off duty.

"Hi, have you had a good watch?"

"Something happened which I have never experienced before. We were on a collision course with the world."

"What!"

"You know, that big ship called "The World", which people live on, in their own apartments. They spend their whole lives just sailing round the world."

I've only vaguely heard of it, but apparently, it is a cruiser-sized yacht made up entirely of privately owned residential units that made its first voyage sometime in 2002. It's a kind of floating city, with every luxury the human imagination can dream up, endlessly cruising the world searching for experiences that will satisfy the restless spirits of those who have everything, and more, who have seen it all and done it all but still yearn for something different. On this ship, more or less the same size as our own, live 130 families, mainly from North America and Europe, the ultimate expression of exclusivity, an extreme version of the gated community, designed to keep out the rest of the world and enabling the mega-rich to meet, converse and socialise with themselves. Here you can see the world without ever leaving your home. It reminds me of a film I saw many years ago in which the elixir of eternal life had been discovered and people went on living for ever. In the end, the promise of eternal fun became a burden. They became so bored, so terminally weary, they were desperate to find a way to die, to relieve the utter tedium of a life that had become completely devoid of challenge and purpose. Ancient people, so old their bodies could scarcely contain them, clung to each other in joyless embrace and rhythmless dance, longing, but unable, to shuffle off their mortal coils.

"What happened?"

"International regulations for preventing collisions at sea state that when two ships are on a crossing course involving the risk of collision, the vessel which has the other on its starboard side, has to keep out of the way. The onus is on that ship to take action to avoid crossing ahead of the other vessel. So they had to give way to us. I like that, the idea of The World having to give way to us."

As he goes down to breakfast, I check our position. 90^0 19' south and 83^0 25' east, somewhere to the south-east of Diego Garcia and right in the middle of one of the deepest areas of the Indian Ocean, the Mid-Indian Basin. Here, there are about 5,500 m (just over 18,000 ft.) of water below us. We are sailing over a wonderful landscape, just as impressive as any mountainous scenery on land. This vast sub-marine basin lies between two great mountain ridges, the Chagos-Laccadive Ridge to the west and on the east, the Ninetyeast Ridge which, as its name suggests, lies almost entirely on the 90th meridian. The Ninetyeast stretches through roughly 30^0 of latitude and in length is about the same distance as from Cape York on the northernmost tip of Australia to Melbourne in the south. At the southern end, it is about 5,000 m high falling to 3,000 m in the north. It also marks the western limit of the West Australia Basin, parts of which are more than 6,300 m. deep. It's an impressive geography over which we are sailing.

CHAPTER 13: Two Hundred

Cigarettes

It's November 25th and shadow hunting day. Janine remains sceptical, but although she demanded proof, she declines to accompany us to see the evidence for herself. It is too far, the air will be disturbingly fresh, and in any case, the sea is rough. Gary, clutching the wine bottle that Janine has thoughtfully just emptied for us, accompanies me to the Monkey Deck.

Janine has a point about the weather. Two days earlier, we received a gale warning for the western area. Overnight, we had caught the edges of this. Now, with force six winds from the south-east and still on course for Fremantle, we are heading almost directly into it. It was a rocky night and there has been no let up throughout the morning. Janine felt queasy earlier and Gary was a bit off colour. As he and I poke our heads above the stairs and step onto the Monkey Deck, we are stopped in our tracks and forced to grab the nearest railing as the full force of the wind strikes us. Up there, it is gale force eight, with winds of over sixty kilometres per hour. With one hand holding onto a railing, Gary places the wine bottle on the deck floor. No shadow! Bingo! We report back to Janine and then check the instruments at the wheel house.

Our position just after noon, is fourteen degrees twenty-four minutes south, almost exactly where the overhead sun is. In fact, we are just twenty-eight minutes of a degree

(28/60ths) short of it, so my calculations were spot on! I think that's pretty good, so we report back to Janine, who greets the news indulgently.

"I think you deserve five hundred brownie points," she says.

The suspicion of a smile hovers over her lips and almost imperceptibly creases the edges of her thin cheeks. Her eyes display a momentary sparkle. It seems that my eccentric preoccupations amuse her. By way of celebration, or perhaps to hide embarrassment at this unusual display of jollity, she lights what must be, judging by the ends in the ash tray, her third cigarette since we left her here twenty minutes earlier. There is a hiss as Gary opens a can of beer, and I follow with a can of lager. Adriaan, already seated in the happy hour corner, puffs contentedly away.

We have left the doldrums and are heading directly into the south-east trades. Here on the open ocean, these winds can build up to considerable strength and persistence. Only twenty per cent of the southern hemisphere is land, compared with nearly forty per cent in the northern hemisphere. Land masses have an inhibiting and distorting effect on winds, and so they are more variable in the northern hemisphere than in the great oceans of the south. South of the Tropic of Capricorn, these unyielding south-east trades, give way to the 'roaring forties', and in the Southern Ocean, they merge into the 'furious fifties' and then the 'screaming sixties'. At school, our geography teacher got us to draw diagrams to show what the global pattern of winds would be like if there were no land at all, with the westerlies and easterlies all blowing in perfectly synchronised formation, without the inconvenience of land to upset the choreography. You get closer to that ideal pattern of global winds in the southern oceans than anywhere else on earth, where land is rare and sea abundant. This is the domain of wind, this is where Æolus really holds sway and we are about to enter his territory. These are the winds my great grandfather, Captain William Royan, made full use of to get his barque, the Kilmeny, from the Cape of Good Hope to this point on his way to New Zealand in March 1882. It took him three months of continuous sailing to get here from London; we have taken just under four weeks, including four intermediate ports of call.

The following morning, a slight feeling of concern mingled with curiosity and perhaps even excitement, runs through our small party when the Captain tells us he has received a warning, which has been sent out to "all ships in passage in East Africa, the Indian sub-continent and South East Asian waters", emphasising the risks of piracy and giving news of recent piratical activity in the area. In Somalia, heavily armed pirates have been attacking ships further away from the coast and all ships have been advised to keep at least two hundred nautical miles from the coast. As we had experienced, this was quite difficult to achieve north of Socotra in a passage which itself is little more than two hundred land miles wide. In the Dar es Salaam area, there have been nineteen piratical incidents since the previous June, and in the Arabian Sea on 12th November, a reefer had reported a small boat approaching to within a third of a nautical mile. The alarm was raised, lights were switched on and the vessel moved away. This brings home to us in a way that didn't quite touch us earlier, how important those extra lights were that had been hung over the side of our ship while we were passing through the Arabian Sea. On 11th November, robbers with knives boarded a general cargo ship at berth in Phu My Port, Vietnam, and the ship's stores were stolen. On 19th November, pirates approached a chemical tanker off Mangkai Island, Indonesia, but were deterred by the alarm and lights.

"I think we are out of the main area as regards the Indian Ocean," says the Officer of the Watch, "and we are not going near South East Asia this time, so we are probably all right."

At lunch, Gary dismisses the threat with a shrug.

"We're well out of danger," he says. "They won't trouble us here."

We all agree, Janine with evident satisfaction and reassurance, but we have a slight feeling of regret, of having missed some excitement. It's an ancient childhood feeling, like when we used to play cops and robbers with the youth club in Reigate Priory grounds. I never wanted it to stop. It was safe, dangerous fun, which in adult life has morphed into wanting to go to the edge and peer over. So here is that old familiar feeling of huge relief tinged with disappointment. I am puzzled by my reaction. I know this is not a game. These incidents are serious, life and death situations. But a small sense of lingering curiosity in me needs to see the kind of human beings who can commit such outrages.

Cooks are sensitive creatures who need to be loved and appreciated, their creations praised. We rarely see Cook, but occasionally catch a fleeting glimpse of him through the momentarily open door when Francis brings us our food. At all other times, that door is kept firmly closed. The galley is Cook's domain, and his alone. What little sight of him we do get, suggests he is always under immense pressure as he struggles to satisfy the tastes of passengers and officers on one side and the crew, who demand a completely different menu, on the other. It occurs to me, that the crew's menu is much more attractive, with its emphasis on spicy South-East Asian dishes. Nevertheless, our European food is good, the menu wholesome and well balanced, with plenty of soups, meat, fish, vegetables, salads, fresh fruit, cheese, and followed invariably by a substantial cooked pudding. It is not haute cuisine, but it is very acceptable.

My problem, however, is that there are too many cooked meals in the day, simply too much food! Each meal arrives plated, so we don't get to choose how much we want. This inevitably means there are leftovers, sometimes quite a lot. This clearly pains both Francis and in particular Cook, who interprets it as a sign that we disapprove of his cooking. But there's another thing. I like to make sandwiches at lunch time. There is always a selection of excellent breads, cold meats, cheeses, salads, pickles, and a good supply of fresh fruit on the table, in addition to all the cooked courses, and this delightful stuff is nearly always removed untouched at the end of the meal because no one has any room for it. So on this occasion, I decide to make myself a sandwich – strong cheddar cheese, tomatoes, green salad, a slice of ham, a drizzle of salad cream. At last, a blissfully simple lunch.

Francis however is puzzled by this. Such strange culinary behaviour bemuses him, and he thinks it is because I do not like what Cook has prepared.

"What will you have after that?" he asks.

"Nothing, thanks Francis. This is fine. This is enough for me."

"Don't you like what Cook prepares"?

"I love it, but I also love sandwiches at lunchtime."

"But you must have something cooked as well."

"No thanks Francis. This will do me fine."

He goes to report on my strange behaviour to Cook. Cook comes out and wants to know that the problem is.

"Don't you like my food?" he beseeches me.

"Cook, I love your food," I tell him. "It is superb. It is so good, so rich, that I cannot eat two lots of it in one day. I particularly love your bread. At lunch time, I like a sandwich, with your delicious bread. I've never tasted bread like it. It is superb. If I don't eat your bread at lunch time when will I ever get to taste it?"

Cook smiles a contented smile, thanks me profusely and returns to his domain, a happy and contented man.

"Smarmy sod," chuckles Gary.

My fellow passengers, however, are not happy. Gary and Janine, and now Adriaan too, have renewed worries about the slop chest. In a few days, we will be arriving at Fremantle and they are giving a lot of thought about replenishing their supplies. The issue, once more, is red wine. Will they be able to get enough there to see them through to Sydney? They decide to quiz long-suffering Francis yet again. When will they be able to place their next order? When will the slop chest next be open?

The Captain had been very specific; the slop chest will open on a Friday, but only then if we are clear of territorial waters. Francis looks agitated. He is caught between the system and their incessant demands on him. He doesn't know how to respond and is flustered. Reluctantly and, I suspect, against his better judgement, he agrees to make special arrangements to open the chest early for them and to allow them to place their orders earlier than usual. He therefore puts their order forms on a side table near the Mess door. It's only Monday so this is highly unusual.

Fired up with enthusiasm, all three have a quick consultation and decide they should go to their cabins and count how many bottles of red wine and packets of cigarettes they have between them so that they can calculate how much of each they need to order. This takes them some time and they forget to tell Francis what they are doing. By now, it is well after 12.30 and Francis' lunchtime duties are officially over. So, thinking they have left the table completely and have changed their minds, he clears everything away, including the requisition form.

The sound of jolly banter in the corridor heralds the return of the trio, evidently pleased with their calculations. On their way in, they pass Francis, laden with bucket and broom, ready to commence his cleaning duties. Pausing at the table by the door, they look for the slop chest order forms. Here their jollity stops abruptly. The forms are no longer there.

"What the hell's happened, Clive?" asks Gary.

"You took so long, Francis thought you'd changed your mind," I said. "So did I."

"Francis had no right to assume that," said Gary and went to the bottom of the stairs.

"Francis, Francis," he shouts, "come back, come back here."

The clang of the bucket as he puts it down resonates along the corridor and we hear the shuffle of his steps as he approaches. In he comes, clearly distressed, red-faced, eyes filling up. I do not want to see this. I go upstairs to the Recreation Lounge to look through the collection of DVDs to select a film to watch this evening. A few minutes later, the others follow and, in subdued mood, we look through them to make our choices. As we huddle over the collection, Janine speaks quietly, to me only I think, but maybe to us all.

"Did you notice that Francis was crying?"

"Yes, I know."

"It was quite reasonable for us to call him back," says Gary.

"He shouldn't have taken the form away," adds Adriaan.

"We don't have to feel bad about it. We had an arrangement. He should have kept to it."

I am angry with them and find it hard not to get involved.

Morning, and I make my customary visit to the bridge immediately after breakfast. Our position at 09:30 is 22^0 54' S and 102^0 09' E, on the south-east edge of the West Australia Basin. We will soon be crossing the southern tropic. Speed remains at a steady twenty knots and we are scheduled to arrive in Fremantle in two days. The south-east trades continue to run straight into us. I check our position at 14:00 hours: we are 23^0 55' south. We have just crossed the Tropic of Capricorn.

Up on F Deck, the trio are huddled together in animated discussion. There is only one topic that binds them together in such angst-laden fellowship, so with a brief greeting, I quickly pass by on my way to the Monkey Deck above them. On this occasion, however, as I am soon to discover, their dismal deliberations actually concern me. In their desperate endeavours to ensure they have all the cigarettes they need to get them through to Sydney, they have overlooked the fact that we will be entering Australian territory long before then, first at Fremantle and then at Melbourne, and that they will be subject to Australian custom rules whilst in territorial waters. They now realise they will arrive at Fremantle with more than their permitted allowance. Even with their voracious appetites for nicotine, they have little chance of using up the surplus in the two days it will take us to get there. This has created a problem for the Captain, who has to make a detailed report about everyone's dutiable possessions. Whether we intend going ashore or not, we each have to complete a signed declaration by the time we enter Australian waters to the effect that we do not carry more than the permitted amount.

"The problem is," says Gary, "that as well as all the stuff we brought on board with us at Tilbury, we ordered enough cigarettes at La Spezia to see us through to Sydney. Forgot about Fremantle and Melbourne. It's stupid, we'll have smoked them by the time we get to Sydney," he adds despairingly. "Dunno what we're gonna do."

That means Gary and Janine envisage getting through six hundred cigarettes in the next ten days, but I can't quite work out if that is each or between them. I suspect it means 600 each; I think they are 60-a-day people. Meanwhile, as the Captain patiently explains, this is Australia and we have to play it by Australian rules. The problem is soon solved for them, however. At dinner the Captain announces his solution.

"As you are over your limit," he says to Gary and Janine, "you can transfer some of your surplus to Mr Robert here, who doesn't have any."

Great, don't bother consulting me. What on earth am I going to do with all those cigarettes? The nearest I ever got to smoking a cigarette was when my brother and I had rolled up a piece of brown paper into the shape of a cigarette and set it alight using a magnifying glass to focus the sun's rays on it and then smoking it. Our pathetic attempts to disguise our uncontrollable coughing and spluttering caught Father's attention, and his reprimand when he found us was quite unnecessary. That was enough to persuade me never to do it again. Now, however, I find myself the very reluctant and hopefully very temporary owner of a huge cache of noxious weeds. I don't even like the smell of it.

"Ah thanks, Captain," says Gary.

This is the thing. He thanks the Captain. Not me, not Mr Robert himself. I am the one compromising the principles of a lifetime to accommodate their craving. Furthermore, I have spent a month trying to avoid their toxic fumes, something of which they have been totally unaware. Now I have been volunteered for this arrangement without any consultation, and Gary thanks the Captain! Just as I am about to lose all faith in human nature, Janine leans across the table and touches my arm.

"Is that all right with you, Clive?"

"Yes Janine," I tell her, "of course it is."

"Thank you. But why did he call you Mr Robert?"

"Oh that's my first name. He thinks it's my surname. All official forms get it wrong. Everyone assumes that you are called by your first name."

Gary, acting for all the world as if a crushing burden has been removed from his shoulders, rushes upstairs and comes hurtling back with ten packs of twenty and I return to my cabin feeling as if I am carrying illicit plunder. I am surprised by how seductive the packaging is. It's like a gift, chocolates maybe, or cream biscuits, a nice treat in front of a cosy fire watching the box on a wintry evening. It rustles with promise as I cast around for somewhere to put it. One thought, however, does amuse me. For twenty-four hours, I am to be the reluctant owner of all those cigarettes. They are mine to do with as I please. Lose them? Throw them overboard? It's a pleasing thought as I shove them in the bottom of the wardrobe.

CHAPTER 14: Cappuccino Strip

The excitement is tangible. When the only land you have seen for a month is from the deck of a ship, the prospect of going ashore and doing ordinary things such as window shopping or buying a paper and reading it over a coffee, is a big deal.

As we approach the great continental land mass of Australia, it draws the south-east trades round to a more southerly direction, and now, on the eve of our arrival at Fremantle, they have veered to almost due south and, at force four, strike us on our starboard bow, enough to make it feel cool, despite a temperature of 23 C.

I am looking forward to a day entirely on my own, moseying along the streets of a city I have not visited before and soaking up the hustle and bustle of normal life. But then, Adriaan asks if he can accompany me for the day. I feel a sudden deadening of my enthusiasm, but it would be churlish to refuse.

"Sure, but there are a few things I need to do on my own, phoning home, emails, and I'd like to find a vegetarian restaurant for lunch."

"That's all okay with me."

Situated between thirty and thirty-five degrees south, this south-west corner of Australia has a Mediterranean climate. It shares this happy distinction with other parts of the world that are similarly situated. To qualify for such a climate, these places have to be on the west coast of a continental landmass and lie between thirty and forty-five degrees north or south of the equator. Other places that enjoy this most agreeable climatic type are the west coast of California, Central Chile, the Cape Town region of South Africa, and a small region of south-east South Australia surrounding Adelaide and facing west across the Great Australian Bight. And, of course, there is the eponymous Mediterranean region itself. All these regions have wet winters and dry summers, with annual temperatures ranging between about 10 C in winter and 30 C in summer. So it never gets really cold and rarely too hot. We arrive at Fremantle on a glorious spring day, beautifully warm, but not uncomfortably so, with a bright cloudless sky and a gentle breeze. Perfect.

We berth at North Quay. It's not good to walk through container ports, even if it were allowed. There's a minibus waiting to take us to Rudderham Drive, from where we pick up the port shuttle bus for the town centre. It's on the south side of the Swan estuary, a ride of about ten minutes. For a moment I'm tempted to get a bus to nearby Perth, which I briefly visited a few years ago and for which Fremantle is the port. It was at the end of a three-day trans-continental train journey from Sydney, and I had arranged to meet an old college friend and look around before getting the flight back to the UK. I'd have liked to see more of the city, especially if, as I expected, Fremantle, being a port city, wouldn't have much to offer.

To my surprise and delight however, downtown Fremantle turns out to be charming. The shuttle bus drops us in the historic centre on the south side of Fremantle Harbour, near a compact and pleasantly pedestrianized zone with a good variety of shops and an aptly named Cappuccino Strip on South Terrace. Adriaan and I agree to meet an hour and a half later, at the telephone kiosk in the heart of the Mall's pedestrian zone. What I feel is nothing short of euphoria, on my own on a beautifully warm day and with nothing else to do than enjoy the bustle of normal life around me. Normality feels strange, simply walking through the town and mingling with others doing exactly the same thing, the kind of very ordinary activity that I do every day at home. But now the ordinary has suddenly become extraordinary.

I buy a phone card and a copy of *The Australian*, put a few coins in a Salvation Army collecting box and ask the lady holding it if she knows where there might be a vegetarian restaurant. She gets onto her mobile phone and asks a friend. Between them they come up with The Istanbul on Essex Street. The Town Hall Information Centre on William Street provides me with a street map. Back at Cappuccino Strip, I study this over a decaff and have a leisurely read of the paper. How can such ordinary, normal things provide so much exquisite pleasure? Adriaan reappears and we set off together for The Istanbul. It's a Turkish restaurant, but with an excellent choice of vegetarian dishes. I opt for mushroom falafel, tabbouleh and rice and linger long over it. Adriaan has a mild chicken curry and whisks through it as if he hasn't eaten for a day.

We decide to have coffee outside, but I should have remembered that this is where smokers congregate, now that they are forbidden to smoke inside. It was a bad move. At one time, one of the most pleasing of all things to do in Australia was to eat or drink on the pavement under a shady awning, lazily watching the world go by. Now that smoking has been banned inside restaurants, the nicotine community have commandeered the glorious outside of even the most delightful of eating places, effectively closing such areas off to non-smokers. It is one of the most infuriating examples of the law of unintended consequences. I realise it has been a serious mistake as soon as we sit down and Adriaan reaches into his pocket for his lighter. But it is too late to go back inside. Our table has been cleared and new clients seated.

Back at the Mall and on my own again, I enjoy a twenty minute conversation with Joan using my $5 phone card, hugely cheaper than if I had used my mobile. She is busy making arrangements to go to Switzerland to stay with son, daughter-in-law and two grandchildren for a short while before they all fly to Brisbane together where we plan to rendezvous for Christmas.

Mid-afternoon and time for another decaff. On our way to Cappuccino Strip, we meet Janine and Gary. There's a look of desperation on Janine's face.

"Have you seen a pub?" she begs. "I must get a glass of wine, red wine."

"Sorry Janine, I don't think I'd recognise a pub here in Oz if I saw one. Wouldn't you just like to join us for a coffee?"

"Well," she says with a shrug of resignation, "I suppose it's better than nothing. What kind of place is this without a pub?"

"Look, see if you can hold out till we get back on the ship soon. Meanwhile, let's all enjoy a coffee."

The first rule when exploring an unknown place is to always look behind you and know your way back. Always work out your return strategy. We didn't do that and relied only on the shuttle bus to get us here. Foolishly, we decide to take a taxi back to the Alexandra Rickmers. Big mistake. We should have waited for the shuttle bus, which would have known the way. Once inside the port complex, the taxi driver doesn't know his way and we have not been sufficiently alert to watch the route he is taking. Something close to panic sets in as we approach five o'clock and we realise we are cutting it a bit short. The ship will not wait. We know that. We drive past endless lines of ten foot high metal railings, but don't know what to look for. We don't remember anything. Everything looks the same; there are no differentiating landmarks. All we have is the name of the ship. The occasional gateway opens onto a quayside alongside of which is any ship but ours. We backtrack and look again, asking with desperation whenever we see anyone, if they know where the Alexandra Rickmers is. But they've never heard of it. Turning round yet again, we try once more. Suddenly Gary recognises an opening that looks familiar. We turn into it and proceed to the control point. There we are met by the smiling look of recognition of the two men on duty, and beyond us, we see the familiar and welcome sight of the Alexandra Rickmers. We breathe easily once more. Mental note: on your way out always plot your way back.

Over dinner, the Captain warns us that we are in for a rocky ride over the next twenty-four hours. I wake up early but need to steady myself as I get up and shower. On the way up to the bridge, I cling to the rails and once there, look out onto a sea that is in great turmoil, with a swell of four or five metres. Paradoxically, the ship's instruments only record a strong breeze, markedly weaker than the wild seas suggest it should be. We are catching the effects of seriously bad weather elsewhere.

By early afternoon, the wind has strengthened to a near gale, but as it is a following wind, it feels like zero. The air is unnaturally still, the sea increasingly turbulent. It doesn't make sense. There's no apparent cause and effect relationship. It's easy to see how, in more superstitious days, this might have been seen as the work of some demonic force, entirely unconnected with anything to do with the natural world, just as Coleridge's ancient mariner had done.

Early afternoon and we round Cape Leeuwin. This marks the point where the Indian Ocean merges into the Southern Ocean, that huge uninterrupted expanse of water encircling Antarctica and sweeping the southern coasts of Australia. There is a lighthouse here, on the most south-westerly tip of Australia, making this, one of the most dangerous shipping lanes on the planet, easier to navigate.

Late afternoon and the First Officer takes us on a tour of the inner chambers of the bow. The men have been looking forward to this, but for Janine it's all a bit too much, so she opts out. Down we go, three, four flights of stairs taking us deep into the belly of the ship, steadying ourselves against her wild contortions. Walls, ceilings, floors are painted a uniform utilitarian grey, but the stair railings, banisters, and uprights are clearly picked out in brilliant white. It is surprisingly clean and tidy down here. I had imagined that it would simply be the place where the anchor is dumped in an unruly heap, wet, slimy and rusting. In fact, it's clean, dry and neatly stored in a separate compartment. The orderliness that is necessary throughout the upper part of the ship, especially the living and working areas, is maintained here also, out of sight but not out of mind.

The size of the anchor chain impresses me. Each section, separated by shackles, is 27.5 m long and weighs between three and four tonnes. There are thirteen such sections in each of the two anchor chains, making each chain 390 m long, almost a quarter of a mile. This is a truly massive pile of iron, lying there in an orderly heap, ready to be released for its smooth tumble out of the hawespipe. Close by are the bow thrusters.

The skin of the ship seems remarkably fragile here. The only thing to separate us from the immense power of the ocean is a thin sheet of steel, hardly enough, it seems, to hold the ship's massive load and to protect us all from the mighty power of the water we can hear battering us on the other side. The beams and joists form the essential rigid structure to which the outer skin is attached. At one time, the First Officer tells us, these beams used to be closer together, resulting in a stronger ship that was more resistant to the brutal pounding of the oceans. But then along came the accountants, who pointed out that money could be saved by spacing the joists just a little further apart. It seemed a good idea. Anything to cut costs and make us all more competitive. But then we are shown a large buckle in this same skin, as if some giant fist has pounded it ruthlessly. It was caused by a particularly high sea which the frame was not tough enough to completely withstand.

Four o'clock and we are just finishing our usual game of table tennis. We are rolling and pitching but seem to have lost momentum. The engines are remarkably quiet.

"It looks as if we have stopped," says Gary, looking out of the porthole.

Rushing outside to look over the edge, we see that there's no doubt about it. On the bridge, the Captain and Second Officer are conferring, just as Number One is about to take over the watch. There's a problem with the fuel injection system. Apparently, we picked up some inferior fuel at La Spezia and as a result, the filters have had to be changed every hour ever since. This time, however, it looks more serious than a filter change. The sea anchors have been deployed, but they only serve to keep the ship steady, not to fix its position. Unable to resist the pull of the cold Circumpolar Current, we are gradually being taken off course.

And then the whole ship shudders as the engineers try to restart the engines. They spring into life momentarily, but then splutter and die once more. Ten minutes and the ship shakes again, and once again they fizzle out. It's like a giant beast in its death throes.

The stillness is unnerving. The occasional clang of metal on metal cuts through the silence as engineers struggle to get us going. We are adrift at the mercy of the ocean, vulnerable, tossed hither and thither. Without power, we will soon be running out of fresh water; for the ship to supply all our needs depends on the ability of the engines to purify and recycle what we use every day. And should the problem last into the night, we will have no lighting. A shiver of alarm. Another judder and another false hope. More silence, more clangs. A few minutes later, another shudder, but it lingers and the tone changes. We wait for it to expire once more, but it picks up its old familiar growl. The water begins to part and our familiar friend, the wake, takes up where it left off.

Early evening finds us passing the old whaling station of Albany on our port side and, thrusting away from it, the promontory of Bald Head at the southern extremity of the Torndirrup National Park. It's a dramatic coastline along this part of Western Australia, much of it national park land. We are at the western reaches of the Great Australian Bight, across which we will make our way over the next three days to Melbourne, where this stage of my journey will be ending. During our evening meal, the wind suddenly drops away to almost zero. The white horses have vanished, but there is still a considerable swell which is likely to continue for the next twenty-four hours. The days are getting longer as we enter these higher latitudes and it is delightful to have an hour or two of sunshine after we have finished our meal, time for a stroll to the prow or the Monkey Deck, my two favourite spots.

Nine o'clock the next morning and we are two hundred kilometres south of Cape Arid, heading almost directly east and making nineteen knots. The instruments tell us there is a strong breeze from the north-west, but on the bridge, it is only a whisper, ideal for walking. There's a ship on the starboard horizon. Cutting short my walk at ten laps, I head for the bridge with my binoculars. The Second Officer looks it up on the Automatic Identification System, it's a class A bulk carrier, the 'Innovator', bound for Rotterdam. A South Korean ship, it's considerably bigger than ours: draught, seventeen metres, compared with our paltry nine; length, two hundred and sixty-nine metres, compared with our one nine five. We continue to make excellent speed under very favourable conditions. With the air uncannily still, we continue to be on the receiving end of much fiercer weather elsewhere. Janine is seasick.

Over our evening meal, conversation turns to Australia and plans for onward travel. Gary and Janine are disembarking at Sydney, where they will hire a car and drive home to Adelaide via the Great Ocean Road and the Twelve Apostles. I will hire a car at Melbourne and drive north to Queensland, visiting friends en route. The Ghan has recently been extended from Alice Springs to the Top End. This is one long train journey that is still unticked on my bucket list. Gary often flies to Darwin on business. He's semi-retired and has time on his hands.

"Have you ever thought of going to Darwin on The Ghan?" I ask.

"Oh no," interjects Janine, "I think I'd find it all a bit boring".

"God, I'd love it. It's one of the great railway journeys I have yet to do. A few years ago, Joan and I went from Sydney to Perth on the Indian Pacific. It was fantastic. We loved being able to get off at various stops on the way and explore. On another train journey from Adelaide to Sydney, we stopped off at Broken Hill and stayed at the YHA on Argent Street.

Everything about the place was so different from anything we were used to."

"But there's nothing there," said Janine.

Gary had to agree at that point.

"Yeah, I have to admit it," he said, "the place was empty. When we went there to get the train, we looked for a pub in the morning but couldn't find one open, so we looked for the casino. And would you believe it? That was closed too! I tell you, there's nothing to do there."

Broken Hill is reeking with history, positively groaning with it. Even the street names yell out its past everywhere you go – Gypsum Street, Mercury Street, Bromide Street, Argent Street, Beryl Street, Silver City Highway, Cobalt Street. I should say fifty per cent of the streets we saw had names reflecting the town's mining heritage. History shouts at you from every street corner, particularly the town's role in the history of the trade union movement and its relationship with the Australian Labour Party.

Janine had a friend who had just lost her husband. She was beside herself with grief and didn't know what to do. Janine invited her to come and stay.

"I said to her, come on, we'll go to the casino and allow ourselves $50 a day and play the pokies. We did that every day for a whole week. That really took her out of herself. It was the kindest thing I could do."

I have seen people going to play the pokies, or slot machines, with their bags of coins. They spend hours there, sometimes all day, and if they run short of coins, there's always an ATM nearby to renew their supply. Sometimes you can see a punter play more than one machine at the same time, transfixed by the flashing lights, the sound of clinking and the lure of the occasional cascade of coins. Many of these machines are to be found in sports clubs, which act as social centres throughout Australia. They generate a lot of money for clubs and for state revenues.

"Yeah, we like the casino," says Gary. "There's one at the local jockey club, where we're members."

"Do you go often?"

"No, not really. Only about once or twice a month."

I go up to the bridge after the meal just as the First Officer is finishing his watch.

"We are due in at Waypoint 197 at about 11:45 on Monday," he says. "That's where we pick up the Melbourne Pilot."

CHAPTER 15: The Big Island

Today is Sunday and it's cooler, with an afternoon temperature of 18 C. The wind is down to a light breeze. Melbourne approaches. Smart clothes will be needed. It's a busy day with the washing machine. Over the evening meal, Janine, Gary and Adriaan invite me to join them for a farewell glass of red wine. There's a card for me at the table, from Janine. "Sorry you're leaving us. We've really enjoyed your company. Come and stay with us any time you like." It's been a long journey. We have learned to accommodate each other's foibles. Affection grows in the most unlikely circumstances.

After breakfast the next morning, I go to my usual place on the bridge, wanting to capture every moment of our approach and of this part of the ship that has meant so much to me in the past few weeks. We're hugging the coast of Victoria, making our way past Cape Otway and Franklin Point, leaving the Great Australian Bight and entering the Bass Strait as we head for Port Phillip Bay. Three hours later and we have lined ourselves up to negotiate the hazardous entrance to the bay via a notoriously dangerous triangle of water known as The Rip. To get to Port Phillip Bay and through that to the Port of Melbourne, all sea-going craft, large and small, must pass through The Heads. Its name derives from three prominent features –Point Lonsdale and Shortlands Bluff on the Bellarine Peninsula, and on the other side, Point Nepean, on the tip of the Mornington Peninsula. These two peninsulas swing round so as to almost completely enclose Port Phillip Bay to the south, leaving just sufficient gap for ships to pass through. Two rocky reefs, Lonsdale Rock and Corsair Rock, make the gap even smaller, but a lighthouse at Point Lonsdale warns of the dangers ahead. The seabed is rocky here and the waters turbulent on account of the powerful tidal currents generated by huge volumes of water pouring into and out of the bay through this restricted channel. It is the lethal nature of these currents that give this area of water its name. The movement of water in rip currents can reach speeds of two metres a second and they are a major cause of fatalities among surfers in Australia, accounting for about eighty deaths a year.[38]

The pilot's launch comes alongside. It is a hazardous business getting the pilot on board. The rope ladder is thrown out as his tough but small craft draws up against our enormous bulk and he hauls himself thirty feet up to the Main Deck. This is hard enough in the calmest of seas, but in rough weather it can be treacherous. His launch has to be kept from smashing into our side while at the same time he has to transfer his footing to the first rung of a ladder that swings wildly. Once on the bridge, he is in charge, not the Captain, as we make our way through these difficult local waters.

When we are through the Heads, we change direction to south-east, away from Melbourne and I wonder what's going on. Officer Ilao explains that we have to make an S-shaped approach because of the configuration of the navigable channel. A series of closely spaced buoys marks our route, green for the starboard side, red for port. Even from forty-five kilometres (twenty-eight miles) away, we can see the city's skyscrapers. Port Phillip Bay is like a small inland sea, seventy-five kilometres from north to south and sixty-five from east to west.

Flags are hoisted to give the port authorities basic information about our ship, the Australian national flag, the green, red and white of the Rickmers flag, a yellow one to show that we are under quarantine, and a red one to show that we're carrying a dangerous cargo. None of us is able to discover what this might be but there is talk of the possibility of something radioactive.

We draw alongside at West Swanson Dock at 16:00 hours. Twenty minutes later, I receive a call on my cabin phone asking me to go to the Conference Room to meet the first lot of customs officials. There are two of them and they want to know if I have any items with me that might pose an environmental threat. I light-heartedly declare a packet of tea, one of two I brought on board at Tilbury, not thinking for a moment that they would take me seriously. It's a cliché that only the English know how to make tea, but of course, it is also true. These are like gold dust to me. I used one packet on the outward journey and have one left for the return. This has remained unopened and is still in its cellophane wrapping.

"We'll have to take that," says one of them.

"But this can't, surely, be a threat to anyone," I plead. "Look, it's air tight. Brand new. Unused. Firmly sealed."

But it doesn't soften their hearts and with unsmiling faces, they confiscate it. Once opened, it might unleash God knows what destruction on the sensitive Australian ecosystem. But what are they going to do with it? Put it on a landfill site? Burn it? Make tea with it? At least when I open it, I'll be in the middle of the Tasman Sea! But they have never forgiven us for the rabbits. They're right, of course, the environment is sensitive, "exceptionally fragile", in Jared Diamond's words, and "the most unproductive continent".[39] They have reason to be cautious. But over a new packet of unopened tea?

In the Mess, there's a small gathering of passengers and officers with glasses already filled waiting to bid me farewell and bon voyage. Janine, however, finds it all too much. She begins to cry, kisses me goodbye and then takes herself upstairs to continue her crossword puzzle until all the excitement has died down. Gary and Adriaan, slightly embarrassed by such gushing, linger to see me off and several of the officers and men also come to shake my hand. I am touched by it all. The euphoria of beginning a new phase of travel is tinged with the inevitable sadness of farewells to temporary friendships. They start and finish on board. I've been with them for 10,738 nautical miles, or 19,887 kilometres, and thirty-four days.

My friend Ken meets me at the port gates at 17:40 and whisks me east along Footscray Road, into Flinders Street and then onto the South Eastern Freeway. I find it difficult adjusting to the speed. This and the noise of the traffic assault my senses. No sooner have I seen something interesting than it is gone. There's no chance of taking in any detail, it's just fleeting impressions. We are heading for Endeavour Hills on the south-eastern edge of Melbourne, Australia's fastest growing city. You can see it in the mushrooming houses. Ten years earlier, when I first got to know Ken and Anita, their house had been surrounded by open spaces as far as the eye could see. Now it is just one among thousands, remarkable only for their uniformity.

Young families have been pouring into Melbourne for a decade or more, and when they get there, they find themselves rootless and in need of a sense of community. In such circumstances, people look for something to belong to, a set of truths and values to hold on to. It is fertile soil for fundamentalist churches to flourish. People caught up in a vortex of rapid change seek certainty, and strong religion offers this. Although throughout most of the western world, church attendance continues its remorseless decline, Pentecostal-type churches are an exception. Offering unambiguous truths and a ready-made community, these fundamentalist, literalist forms of religion are experiencing rapid growth. Their churches are often very big indeed.

On Sunday, I am taken to one such mega-church in the midst of Melbourne's housing mushroom. Waverley Christian Fellowship is unlike any other church I have ever been in. The music hits me long before I enter the doors. In the reception area, a team of half a dozen smiling faces and outstretched hands are poised, ready to welcome me. Inside, row upon row of soft velvet blue, comfortably upholstered chairs, reach to the far end of an impossibly large auditorium and form an arc around a massive stage. This holds the band – three pianos, half a dozen guitars, a full set of percussion instruments, several flutes, a couple of clarinets. Soft, tranquil, emotionally charged gospel music is playing. There are a thousand people in the congregation. Two more such services will be held in quick succession that morning, with a thousand at each. As the service proceeds, those who are too far away to see what is going on, can get the detail from two giant television screens strategically placed near the far ends of the auditorium. When the preacher gets up to deliver his sermon, you can catch every nuance of his impassioned face from these same screens.

The theme is outreach, preparing the assembled believers to take the truth to those who haven't yet heard the good news and to deliver those who belong to other faith traditions from error. A series of dramatic enactments takes place, with appropriate costumes, to demonstrate the absurdity of other religions. It begins with Buddhism. "Buddhists believe you must be born again," a young man dressed in an orange robe declares. There is a suitable pause for the words to sink in, for Christians too believe in being born again and the pronouncement is greeted with a suspicion of respect. "And again" the actor continues, and this time a ripple of laughter goes through the auditorium. Then we have the punch line. "And again, and again," the young man declares triumphantly. Then a torrent of laughter thunders through the hall. Having demonstrated the absurdity of Buddhism, we move on to Islam, Hinduism, Jainism. Each one is shown to be ridiculous and in error. There will be training courses during the coming months to prepare volunteers for missionary service, to take the true truth to those who do not yet possess it.

The next day, I hire a car and set off, meandering slowly through Victoria and New South Wales. Jacaranda trees are in full bloom and line the centres of small town Australia. Through the rolling green grasslands of The Riverine, my route takes me over the Murrumbidgee River and on past Gundagai, the western gateway to the Snowy Mountains and Mount Kosciusko National Park. The Great Dividing Range separates the coastal regions of eastern Australia from the high Tablelands. I like these inland plateau areas. The land here is vast and so also are the skies. It reminds me of Central

Africa and the gently undulating savannas. But most Australians do not live here. If only, Bruce Chatwin, suggests, it had been people from Eastern Europe who were used to wide horizons and knew how to cope with them, who had settled Australia[40]. They would have known how to love the land and make it truly theirs. Whereas in fact it was colonised by island people who didn't choose to go there, were not used to and never understood the wide spaces and large skies, may even have been afraid of them, and so confined themselves to the narrow coastal region on the east of the continent, as if to disown the rest of this huge and intriguing land, as if to demonstrate they did not belong to it. I am not sure that the same is true of the Tasmanians, however.

The inhabitants of this island state see themselves as the real Australians. They inhabit their island more fully and lovingly than their northern neighbour. What the rest of the world thinks of as the real Australia, they refer to as The Big Island. There is some justification for this view of things; for unlike Tasmania, the big continent of mainland Australia is not really fully inhabited by the people who call themselves Australians and it is only recently that the Australian people have woken up to the fact that they are part of Oceania and the Pacific Rim countries and that it's here where their destiny lies. It's as if they have wanted to be part of Europe rather than of the Far East, and this may be because they did not voluntarily seek out this continental island and enthusiastically colonise it as the European migrants to America did. They must surely have resented being here, and it would be unsurprising if they did not consider Britain as their real home.

The people of this big island cling precariously to its fringes, mainly in the five cities of Melbourne, Sydney, Brisbane, Perth and Adelaide, all of them outward looking port cities, as if not daring to own what they see as the harsh, threatening, hostile interior. Its mysteries lie outside the compass of their real lives. It is a legacy of the fact that the early settlers found the Australian environment alien and so tried to adapt it to accommodate animals and crops that they were more familiar with, such as wheat, sheep and cattle, even rabbits and foxes. "Most Australians," says Jared Diamond, "don't depend on or really live in the Australian environment."[41] They have created an environment more like the one they knew back home.

True islanders have a special relationship with the rest of the world that the rest of the world identifies as insular. But whilst living contained lives, most islanders are also outward-looking. So although the British have been described as an island nation, hesitant to throw in their lot with the European mainland, this same insularity has moulded their sense of destiny, making them the maritime people that they became, a nation of explorers, traders and colonisers. But first of all, they inhabited their island well. Insularity gives you a particular view of the world. Islanders tend to regard theirs as the real world, considering what goes on beyond their shores as but pale imitations of reality.

To familiarise ourselves with the interior land of mystery that Australians have so strenuously avoided, Joan and I once travelled there by bus, along with a small group of other people, making our way along dusty roads by day and pitching our tent each night under skies heavy with stars until, some nine days later, we reached the 'Red Centre', Uluru, the sacred heart of a not very well understood world. We were the only Brits on that visit. The rest of the party were Australians for whom this was the trip of a lifetime, something for which they had been saving up for years. For them, it was like a visit to a foreign country, a venture into the unknown. So whilst the Tasmanians inhabit their little island fully, and know it in its entirety, their cousins on the 'Big Island' next door, cling hesitatingly to the edges of their vast land, not quite knowing how to take possession of it completely.

The peripheral inhabitants of Australia refer to this area as the Dead Heart, but to the Indigenous Australians, it is sacred, for it provides both spiritual and physical nourishment. The incomers for whom this is the Dead Centre, however, see it as threatening and a place to be visited only out of curiosity. Americans on the other hand, have no hesitation in celebrating their continental interior. It is acclaimed in Oscar Hammerstein's much-loved musical *Oklahoma*, set in the deep interior of the USA just before Oklahoma achieved statehood in the young United States of America. In it stockmen and farmers, although rivals in the different ways they used the land, joyfully asserted their proud sense of belonging to it.[42] The Americans inhabit their land well and fully. After all, they went there voluntarily and with an enthusiastic gleam in their eye.

Before them, the First Nation Americans also inhabited their land well and fully. In the nineteenth century, as Chief Seattle saw the land he and his people had lived on for generations slipping away from them, he made his famous speech. Every part of their soil, he declared, had been sacred to them. Hills, valleys, plains and groves, even the rocks, had all been made holy by the events of lives lived in close intimacy with the land. As they walked on this land, they felt a deep spiritual kinship with it, unlike the strangers who had taken possession of their land but who had little understanding of what belonging to the land really meant.[43]

The First Nation People of Australia had a similar spiritual bond to the land. According to Bruce Chatwin, the Aboriginal version of the creation story is that their ancestors sang themselves into existence as they strode across the earth, marking their route with songs. These totemic ancestors left their imprint on the land in the form of a network of songlines which are, to the Indigenous Australians of today, what footpaths and signposts are to us. That's how First Nation Australians find their way across the land and link up with members of their own tribe, by following these ancient songs. Their religion is about treating the land as sacred, and they worked out a way of living on it without threatening its delicate ecological equilibrium. [44] We in the West, on the other hand, tend to do our religion by transcending the natural world and looking for paradise somewhere up in the skies, beyond this world and after this life. For First Nation Australians, however, there is no distinction between the physical world of the here and now and the world of the spirit in the hereafter. For these people, as well as for the North American Indians, the spiritual and physical worlds are synonymous, geography and divinity in total accord.

CHAPTER 16: Illegal Visitor

George, the Port Agent, was born in South Australia but is in love with England. Most people in Australia have some very personal link with the Old Country and treat visitors from it with a mixture of good natured gloating that they, the new Australians who went there voluntarily (or who are sufficiently distant from their convict ancestors to be able to acknowledge them with pride), have had the good sense to escape, and gentle disdain, that the rest of us haven't. They are particularly boastful of their climate and the year-round outdoor life it makes possible. They therefore have a tendency to look on us Poms with pitying condescension because of our grey skies, drab summers and cold winters, and grudging respect that we are still there. Nevertheless, we tend to be treated as the boring stay-at-home older brother, whereas they act like the get-up-and-goers who had the good sense to leave.

"It's not what it used to be," they say of the Old Country. "Come out and join us. You can have barbies and swim every day."

But their jovial mockery disguises a very real affection and conversation is easy. They are more at home, it seems, with us than with the original inhabitants. That is one thing they need to sort out.

George is the operations manager for the port of Brisbane. I had phoned him about the whereabouts of the CMA CGM Manet, my next ship. He says he will let me know when it comes in, but I need to be on hand, ready to go as soon as possible once I get the call. So I've taken a small unit for a couple of days on Charlotte Street. It's a good place to wait and there are one or two things I want to do in Brisbane. One is to walk through the Botanic Gardens and beside the Brisbane River, along the boardwalk that cuts through the mangrove swamps.

Mangrove vegetation flourishes on strips of land that are intermediate between land and sea. It thrives in tidal areas where there is insufficient water to wash away old, dead vegetation and where mud and silt accumulate. In such conditions, where the ground is often unstable, trees and shrubs grow vigorously, sending out long shoots which germinate before they break away from the parent tree and dropping into the mud as ready-made plants. The black, slimy mud is littered with these tiny perpendicular shoots, hungrily thrusting upwards to grab their share of the meagre light. Larger trees grow stilt roots to keep themselves upright, looking for all the world like long, majestic flying buttresses propping up the walls of a cathedral, or like triffids, sending out hesitant, slender legs with half a dozen elegantly spread toes, treading ever so lightly as if reluctant to make contact with the oozing mud. Every so often, surreptitious movements catch my eye as mangrove crabs forage for leaves. The smell of hydrogen sulphide hangs heavily in the air, the characteristic rotten egg odour of layer upon layer of vegetation, rotting under anaerobic conditions. But above all, on this sultry, stiflingly hot mid-summer's day in early January, there is the welcome relief of shade and cool damp air. Long branches arch over the boardwalk forming a magnificent arboreal sunshade as they gracefully reach over me towards the sunlight that glistens on the river ten metres to my left. I take my time here and let it wash over me, before returning to the noise, heat and bustle of the city.

The walk round the loop of the Brisbane River brings me to Goodwill Bridge, and over this, to the parklands for a cooling ice-cream and a gallon of water at an artificial seaside beach, where children play in the sand and parents lounge in deck chairs, all protected from the sun by large multi-coloured awnings and a fortune's worth of sun screen. A brochure I picked up at the Information Centre, has directed me to a promising Turkish restaurant, and although it's hot, I think it will be worth the walk. A dismal sight greets me, however. It is closed, furniture is piled high against the floor-to-ceiling windows, and a large hand-written notice on the door announces that the lease is up and anyone who has equipment there has to stake their claim now through the appropriate channels, or risk it being sold off.

I beat a disgruntled and muttering retreat, get back to the other side of the river and find an excellent meal in the middle of Queen Street, which I eat alfresco in the cool of the evening. On my way back to Charlotte Street, the heavens open without warning and a deluge falls like a power shower. Keeping to the inside of the pavement to shelter under the overhanging departmental stores, I manage to find a shop to purchase an umbrella for six dollars. It doesn't function properly, blowing inside out with every gust of wind that hits me at street intersections, or collapsing under itself with the sheer volume of water falling on it. But it keeps me dry to knee level, which is all that's necessary in this land of shorts.

Back in my rooms, there's a telephone message from George.

"The Manet is leaving tomorrow afternoon, Clive. You need to be on board early. I'll call for you at eight-thirty."

I travel as light as possible, with just one case and a small daypack, which today is stuffed with as many newspapers as I can get my hands on. George arrives punctually.

"Good to see ya mate," he says as he shakes my hand.

"Good of you to give me a lift, George."

"It's nothing," he says, "I live nearby and you're on my way to work. Couldn't be easier."

The first thing he wants to talk to me about is Whitley Bay, which he visited twenty years ago. He remembers the metro system, Spanish City, St. Mary's Island and the lighthouse, and the Collingwood Statue at Tynemouth from where he watched ships sail up and down the Tyne. The borrowed nostalgia for what was never actually his, oozes from him.

George smoothes my way and sees me through the security procedures with consummate ease. It is becoming familiar now, this cubic, metallic land of busy precision with straddle cranes, and orange-clad men in hard hats. As the shuttle bus approaches the quayside, my ship rises up solidly in front of me, its name, CMA CGM MANET, proudly displayed in white across the blue of the stern. It's a nice ship. Built in 2001, it is, at one hundred and ninety-five metres long, the same size as the Alexandra Rickmers. The French CMA CGM group is celebrating its thirtieth anniversary this year and I wonder what influence, if any, its French provenance will have on the cuisine.

Bill and Amanda are going ashore as I board. Bill is a large, amiable, slightly bewildered looking man, comfortably but carelessly clothed in well-worn baggy jeans, loose brown shirt and a light, crumpled jacket. Amanda is dressed rather more smartly in satisfyingly trim, faded blue jeans, glistening white blouse and with a light blue jumper draped round her shoulders. Her attractively greying hair falls to just above her shoulders in a neat bob. She looks business-like, in control, knows what she's about. They've been on the ship from Tilbury, they tell me, and are off for a day in Brisbane. I wish them well and set about settling into what is to be my home for the next six weeks.

This ship has a lift. Eduardo, the steward, uses it to take my case up to E Deck. There's only room for him and my case, so I take the stairs; one flight of sixteen and eight flights of eight. It's a good way to get to know the ship. My cabin is on the port side of E Deck, looking astern. Like my previous one, it is well-equipped and comfortable. I accept philosophically the containers in front of the porthole.

Bill and Amanda are already seated when I enter the Officers' Mess for dinner at 17:30. They are from Wales but not Welsh. We are joined by Maritje, who embarked at Rotterdam and is returning to Rotterdam, having come out via New York, Norfolk (Virginia, USA), Savannah (Georgia,

USA), Manzanillo and the Panama Canal, Papeete (Tahiti) and Noumea (New Caledonia). She's Dutch and a demi-veg, that is, she will eat fish but not meat. I will eat poultry as well as fish and avoid red meat, so that makes me one-quarter veggie. Our Dutch companion is a small but tough looking woman who, I guess, is in her late fifties or early sixties and keeps herself fit. She loves the sea. For fifty years, she tells me, she had her own yacht, but on account of advancing years, had to let it go.

"I'd love another one though, perhaps, one day," she says. Fifty years is a long time to own a yacht. Maybe she is older than she looks. Could the tai chi exercises which she performs on the Monkey Deck each day, be hiding her years?

Captain Stjepan Ivanović enters and comes over to introduce himself. He is Croatian and an unassuming slightly built man of about my height, who speaks quietly in slightly halting English. His neatly trimmed black hair, parted on the left, shows a suspicion of grey at the temples, and his finely chiselled face is smiling and friendly. I stand to greet him as he takes my hand in a warm shake, but I have a little difficulty understanding him and have to focus carefully. I get the gist, though. The good news is that there is an open house policy as far as access to the bridge is concerned. We can go there at any time of the day or night, except of course when pilots are aboard, but even then we can stay on the bridge wings. This is good news indeed. I regard time spent on the bridge as by far the most interesting part of a freighter voyage. Captain Ivanović is also a vegetarian, so the chef is pretty used to quirky food requests and doesn't mind when I ask for fish instead of red meat. Two other officers also enter and introduce themselves – Second Officer Patrik and Third Officer Dragomir, both Croatian. Wine is on the house for both lunch and dinner. I am astonished. Such largesse on a container ship I have not come across before. Is this the French influence, I wonder, or a celebration of the company's thirtieth birthday?

I ask Bill and Amanda if they have had a good day.

"Not really," Bill says. "It was a bit boring".

"Where did you go?"

"Brisbane Airport. We just went to get a paper and have a meal. Horrible airport food."

"You mean you didn't go to the city?" asks Maritje.

"No, I asked the taxi driver where we should go and he took us there. Then when I asked if there was anywhere else he'd recommend, he suggested the other airport, so we stayed where we were. Anyway, we were told Brisbane was a bit boring."

"So was the first half of your voyage good?"

"Not really," he replies, "The weather was bad and there's nothing to do."

"So how do you spend your time on board?"

"Reading, crosswords – what else is there to do? I get fed up with reading. The evenings are the worst part. I like to go to bed about 2:00 a.m. and when I've watched one DVD it's still only 9:00 p.m. so I watch another."

"Yes, well that's because you sleep too much during the day," intersperses Amanda. "You'll probably not touch another book for six months or more when we get back."

"Well," he responds, "there's no time to read a book at home, is there. I mean there are the papers, television, the telephone. What time is there for reading books? And you don't play golf in the winter, do you?" he says to Amanda.

"Actually I do," she answers, flashing an indulgent smile round the table.

"Are you staying on board 'til we get back to England?" I ask them.

"No, we get off at Melbourne," says Amanda, "and then fly back to the UK."

After the meal, the Admin Officer, Dakila, also known as Sparkie on account of his electrical skills, asks me for my ticket. I produce all the documentation I have with me but it doesn't seem to be what he is looking for. It's not a proper ticket, he says. Satisfied with my documentation for the time being, however, he tells me with a smile that I can stay on board. I hasten to my cabin and send a frantic email to my agent in the UK. "You don't need a ticket," she tells me, "Your documentation *is* your ticket."

It's good wandering down the east coast of Australia; knowing that we will be going ashore at Sydney in just over twenty-four hours and then Melbourne two days after that, lightens the mood. It feels more like a coastal cruise. There's a feeling of anticipation in the air. I spend the evening watching *Desperate Justice*, the first of three DVDs Bill has lent me to watch before he and Amanda disembark at Melbourne. It's a sobering movie, dealing with the harrowing subject of child rape and summary justice, and not the most relaxing way to end the day.

It takes us thirty hours to cover the five hundred and two nautical miles to Sydney, where we berth at 06:00 at the Botany Bay container terminal. The Port Operations Officer arranges a taxi for us and we are off the ship by 08:00. Bill, Amanda and I share it to Circular Quay, where we agree to meet at the end of the day. This is a well-known spot for me, reminiscent of the many times Joan and I have landed at Sydney early in the morning and had an early breakfast here, before taking the Country Link train north on our periodic visits to see the grandchildren. So for old times' sake, I have a leisurely coffee, watching the ferries come and go. Circular Quay is magnificently sited between the Opera House and the Sydney Harbour Bridge and whatever ferry you take, to Manley, Garden Island, Balmain, Kurraba Point, Taronga, or beyond, you will get superb views of both of these iconic structures. These ferries operate a regular service for shoppers and commuters as well as for tourists. No wonder the place is brimful of people, happily so, abundantly so.

And so to Pitt Street and the internet café, where I search anxiously for an email from my agent hoping to clear up this business of the ticket I didn't need to have but should have. It's there, she has sent one, but I can't resist replying to say that I have already boarded the ship and that under the circumstances maybe I should have had it earlier. Much relieved, I continue along Pitt Street and into Market Street in the direction of Darling Harbour and the Pyrmont Bridge. This whole area is a celebration of city life. It is a delight to saunter here. It is still school holidays of course and so there are lots of families just enjoying being out together, and the sheer busyness and colour intermingling with land and water, make this a lively and enjoyable place to be, especially in dry weather. It is where people congregate to have fun, to eat in one of the zillions of restaurants and cafés that congregate here, to soak in the abundance of light and warmth, and to people watch. I seek out one such eating place and luxuriate in a truly slow lunch and being surrounded by happiness.

There's time for a stroll along Cockle Bay Wharf to Tumbalong Park and the Chinese Garden. There is something magical about Chinese gardens. The juxtaposition of very elemental things – water, rock, trees – in a three dimensional landscape has a very calming effect. It seems very Taoist. I love it. It is well worth the six dollars it cost me.

And then the slow walk back, this time along George Street, taking in the famed Queen Victoria Building, and a quick visit to Woolworth's to get some Rooibos tea. This is the favourite drink of Mma Ramotswe, heroine of Alexander McCall Smith's *The Number One Ladies' Detective Agency*, which is set in Botswana, so as well as being naturally caffeine free, it has the added benefit of bringing back pleasant memories of a part of the world I used to know well. Woolworth's here should not be mistaken for the brand we used to be familiar with in the UK. Here, it is a very large supermarket chain. It and Coles command most of the food and grocery supermarket business in Australia. Then out onto The Rocks – a delightful area of craft shops and eateries set on a ridge of land that separates Sydney Cove and Circular Quay from Darling Harbour and Cockle Bay. Finally, there's a welcome shaded seat at First Fleet Park at the bottom of The Rocks and overlooking Circular Quay. Here, I buy an ice cream, read *The Sydney Morning Herald* and wait for Bill and Amanda to join me.

Given my first encounter with them, I am amazed and somewhat relieved to discover that Bill and Amanda have also had a pleasant day, shopping for items they will need for their return journey from Melbourne.

"I wonder why Maritje didn't want to come ashore today," I say to them as we settle down in the taxi.

"Oh, she's a strange woman," says Bill, "and not one to be crossed."

"Really. Why's that?"

"There was this guy, John, who got on board at Papeete. The first morning he came down for breakfast, he saw a bowl of nicely prepared fruit on the table, thought it was for everyone, so helped himself to a portion - as you would, wouldn't you? Well, then she appeared. Took one look and shouted at him for taking her breakfast. Furious with him, she was. They never got on for the whole time he was on board. They never spoke again."

"Good grief. What was it all about?"

"Well, she's a vegetarian, you know. Never has a cooked breakfast. She'd come to an arrangement with Eduardo and the cook to always have a bowl of fresh fruit cut up for her, ready to eat. It was done especially for her, difficult, fussy woman, manages to get people to organise things for her. Anyway, there it was in the middle of the table. Poor fellow, he wasn't to know. He just helped himself. I bet he was pleased he was only on board for a short while, left us at Noumea."

It's dinner and Cook bursts into the Officers' Mess.

"What the hell is going on?" he yells. "I don't work miracles. There *is* no chicken. It's all *gone*. You've *eaten* it all. Gone. Finished. Leave me alone. *Please*, stop pestering with impossible demands."

Complete silence greets his outburst. No one gets up to remonstrate or to pacify. He is allowed to have his say, after which he disappears into the galley. It seems that one of the engineers had complained that chicken was not on the evening's menu when he had been expecting it.

The officers finish their meal and leave the table. On our way out, the cook, who has been lurking behind the door, waylays us one by one, just as we are about to go upstairs.

"Please help me," he pleads. "Come and look at my store. See what I have. See how empty it is. Please understand me."

Bill and Amanda say they are leaving in just over twenty-four hours so there is no point. Maritje slips away quietly. I am cornered. The unhappy man leads me to his store.

"See. It is empty. I have no more supplies. There is no chicken. We are short of bread, cheese, fruit, everything. It's all gone. What can I do? What am I supposed to do?"

Admittedly, his stocks do look pretty meagre. But he knows he has enough for the next twenty-four hours, by which time we will be in Melbourne.

"You'll be taking on more stores there, won't you?" I suggest.

"Yes, I suppose you're right," he says.

I'm embarrassed dealing with this. It's not my business. It's dangerous to get involved in things of this kind. Working relationships in the intense atmosphere of twenty-three men living in this closed environment can be delicately poised and it is well to keep clear of them.

Rounding the coast of Victoria the next day, our course is now more or less due west and with a following wind of twenty knots from the east, we make good time. Officer Patrik, however, says there is poor weather ahead. We are going to be caught between two low pressure systems. As it's likely to be further out at sea, though, there's a chance that we may get to Melbourne before we hit it.

Maritje has been getting excited about Melbourne. She has a sister, Greta, living there whom she has not seen for several years. Our schedule allows for a full day and night in port and on this basis, Maritje has made arrangements to spend the whole day with sister Greta and booked into a smart hotel for the night. She wants a taste of luxury, she says, after nearly two continuous months at sea.

In the chart room, however, all is not well. Patrik has a face like stone. Massive displeasure is written on Maritje's face.

"I've made arrangements," she says. "My hotel room is booked. It's cost me money."

"Sorry, Maritje," he says, "but the schedule has changed. We arrive in the morning and must now leave the same day. It's the cargo, you see. It must come first, very sorry."

We step outside onto the bridge wing and Maritje is consoled a little by the magnificent views of Anser Island and the cluster of other small rocky outcrops that gather round it. They're an extension of Wilson's Promontory, Victoria, the tip of which is the southernmost point of the Australian mainland whose lighthouse has been in continuous operation for a hundred and fifty years. It's teeming with wildlife here. The Promontory, notable for its rainforests, is a National Park and together with the granitic islands and the water surrounding them, it forms the Wilson's Promontory Marine National Park. Rodondo Island, on our port side, is the northernmost point of the state of Tasmania. This too is a nature reserve and is famous for its colony of short-tailed shearwaters. We pass between these two islands, Anser and Rodondo, and these two states, Victoria and Tasmania, at about 18:00. But it doesn't stop there. There's the Kent Group, the Hogan Group, the Curtis Group, the Glennie Group. They all rise out of the Bass Strait at 90 degrees like dumplings floating on top of a gigantic casserole. It's as if they have been newly dumped there before the sea has had any time to soften their outline.

We arrive at Port Melbourne early the following morning. Maritje and I take a taxi in the cool of the early morning to the Central Business District, the heart of the city, where we go our separate ways. It is hot, very hot, swelteringly hot, well into the forties. It's best to keep to the cool sides of the streets and the best place to be is the Ian Potter Centre (part of the National Gallery of Victoria) in Federation Square. This focuses entirely on Australian art, from the colonial period to contemporary art, and including galleries set aside exclusively for Aboriginal and Torres Strait Islander art. All this is housed in an ultra-modern building that contrasts superbly with the colonial style buildings that surround it. I enjoy a salad and another gallon of water at one of the many cafés and restaurants in Federation Square and manage to find a cool seat under one of a cloud of awnings erected for that purpose. After lunch, I take a cruise on the River Yarra to Williamstown, passing the CMA CGM Manet on the way. It's a strange experience seeing my huge ship from this tiny river boat. It makes me feel disconnected from my fellow passengers. All around me, people comment about how big the container ships are and, how ugly, and I think, that's my home, that's where my bed is, that's where I'm going back in a little over an hour from now.

At Flinders Street Station, I take a taxi back to my big, ugly, but familiar and comfortable home. We must be back by 17:00 so that we can be processed by the customs and immigration people. I arrive at 16:00, just in time for a shower before reporting to the Officers' Lounge, where the officials are gathered. I hand my passport over. The Immigration Officer studies it for what I think is an inordinate amount of time.

"There's a problem," he says.

"Oh really?"

"Yeah, you've already left the country."

"Well, yes, I thought I'd left at Brisbane."

"That's what it says here. Now you want to leave again, but you've already left. What've you been up to?"

"I disembarked at Melbourne on December 3rd, drove to Queensland to spend Christmas with family, and boarded this ship in Brisbane on January 6th."

"Oh dear. They stamped you as having left, whereas technically, you never left, been inside territorial waters all the time. You've been in the country illegally, mate."

"What're you gonna do? Lock me up?"

"We'll have to think about that," he says with a grin.

The officials get into a huddle and confer for a few minutes, before my interrogator returns.

"Ok," he says, "this is how it is. Your passport says you've already left Australia, so we can't stamp it again, which is what we're supposed to do. But you'll have to sign a form declaring your departure from Melbourne. We're gonna have to live with conflicting documentation. I think we might be able to do that," he says with a chuckle as he shakes my hand warmly. "Have a good journey."

Bill and Amanda have been waiting all day for the immigration people to clear them. This has not made Bill a happy man. Nothing, however, can dampen Amanda's high and always cheerful spirits.

"Hope you've had a pleasant voyage."

"It's been brilliant," says Amanda.

"Well, there've been some positives, but they've been outweighed by the negatives," mumbles Bill, with the merest hint of a mischievous twinkle in his eye, which I had not spotted before. "Anyway, I've enjoyed your company. And you can keep the DVDs I lent you and the book. Hope you like it. I did."

It's a good book, Paul Theroux's *The Great Railway Bazaar*. If Bill can enjoy reading a book like that, there's got to be more to him than meets the eye, and much more than the sour demeanour he presents to the world. That twinkle makes me wonder whether it hasn't all been a bit of an act, a deliberate attempt to downplay what he and Amanda clearly love doing together, travelling slowly.

"Why, thank you Bill," I say as we shake hands. "Have a good flight home."

And off they go. I stay on deck, wanting to see our departure, the slow drift away. Departure time is set for 22:00 and I hang over the railings of the Monkey Deck hoping to detect the first sign of movement, the throwing of the last rope, the almost imperceptible distancing of ourselves from land. Maritje joins me in companionable silence. At 23:00, we are still in dock, still looking. Just after midnight, Maritje asks

Officer Dragomir, who has just come off watch, what the problem is.

"The containers were too hot to put into the hold on the lower decks," he tells us. "With temperatures in the forties, you could have fried eggs on them - could have been dangerous, had to leave them to cool down."

We eventually pull away at 07:15 the next morning, and Maritje wonders, a little crossly, whether she could have stayed in her hotel after all.

CHAPTER 17: Sparkling Waters

It is not a good idea to be ill on freighters. The number of passengers is limited to twelve for a reason. Any more than this and there would be a requirement to have a doctor on board. This would be expensive. You need to be in good health and well insured to travel this way. This includes deviation insurance. If things go seriously wrong with you and the ship needs to divert to get you to a doctor, it could cost the carrier hundreds of thousands of pounds. You need to be able to indemnify the company against this potential loss. There is normally, however, an officer on board who is trained in first aid, and that usually suffices. It does, fortunately, in the case of my troublesome tooth, that and the convenient fact that we are only days away from a port.

We are passing through the Bass Strait, the sea is beginning to cut up rough and we are caught between a low to the north-east over the Coral Sea and another one to the south-west over the Southern Ocean. Between the two is a high pressure system. Through the Strait we set a course of seventy-five degrees for Auckland. Gale force winds hit us, Beaufort force nine. The high pressure system into which we are headed, extends towards New Zealand and as we are on its western edge, we are getting the full force of the northerly and north-easterly winds. Contrary to the pattern in the northern hemisphere, winds blow anticlockwise round high pressure systems here in the south.

Out of the Bass Strait we begin to cross the Tasman Sea, close to where the Kilmeny and all her crew perished. It's more than a hundred and twenty years since my great grandfather perished somewhere in these waters. No one knows the exact position, but all the evidence suggests it was in the Tasman Sea. The knowledge that he and all his crew are lying below me, gives an edge to my natural curiosity. It makes these waters personal. Beneath them lie the bones of a kinsman to whom I owe my very existence. It is hard to imagine the hardships they must have endured, relying only on the wind to drive them.

Then the toothache hits me. I need my emergency antibiotic. What I absolutely do not want is the prospect of two weeks crossing the Pacific Ocean with an abscess and no prospect of dental help. I can deal with discomfort, but not that kind of pain. We are scheduled to spend a day at Napier and that's a perfect opportunity to get professional attention. Using the expensive ship's system, I get an email to Joan. Will she ask Phil, my dentist, for advice? Almost immediately, he replies.

"Start using the antibiotic immediately to quell the infection and then, if necessary, have it extracted. We can decide what to do about the gap later."

Sparkie radios ahead to make an appointment for me.

"The only problem is," he says, "we get in late at night and depart early in the morning. The timing's going to be difficult."

"Why? Has the schedule changed? I thought we were arriving early in the morning."

"That's Napier. I've made an appointment for you in Auckland."

"Sorry, there's been a misunderstanding. Auckland will be too soon. It's important I get through the course of antibiotics before treatment, otherwise the infection could spread when the tooth is taken out. So I need it to be done in Napier if at all possible. Is it possible to change it?"

The amoxycillin is at work, holding the pain at bay. The wind has all but disappeared. The nearer we get to the centre of the anticyclone that has been defining our weather, the quieter it gets. It is now Beaufort zero point five, technically a calm. Skuas are dipping and diving over the surface of the water, which is so calm that it has become like a mirror. Each bird is accompanied by its reflection, the distance between them varying with the height of the bird. From time to time, the two of them, bird and reflection, almost coincide as one of them skims the surface. Whole clusters of them sit lackadaisically on the surface, waiting until the very last moment before nonchalantly lifting themselves out of harm's way, and even then, a defiant band of laggards almost decide it is not really worth the effort. Just in time, they change their minds, scarcely making it into the air before we plough into them, leaving a violent wake where tranquil waters had been. It is now dappled grey, green and blue.

Auckland straddles the north-western peninsula of North Island. We approach it from the east, past the volcanic island of Rangitoto, which appeared out of the sea some six to seven hundred years ago. Two hundred and sixty metres high, it came into existence when a couple who lived on the North Shore started cursing the fire goddess, Mahuika. She was so upset by this that she asked Mataoho, the god of earthquakes, to destroy them. Trembling with wrath on her behalf, he set off a great earthquake, right under the blasphemous couple's home. This opened up a huge hole which then filled with water and became what is now known as Lake Pupuke. As they saw their home being swallowed up, they watched in disbelief as Mahuika, still smarting with indignation, rose in fury from the depths of Hauraki Gulf, spat out fire and ash as she did so and left behind Rangitoto Island as a permanent legacy.[45] This was but the latest in a long line of Mahuika's temper tantrums, however, for there are over fifty such volcanoes in the Auckland area, known collectively as the Auckland Volcanic Field. Rangitoto is the youngest. It's never good to annoy the gods. They mess around with our geography quite inconveniently at times. You may not believe in them, but don't upset them.

Past Rangitoto Island, we then glide through Rangitoto Channel before entering Waitemata Harbour, the Harbour of Sparkling Waters. This is an apt description, for the waters do indeed sparkle as the shimmering light plays on island, rock and sea, transforming the water into tantalising shapes and colours. It is early evening and we take a circuitous route through the green and red marker buoys that show us our way. The air is quite still and the ship, together with passing small craft, create a myriad of criss-crossing patterns on the surface of the water. They linger there for almost as long as the eye can hold them, as if some waterscape artist has been commissioned to etch abstract designs on this watery tabula rasa.

The Sky Tower dominates the skyline. At three hundred and twenty-eight metres, it is the tallest building in New Zealand. It is late by the time we are alongside but it is too good an opportunity to miss. I ask Maritje if she is interested in walking in with me.

"Last time I was here it was all rather boring," she says. "Dead at night. Nothing goes on."

"Well, it's my only chance to see anything of Auckland. I've never been here before and will probably never be here again. I'm off. Do you want to come?"

We are berthed at Mechanics Bay, a mere twenty minute walk along Queen Street to the edges of the downtown area. As we step off the gangway, a new passenger, Jörg, is just about to come on board. He will be with us all the way to Europe, so there will be three of us now.

"You can walk to the gate," the Port Agent tells us, "but keep to the yellow walkway. It's very clear."

Half way along, our passage is blocked by a massive straddle crane, so we divert and begin to cut across to the port gate. We are spotted and a shuttle bus sprints up to us. The driver leans out.

"You shouldn't really be walking here," he says. "Jump in. I'll take you to the gate."

"We were told it was okay to walk."

His radio crackles. "Yes, I have the visitors."

I often feel I could slip into the way of life here in New Zealand quite unobtrusively. In Australia, I feel more exposed, my very English accent contrasting so vividly with the sharpness of theirs. It seems to me that New Zealand is a gentler country, more at ease with itself and with its first nation population. It all feels very familiar.

It's balmy warm, like the kind of English summer I used to love as a boy in Surrey but which I rarely experience now in the far north of England. Light slacks and a summer shirt will do. We find our way to Princes Wharf, where there is a delightful array of restaurants, bars and coffee houses which, despite the fact that it is late on a Monday evening, are all humming with activity, heaving with customers. We stroll for an hour. It's a time and place for young people. There is happiness all around, excited chatter, laughter, meetings and greetings, goodbyes until the next time, huddled conversations, couples canoodling, togetherness. We stop for a quiet drink and take it in, saying little, just watching. It is enough to do this.

"It was better than last time," Maritje volunteers, as we make our way back to the Manet. She is interesting to talk with, but only if one happens on the right topic, especially the sea and sailing. Small talk does not come easily to her. So we sit for long periods of silence at the meal table. But it is a companionable silence.

Morning and we depart Waitemata Harbour, so this time we have the red buoys to starboard and the green to port. Auckland's CBD begins to fade into the distance, its gleaming white sky scrapers perfectly reflected in the utterly motionless water through which we carve an ugly scar. It is beautifully warm and sunny but, as ever when we have been stationary for some time, the upper decks are littered with lumps of soot which only clear as we gather speed. At breakfast, conversation sticks. Maritje needs a topic that interests her, sailing, tai chi, marine literature, Flemish art. I don't always want serious talk. Jörg has very limited English and I have no Dutch. I begin to miss Gary, Janine and Adriaan. I crave small talk. Simple chitchat.

We cross Hauraki Gulf and make towards the tip of the Coromandel Peninsula. A fresh breeze blows from the west and by mid-morning, we round the head and pass through the Colville Channel, with the tail end of the Moehau Range to starboard and Great Barrier Island to port, so named by Captain Cook because it protects Hauraki Gulf from the worst of the storms and powerful currents of the South Pacific which batter the coast here. We turn south-east and run between Cuvier Island and the Mercury Islands and begin our crossing of the Bay of Plenty. White Island, an active volcano, looms on the eastern horizon. Tauranga, where Joan and I boarded the Tasman Discoverer less than a year ago for our voyage to Shanghai, lies to the south of us.

In New Zealand, the earth's crust is insubstantial, vulnerable, thin. At Rotorua, a few miles to the south of Tauranga, it is so thin you can slip through it, if you are not careful, and drop into a fiery pit of molten rock from which you'd be lucky to escape with your life. Some time ago Joan and I took a walk in Kuirau Park, in Rotorua, and came across a mini smouldering volcano, about two metres high. It had appeared suddenly on Friday 26th January 2001 at half past three in the afternoon, the eruption lasting for about a quarter of an hour. Mud, steam and debris were thrown two hundred metres into the air. As we continued our walk, we saw other little puffs of smoke seeping out from shrubberies or the edges of the grass, a few metres away from where we were walking. Any moment, we thought, we could fall through. We were told of a professional volcanologist who, in his enthusiasm to explore a particularly good example of a mud volcano in Whakarewarewa Thermal Village, forgot the warnings about keeping only to the marked path and fell into a bubbling crucible of superhot mud just inches below the innocent looking surface, giving him third degree burns up to his waist. A helicopter pad is now provided to get such errant tourists to hospital. Whakarewarewa is, of course, one of the great tourist attractions of North Island, but these geothermal springs and geysers had been on my to do list for half a century, ever since as a schoolboy, I had learned about Rotorua in my geography lessons. It was well worth the waiting and the Lady Knox Geyser did not disappoint.

The problem for New Zealand is that it is right on the edge of the Indian-Australian Tectonic Plate, which is on a collision course with the Pacific Plate. It is not good to locate a country where two plates are smashing into each other; it makes for great geological instability. One plate will always be pushed under the other in a process called subduction, making the whole region prone to earthquakes and volcanoes. In the north of New Zealand, it's the Pacific Plate that is being sucked under the Indian-Australian Plate, while to the south, the opposite is true. Here, it is the Indian-Australian Plate that is being sucked under. This means that pretty well the whole of New Zealand is a colossal subduction zone. North Island has a line of volcanoes cutting right through it, from Tongariro, Ngauruhoe and Ruapehu near the centre, northwards to Whale Island and White Island in the Bay of Plenty. It is known as the Taupo Volcanic Zone after Lake Taupo, itself a giant flooded volcanic caldera.

This fiery chain goes out beyond the North Island's Bay of Plenty to the Kermadec Islands, one thousand kilometres to the north-east of New Zealand. This uninhabited outpost of New Zealand is part of a volcanic arc, extending to Tonga. Immediately to the east of these islands, are some of the deepest areas on earth. The geography of the ocean bed is much more dramatic than that small portion of the earth's crust on which we happen to live. The Kermadec and Tonga Trenches, for example, are both more than ten kilometres deep, five and a half times deeper than the Grand Canyon and deeper than Mount Everest is high. From Tonga to Tongariro, from the deepest ocean to the highest point on North Island, the earth's crust has been ripped apart in one almost perfectly straight line. This axis of vulcanicity is part of the great Pacific Ring of Fire. Wherever the Pacific Plate collides with the continental plates of Indo-Australia, Eurasia and North and South America, lethal energy is periodically released, killing hundreds, destroying towns and cities.

These too are zones of subduction, where the Pacific Plate is being sucked down to enormous depths, exposing great lines of weakness. Any decent atlas will show them; lines of deepest blue for deepest depth, which continue round almost the whole of the western Pacific and including the Mariana Trench to the east of the Philippines, the Izu and Japan Trenches, the Kuril Trench, which forms the eastern boundary of the Sea of Okhotsk, and the Aleutian Trench, guarding the entrance to the Bering Sea. From New Zealand to Alaska, the western rim of the Pacific is a subduction zone, creating a huge semi-circle of geological instability.

Fire spitting mountains are scary. Geological science has come a long way and we now know how volcanoes work, but this does not stop them stirring up feelings of awe, fear and wonder. Knowing the science does not stop them being revered and this volcanic core of North Island is treated with great respect by the Maori people. These sacred mountains remind them of the time when, in the deep mythological past, the high priest Ngatoroirangi led the Great Migration from the mystical island of Hawaiiki in the sacred canoe Te Arawa as he looked for a place where his people could settle. Those who accompanied him on this great migration had for their guide, a long white cloud by day and at night a long bright cloud[46]. The Maori word for long white cloud is Aotearoa, which is also the Maori name for New Zealand.

On the opposite side of the world, the Children of Israel, when they too were on a journey in the wilderness looking for somewhere to settle, had a similar pillar of fire to guide them by night and a pillar of smoke by day, a clear sign of volcanic activity. From the moment Ngatoroirangi and his band of migrants made land on the shores of the Bay of Plenty, they saw fiery Tongariro in the distance. It beckoned them, and as they got closer, Ngatoroirangi understood that in order to fulfil his sacred mission of claiming the lands of Tongariro for his people, he must first climb up the volcano to its highest peak. Leaving his party by the shores of Lake Taupu, he continued up the mountain of fire with his slave. There he was so cold that he pleaded with his sisters Te Pupu and Te Huata on Hawaiiki, to send fire to warm him. They responded immediately by sending a straight line of fire, direct like the flight of an arrow, from Hawaiiki through White Island in the

Bay of Plenty, on to Rotorua, then to Taupo and finally to Tongariro, where he was standing[47].

The resemblance to the story of Moses climbing fiery Mount Sinai, where he spoke with God and received a set of commandments before leading his people to the Promised Land, is striking. The Children of Israel were drawn to a mountain that was "wrapped in smoke, because the Lord had descended upon it in fire"[48]. The Maori name for their God of volcanoes was Ruaumoko, the god of volcanic energy. Yahweh, the God of the Old Testament, was, in one of his guises, the God of Fire. Even Hawaiiki, the paradise from which the Maoris believe we all came and to which we will all return at death, has its parallel in the Garden of Eden for Christians, and the Happy Land of Matang for the Gilbert Islanders.

We need stories to help us make sense of the world, especially stories about beginnings and endings. However much we believe the science, we still need the mythology. In his mammoth study of global patterns of mythology and religious belief written at the end of the nineteenth century, Sir James Frazer looked at the way in which similar religious ideas seem to have appeared quite independently all over the world. The cult of Mithra, for example, was astonishingly similar to Christianity, as was the worship of the Aztec god Tezcatlipoca. Frazer suggested that these remarkable coincidences of religious belief patterns must stem from "the independent workings of the mind of man in his sincere, if crude, attempts to fathom the secret of the universe, and to adjust his little life to its awful mysteries."[49]

Joan and I saw Christchurch a couple of years before it was laid waste by earthquake. We had driven south from the ferry landing at Picton along the spectacularly beautiful stretch of the coast road that takes in Kaikoura, where we stayed as elderly guests at the Kaikoura Mani Youth Hostel. Here the sea washed up almost to the front door and we looked out onto a bay of emerald green water, beyond which blue and purple mountains rose through a white layer of low-lying cloud, and above which a proliferation of ominous storm clouds hung heavily, but far enough away to leave us clothed in sunshine.

At Christchurch, the annual 'World Buskers Festival' was in full swing in Cathedral Square, with the grey stone cathedral itself at the very centre, its slender spire reaching up to a clear blue sky. Symbolic of enduring values and solid continuity at the heart of this delightful antipodean city and surrounded by neat lawns and flower beds, cooled by the dappled shade of sweet smelling lime trees, it all seemed so utterly English. Nearby, people of all ages stood thoughtfully, arms folded, considering their options as they watched two young men absorbed in a giant game of pavement chess. A clown on a unicycle mingled with the slow moving traffic as if it were the most normal thing in the world to do. A helmeted young man, small rucksack on his back, dressed in smart black shorts and light blue shirt, rode purposefully past us on what looked like a brand new, yellow-framed penny farthing, with the air of a man on his way to the office. Crowds gathered round buskers, jugglers, circus acts, and occasional spatterings of applause showered us all with contentment. Beside the cathedral, stood the proud silver Chalice, an eighteen metre high metallic sculpture, built to celebrate the millennium, woven with a multitude of different kinds of plants native to New Zealand. Among them was the Silver Fern (Cyathea Dealbata), one of the best known of New Zealand's national symbols. It is easily recognised by turning over the fronds. Of the seven tree ferns in New Zealand, this is the only one whose fronds are pure white or silver underneath. The Chalice seemed to symbolise a society at ease with itself, and with its two cultural traditions, European and Maori. A plaque nearby celebrated 'The First Peoples – Waitaha to European in Christchurch'.

On the southern fringe of Christchurch, if you climb the hill on the Banks Peninsula, you can look down on the port town of Lyttleton. A suburb of Christchurch, it is built round Lyttleton Harbour, which is a drowned volcanic caldera, another reminder of New Zealand's structural fragility.

Lyttleton was severely damaged in the earthquake that destroyed parts of the central business district of Christchurch, killed almost two hundred people and irreparably damaged the cathedral.

If you travel west and south-west from Christchurch, you cross the Canterbury Plains. I first got to know about them through school geography and the New Zealand roast lamb we ate every Sunday. They roll gently, these plains, and the character of the small towns through which you pass reflects the agricultural emphasis of the region, Bankside, Rakaia. The larger towns, like Ashburton, are littered with industries that support farming – plants for processing meat, arable crops, dairy produce – as well as businesses related to agricultural machinery maintenance, particularly irrigation equipment. But ahead of you, as a constant backdrop to the gently undulating plains, are the Southern Alps. Magnificent as these are, they also are a sombre reminder of New Zealand's thinness. These mountains have been, and continue to be, thrust upwards by the relentlessly slow collision of the Pacific and Indian-Australian plates.

In South Island, it is earthquakes rather than volcanoes that are the norm. There are literally thousands of earthquakes in New Zealand every year, most of them scarcely noticeable except by seismograph. Some of them are, however, strong enough to be felt and some catastrophic, to which the tragedy of Christchurch in February 2011 testifies. The fragility of the earth's crust is writ large in the landscape of New Zealand. In recognition of this, Australians sometimes refer to New Zealand as the Shaky Isles.

It is a spectacular drive north along the west coast on State Highway 6, through Mount Aspiring and Westland National Parks. I wanted to see the Fox and Franz Josef glaciers, because here you can see the way in which, at the same time as mountains are being built, they are also being worn down by rain and ice. The Fox Glacier is the largest of the West Coast glaciers, and the average precipitation is 9,000 mm per annum (that's over three hundred and fifty inches per year, compared with London's twenty-three). This rain and snow is continually feeding the glacier, which is scouring out the valley down which it is slowly grinding its way. You can see this too at the Franz Josef Glacier, twenty-five kilometres further north.

It's a good walk to the Fox Glacier from where we are staying, but before we set out, we checked in for a coffee. Here, we met Richard and Carol. He was ex-New Zealand Air Force, she was Australian. A short greeting was all that was needed to get them talking.

"We're a Christian family," said Richard, "Bible believing Christians."

"So are you just travelling round, enjoying retirement?" I asked.

"Oh no, we're buying, refurbishing and selling houses as a way of making money. We've just finished one and sold it. Got a very good price. God really does answer our prayers."

"And I'm writing a book about health and diet," said Carol, "from a Bible-based point of view."

We left them there and walked to the snout of the Franz Josef Glacier. Here, I was interested in a particularly striking rock formation. It had been formed by layers of sand and sediment laid down horizontally, year after year for millennia, each layer veneer-thin but clearly visible, like minutely thin pancakes. The accumulated weight of geological aeons had compressed them all into solid rock, but the original layers were still spectacularly evident. By now, however, orographic forces had pushed it all up and tilted these layers, so that they now lay on their edge, making what were once horizontal stripes, into vertical etchings on these massive rocks at the nose of the glacier.

Richard and Carol found us there taking photographs of this rock. He wanted to know why I was so interested in it.

"I used to teach geography," I said. "You can see how the landscape has evolved here. Mountains are built, water, wind, ice wear them down. It's terrific, fascinating stuff."

"Well," he replied, "I look at it this way. You only have to look at this to realise that Darwin was way off beam. What you see here totally disproves everything he said. We even see the sun and moon together now during the day. That shows how wrong our world is. In biblical times, God made the sun to shine by day and the moon by night. When God made the world, everything was good. The sky was always blue and there were never any clouds. And then man sinned and the flood happened and the world changed into what we know now."

That was a year ago and I am reminded of all this as the Manet puts into port, and once again I arrive at Napier, although this time Joan is not with me. It is tooth extraction day. My appointment is for the afternoon, so I spend the morning revisiting a few places we had seen together. Then I had thought that that would be my first and only visit to New Zealand; you never know where life is going to take you. Now here I am again and I realise how good it is to know my way around.

Time for a quick walk up to Bluff Hill Lookout. From here, I look down on the sweeping waters of Hawke Bay with a necklace of white foam as Pacific Ocean waves crash silently onto the beach. White timber houses, each one different from its neighbour and built on stilts to accommodate the steepness of the slope, have magnificent and expensive views over to the other side of the bay, towards where Cape Kidnappers fades into the far distance.

This is the Art Deco Capital of the World. There are other contenders. Miami, for example, and even New York, largely, it seems, on account of the fact that the Empire State Building has an art deco hat. Napier, however, is pretty well all art deco, and this is because of the devastating earthquake, registering seven point nine on the Richter scale, that struck it on 3rd February 1931. Napier and its neighbour to the south, Hastings, were destroyed, and two hundred and fifty-six people killed. Hillsides disappeared and great fissures, kilometres long, scarred the landscape. Near famine conditions resulted as about thirty thousand people went short of food and water, whilst electricity, telephone and transport communications were destroyed[50]. The city fathers decided

Napier should be rebuilt in the style of the era, art deco, and a stroll through the heart of the town, takes you right back to that time. From the Sound Shell on Marine Parade, to the Art Deco Masonic Hall on Tennyson Street, Charlie's Art Deco Restaurant on Emerson Street, the ASB bank and the Aqua Seafood Restaurant, the whole city walks, talks, thinks and feels art deco. You can even take a ride in a magnificent red 1934 Buick Sedan and view everything in art deco style.

It's good to see all this, to refresh memories, to make me feel at ease before my rendezvous with the dentist at two o'clock. The anticipation of what is to come, dulls the edge of my appetite, so I have a meagre lunch – a bowl of soup and a light salad – somewhere on Emerson Street. Then off to the dentist. As I am expecting, the tooth has to come out. This makes the walk back to the ship an uncomfortable business, but the turquoise of the sea lifts my spirits, and after another meal of soup, I retire early and nurse my wound. Eduardo provides me with a supply of salt so that I can make a mild disinfectant to rinse my mouth with every few hours.

It is morning and I am feeling better. There are no straddle cranes here and no mobile overhead cranes, so we have to use the ship's jib crane for getting containers on board. These are not so controlled in their handling of the containers and there is therefore less precision. It is disconcerting to see these huge boxes swinging as they are lifted to clear those already on board and lowered into the appropriate gaps. One container crashes into the side of another, the first of a row of three. All three tilt alarmingly as if about to set off a domino chain of falling boxes but just in time, they manage to straighten themselves.

It is 30 C in the shade and the sun is shining out of a clear sky. Two tugs are tied up alongside and at 10:15 their engines roar into life as they begin to drag us away from the quayside. We are already facing towards the open sea so their work is soon done and the ship's engines can take over. The pilot leaves us about an hour later and I make my way to the wheel house to find Patrik plotting a route that will take us in a more northerly direction than that already planned. The Captain has given instructions to avoid an occluded front that might give us bad weather. We pass the Mahia Peninsula, which marks the northern limit of Hawkes Bay. New Zealand disappears over the horizon. It is probably our last sight of land for fourteen days.

CHAPTER 18: Groundhog Day

Morning and we are on the edge of a typhoon to the north-west of us, off the coast of New Caledonia. All night we have been buffeted by heavy seas, but have avoided the worst of it because of yesterday's adjustment. The wind is surprisingly moderate, however, a mere fifteen knots. But still the buffeting continues. It's from the typhoon; angry water travels a long way.

We are heading almost due east to correct for yesterday's deviation. Afternoon, and fierce winds begin to batter us from the north, striking us on our port bow. Every few minutes, the ship judders as mighty waves smash into her in a vain attempt to push us off course. The view from the bridge is stupendous. As each wall of water thuds into her, the prow is momentarily jolted over to starboard. Great mountains of white foam rise up out of the ocean and wrap themselves over the whole of the fo'c'sle, covering it with furiously agitated water. But almost immediately, the ship lifts herself up with a nonchalant shrug, shakes the water off, and then, as the automatic system engages, defiantly pulls her prow back on course, quickly repositioning herself before the next onslaught challenges her authority.

Astronauts tell us that we inhabit a blue planet. This is because more than seventy per cent of the earth's surface is sea water, and most of that is in the Pacific, Atlantic and Indian Oceans. Of these, by far the largest, is the Pacific Ocean. This one ocean spreads itself over more than one hundred and eighty million square kilometres. The Indian

Ocean is a mere puddle in comparison, with just seventy-five million square kilometres. This vast surface area with practically no land to impede their flow, means that winds get up to colossal speeds over the Pacific. They have a huge uninterrupted run over which to accelerate.

In much the same way, powerful ocean currents also develop, driven by the prevailing winds. The relationship between winds and currents is an intimate one and it is particularly pronounced in the Pacific. The north-east and south-east trades drive the North Equatorial and South Equatorial Currents respectively, pushing colossal amounts of water over to the west. This surplus water is then taken back east by the Equatorial Counter Current, which runs between them on the equator. A pronounced circular pattern of currents has developed over the oceans, particularly the Atlantic and Pacific, powered not only by the winds but also by the Coriolis Effect. This is an apparent force that causes winds and currents to be deflected to the right of the direction of flow in the northern hemisphere and to the left in the southern hemisphere. This creates a large clockwise circulation of water in the north and a counter-clockwise pattern in the south. In the Pacific, these are known as the North Pacific and South Pacific Gyres. They have their counterparts in the Atlantic Ocean, while the Indian Ocean only has a southern gyre on account of the Asian landmass blocking its development in the north.

We continue east, following the thirty-sixth parallel and have moved just one degree of latitude north since leaving New Zealand three days ago. This means we will be slicing right through the centre of the South Pacific Gyre. Large amounts of debris often gather here, in much the same way as autumnal leaves collect at the centre of swirling eddies in the back garden. It has been estimated that as much as one hundred thousand tonnes of plastic waste may have accumulated in the central area of the North Pacific Gyre, with more than three hundred thousand individual pieces of trash for every square kilometre.[51] This would explain the clumps of plastic bottles I can see here in the South Pacific, pieces of wood, the occasional child's beach ball, a half deflated pair of water wings, even a deck chair that someone must have left on the beach and the tide removed. It all floats listlessly past us in dejected looking clumps, sad and lonely there on the still water, the abandoned detritus of a summer's day at the seaside, carrying the wistful echoes of children's laughter and adult carelessness. All drawn together as if by magnetism and wandering the oceans waiting to suffocate or poison some hapless marine creature, clogging up this last remaining wilderness, rich in life, nutrients and human detritus.

It is the morning of Friday the 18th January. During the night, we crossed the 180th meridian and entered the western hemisphere; it feels strangely consoling. It's not so far to go now, not so far from home. For much of its length, this is the International Date Line (IDL), but it kinks out to the east in places to accommodate some of the far flung islands belonging to New Zealand, such as the Chatham Islands, about 800 kilometres east of Christchurch, and the Bounty and Antipodes Islands, which get their name from the fact that they are almost the exact antipodes of London.

A vast kink in the International Date Line is necessary to accommodate Kiribati's enormous territory. This Micronesian state has a population of just over one hundred thousand people on a land area of roughly eight hundred square kilometres, but it is spread over some five million square kilometres of ocean and three time zones. Consider that the population of Oldham in the UK has the same population on a mere sixty-seven square kilometres, one twelfth of Kiribati's land area and seventy-five thousand times smaller than its ocean area. The UK has a population of more than sixty million (six hundred times more than Kiribati's) on an area less than half that of Kiribati's oceanic area. So, to make sure that everyone living in this fragmented island state can go to work or school on the same day of the year, if not the same hour, the International Date Line almost totally encloses it by swinging east to the one hundred and fiftieth meridian west.

First Officer Radimir Kovač makes the announcement from the bridge, in the middle of the dog watch.

"Tomorrow, today will be repeated. Today is Friday the 18th January. Tomorrow will also be Friday January 18th."

I now get back the day I lost when travelling the other way two years ago, a Monday. On that occasion, a fellow passenger was tied up in knots over what to do about taking her pills when we crossed the Date Line. It was a once-a-week pill and as Monday was about to disappear, she wanted to know whether she should take it on Sunday or Tuesday or not at all that week.

At two o'clock in the afternoon, another announcement; we are asked to put our clocks and watches forward by one hour. Jörg does not turn up for dinner this evening. He forgot to adjust his watch. He makes it just in time to snatch a bite before it is cleared away.

There's a well-stocked library next to the gym, which isn't well-equipped. I have just finished Sue Townsend's *Number Ten*, a brilliant take-off of Tony Blair, and Tim Binding's *Island Madness*, about the wartime occupation of the Channel Islands, both most enjoyable reads. The recreational facilities, however, are not good. In a recent issue of *The Sea*, published by the Mission to Seafarers, there is an article about this. It says that with a major manning crisis looming in the shipping industry, it needs to do more to provide for the comfort of the crew. I am only here temporarily so it is not a big deal, but for the men who spend their lives here, it is vital. There is no swimming pool on this ship, and the apology for a pool that was on the Alexandra Rickmers, was tucked away in a dark pokey room that would have been rather like swimming in an unlit cellar. It seems to suit naval architects, the article suggests, to plonk a tower block on the deck of a ship with no further consideration for the human needs of the people for whom it is to be their home. There's no space for the men even to sit out in the sun. The superstructure is sited where it is least likely to interfere with the cargo, and this means as far back as it can go, towards the stern. In every other area of life, a great deal of concern is shown about providing decent living environments except, it seems, at sea. When these courageous and magnificent guys are expected to live with such inadequate recreational conditions, it is scarcely surprising that there is a manning crisis.

It is Groundhog Day, January 18th for the second day in succession. I wake to a fresh breeze from the north-east buffeting our port bow. This makes it too risky to walk on the Main Deck, so I try the exercise bike in the gym. It's a tough old thing and I can see no way of adjusting the gear ratios, so it's rather like cycling up a very steep hill in top gear. Just as I finish this, the Captain tells us to expect an emergency drill, the strangest I have experienced.

"When the signal sounds, you should all assemble on the bridge," the Captain says to us three passengers.

"Should we take anything with us?" asks Maritje. "Immersion suits, life vests?"

"No. Just come to the bridge. You need bring nothing with you."

And so we play no part at all in this drill. It just goes on below and around us while we look out to sea and wonder what we would do in a real emergency. Don't we also need to know how to deal with an emergency? Would not our lives also be at risk?

"We are just here to keep out of their way while they do the drill," said Maritje.

In the morning, the wind has veered to the south-east, a strong, fresh breeze and we too have changed course, to the north-east, sixty-four degrees. Our speed through the water is a mere nine knots, but our ground speed is nineteen knots. The South Pacific Gyre is helping us along. We are making good time and I feel I am on my way home. New Zealand is five days behind us now. The deeper waters of the South West Pacific Basin, where the Pacific Plate is being sucked under the Indo-Australian, have now been left behind and we find ourselves over the East Pacific Rise. There are islands nearby, French Polynesia and, further over to the east, Pitcairn. Further north and almost directly on our route, are the

Galapagos Islands. We are pushing through an anti-cyclonic system that extends all the way to Panama and promises relatively fine weather to accompany us.

"We're taking the rhumb line route," Captain Ivanović tells me, "not the great circle route. It's more practical."

The rhumb line is a straight line route on the map, the great circle a straight line on the globe, which is an arc on the map. The advantage is, he tells me, that the rhumb line is more flexible. With the great circle, you have to keep changing course to keep on the arc, whereas with the rhumb line route, you can set the course and just keep going in a straight line, which is what we have been doing. This means that if deviations are needed, for example to avoid a storm, it is easier to do this and then adjust back on course again. Sometimes, the saving in distance on the great circle, can be considerable. For example, crossing the North Pacific from Panama to China, can save three hundred nautical miles, but from Napier to Balboa, on the southern entrance to the Panama Canal, the difference is just twenty-two nautical miles, and from Philadelphia to Tilbury, it is only twenty. So we take the practical rhumb line route, sixty-four degrees.

We enter the territorial waters of French Polynesia, an overseas territory of France consisting of one hundred and thirty small and mostly volcanic islands, although some are coral atolls. Tahiti is the largest and highest and contains the capital, Papeete. Scattered over the south-western part of the East Pacific Rise, they lie mid-way between South America and Australasia. These are some of the most remote places on earth. Up on the bridge and using the most powerful binoculars I can find, I search the horizon in the forlorn hope of at least seeing land. Is this the onset of cabin fever? The strength of my desire to set eyes on land surprises me. The Monkey Island, forty metres above the level of the ocean, gives me a visibility of almost twenty-three kilometres, just over fourteen miles. I scan the horizon through three hundred and sixty degrees. Nothing. One hundred and thirty islands all around me, but not one to be seen. They are scattered over four million square kilometres of ocean. What hope, realistically, is there of seeing land?

Pitcairn, whose waters we enter the next day, is even more remote. It is a tiny volcanic rock in the middle of the vastness of the South Pacific, with a total land area of just under five square kilometres, or less than two square miles, and inhabited by about fifty descendants of the Bounty mutineers. In fact it's a cluster of islands known as Pitcairn, Henderson, Ducie and Oeno. Only Pitcairn is inhabited. They are administered from Auckland, more than five thousand kilometres away, though final responsibility lies with the British government through the UK High Commissioner, who is based in Wellington.

The sheer scale of Pitcairn's isolation is stupefying. More than two thousand kilometres from Tahiti, six and a half thousand from Panama and almost six thousand from Peru, ten days' steady sailing across open ocean from Valparaiso and with no airport, it is one of the most remote places on earth. I could contemplate the idea of living there for six months, perhaps even a year. That would be interesting. But beyond that, I think I would find it hard. The length of the island is equivalent to a walk to my local shops and back. Its breadth is even shorter. I know from experience that I need more than that.

We pass within one hundred and seventy-seven kilometres, too far away to see. Supplies are sometimes taken there by container ships like ours, en route from New Zealand to Panama. Two years ago, I was close enough to take in more detail. My immediate impression was of a huge lump of black rock rising almost perpendicularly out of the level calm of the Pacific. It was difficult to comprehend how such an island, with practically no shore to speak of, could possibly have been regarded as a place to settle, except, of course, under the extreme circumstances of the mutineers. Its forbidding cliffs gave the appearance more of a fortress than an abode. Everyone lives in the little town of Adamstown, but in reality, it struck me as not so much a town as a scattering of dwellings, each within its separate forest clearing, insulated from its neighbour, as if being in the most remote place on earth weren't enough and they had to hide from their neighbours. Even this one solitary settlement can only be reached by a stiff climb from Bounty Bay up the Hill of Difficulty. Added to this, actually disembarking from any vessel can be a problem; if the seas are rough, it is not unknown for aspiring visitors, having travelled there by sea, to be unable to set foot on the island.

Attempts have been made from time to time to settle the occupants elsewhere, but they have always moved back. The outside world, with all its hustle, bustle and busyness must, I suppose, be unnerving for people who know only such small scale living. The power of the familiar, however limited or perhaps even dysfunctional, to override the unfamiliar should never be underestimated. Maybe it was the power of belief that drew them back. The population of Pitcairn is one hundred per cent Seventh Day Adventists. They believe in the literal truth of the Bible, that the world was created in six days less than ten thousand years ago, and that they should avoid 'worldly' pleasures. Isolation, it seems, is not severe enough. Even on this, the remotest inhabited spot on earth, one must not be tempted by 'the world'. The quest for salvation in the next world can exact a very heavy price in this one.

Pitcairn is a curious anachronism, a tiny remnant of the Britain Empire, almost unattainably remote, a curious relic and unanticipated consequence of the harsh naval practices of a bygone era, an accident of history.

I once lived in the central African bush for a few years, marooned on an ocean of savanna between the Atlantic and Indian Oceans. While the novelty of the first year or so was exciting, I eventually found the isolation and limited horizons hard to bear. But I was at least able to get in a truck half a dozen times a year and drive over dirt roads to Harari or Bulawayo for some contact with friends, a sociable meal, touching base with normality. And I had neighbours whom I could talk to over the garden fence. But it does something to your mind, that kind of isolation. It deprives you of sufficient stimuli to give you a healthy balance of interests. I wonder if there is a critical size below which communities might be in danger of falling in on themselves. A few years ago, some adult members of the island community of Pitcairn were found guilty of various sex offences, and the British built a prison for them on the island. It is difficult to see how this differed greatly from how they were already living – in a prison within a prison.

This is the nearest we have been to land for a week and the nearest we will be to land for another week. Days pass, the pattern repeats, breakfast, lunch, tea, bed, ocean and yet more ocean. Mealtimes map out the day, provide a welcome structure to long hours looking out onto vast unchanging oceanic vistas. The fo'c'sle, although a jumble of winches, drums and coils of rope, provides a refuge from the noise of the engine, a mighty roar at the stern, a grumble mid-ships, a hum in my cabin, but at the bow stillness and a gentle swish.

Today, however, sounds of commotion come up from below, like children at play. I look over the side. A small pod of dolphins has befriended us. They weave in and out of the bow wave, ride its crest and then veer off, making way for companions. They take it in turns. Apart from weasels, young lambs and kittens, I have not seen other creatures so obviously enjoying play. Are they playing or are they merely being pragmatic? Have they simply worked out how to use us to give them a boost so as to increase their own speed, get them on their way? Are they piggy-backing on us? Just at the point of turn, as each one is about to swoop round for another go, I swear that they turn to look at me, smile, and then take their momentary leave, their eyes twinkling with laughter.

On my daily walk round the Main Deck the next morning, I meet a crew member, Benjie, with a frozen decapitated sheep's carcass over his shoulder. He takes it to the Poop Deck, where he proceeds to hang it up by its hind legs with a piece of cord, a few inches from the stern, almost immediately above the foaming water being churned up by the propeller. There it stays until mid-afternoon, swaying in a macabre dance with the rolling of the ship and accumulating a thin coating of saline spray. It is destined for a barbecue which will take place this evening. It's an efficient way of thawing it and the salt will help it to crisp nicely on the spit.

At 18:00 hours, I accompany Maritje and Jörg to the Poop Deck to see how things are progressing. Half an oil drum filled with red hot coals serves as the barbecue and above it is a metal spit on which the now well-thawed carcass is being slowly turned by Second Officer Patrik. It is already looking and smelling pretty good. We all hang around, taking it in turns to work the spit. Every so often, Captain Ivanović pours some of the contents of a can of beer over the golden, crisping flesh. Maritje and I put in an order for barbecued fish, but I intend having some of the lamb as well. I am not doctrinaire about vegetarianism and I have, after all, helped to roast it. It seems to be very much a Croatian way of doing things.

"Filipinos do not like lamb very much but prefer pork," says Maritje. "At Christmas, a lamb carcass was prepared in the same way, but a pork carcass for New Year. So everyone was happy."

It's a lively barbecue, good spirited and fun, a necessary break from the otherwise monotonous routine of isolated lives. The Filipinos, as usual, entertain us with their soulful singing. The karaoke is a way of life for them. Every one of the Filipino crew has to have a go. They breathe music. As it comes to an end, I go up to the port bridge wing, soulful songs hovering over the still night air. Here I watch another day end. Looking aft to the west, the tops of a low bank of cumulonimbus clouds go through a change of colours from yellow to gold to blood red. Away to the south, a band of turquoise sky positions itself between storm clouds and altocumulus. Turning to the fore and looking east, is a full moon, ever so slightly veiled by a thin layer of salmon pink cirrus, delicately poised in transit to the high heavens, waiting for the day to properly end and her thin veil to be lifted to reveal the full extent of her glory. Here we are, twenty-six souls on board this metal warehouse, noisily thrusting itself through the middle of the world's biggest ocean, surrounded by nothing except water and sky, and still there are scenes to amaze the eye and warm the spirit.

The fragile splendour of the level sea,
The moon's serene and silver-veiled face,
Make of this vessel an enchanted place
Full of white mirth and golden sorcery.[52]

We are back in the tropics, the air is warm and calm, the water still. The sky is clear blue with an occasional brush of high cirrus clouds, but all around, stretching as far as the eye can see, are fair-weather cumulus, squat and wide with only limited vertical extent, sitting in the sky like randomly scattered puffs of cotton wool. They are sometimes known as humilis, from the Latin for humble – an apt description, for they do not aspire to the heights, preferring to spread horizontally. One or two in the middle distance, however, have shot to enormous altitudes and have developed their characteristic black bases, in classic storm cloud formation. Below each can be seen the tell-tale thick grey column, slightly tilted according to the direction of the wind, a sure sign that there is a raging storm below. The candy floss tops are in turmoil, towering rapidly and perpetually changing shape as they escalate at enormous speed to the edge of the stratosphere and then begin to level out into their signature anvil head. You can see weather being made here. One particular monster is off our port bow. We have been edging towards it for the past hour, but it looks as if we will miss it.

It's the afternoon watch and Second Officer Patrik has a bit of a sniffle. He's the second of the officers to have it. A cold is going round and I try to keep my distance. It's difficult, though, for the bridge is a companionable place and informative. I want to be there. We bend over charts, watch the seas, read the screens. It's impossible to isolate oneself. A few days later, I feel the warning itch at the back of my throat. The air conditioning has circulated the air nicely, making the spread of the ship's cold inevitable. It travels through the crew and officers alike like wildfire, but there is little slack for taking sick leave. Work has to continue.

Large brown birds with long yellow beaks seem to be following us, hovering over the sea and then swooping down towards the prow, an aeronautic sequel to the dolphin show. Sometimes, they hover high and close enough for me to be able to make out their yellow legs, tucked neatly under black tail feathers. Their gleaming white bellies and underwings form brilliant crosses, dipping and diving, swooping and swerving, each bird intent on its purposeful business. These are brown boobies. But it is not a game they are playing. It is a grim dance of life and death that I am witnessing. I walk to the f'o'csle once more to take a closer look. More commotion over the bulbous bow. Below me a shoal of flying fish collides with the bow and, frantic with fear, they take off in panic, pectoral fins whizzing like humming birds' wings, carrying these fascinating marine creatures to safety, or so they believe. But in fleeing an imagined giant predator, they unsuspectingly present themselves as food to real unimagined predators above them, who swoop down as soon as they leave the water and carry them away, swallowing them whole as they go, before turning steeply for another mouthful. Brown boobies are moderately large birds, with a wing span of about one and a half metres. As they hover, waiting for their luckless prey, their bullet shaped bodies bend themselves into smooth right-angled curves of perfectly poised concentration, quite beautiful to behold, beauty and blood in perfect oceanic symbiosis.

CHAPTER 19: Dark Skies

Great disappointment. The revised schedule has been posted. We arrive at all of the major ports on the remainder of our itinerary (Manzanillo, Savannah, Philadelphia) late in the evening and depart early the following morning, so there is no chance of spending any time ashore at any of these places. The best we can hope for might be a quick evening walk at Savannah, like at Auckland. But right now I am looking for a quiet, warm and comfortable place to sit on deck. The anticipated cold has matured; hacking cough, sore throat, headache, sleeplessness. Patrik has become the medical orderly, dispensing emollients, making sure everyone can carry on regardless. He gives me something that looks and tastes like Lemsip to ease the symptoms, and it does so, quite agreeably.

"It's not called Lemsip," he tells me, "but it's the same."

Hmm. Maybe a bit stronger, for it is remarkably effective.

It's not easy finding a quiet place today. The Captain is taking advantage of the calm conditions to set up a painting programme. It always needs doing, scraping blistered paint, treating rusty patches, renewing heavily worn areas. It all takes a mighty battering from the relentless salt-laden spray and the march of feet. Three men have been deployed and great progress is being made. I find a spot on F Deck, far away from all this, to sit and read.

At night, I get up and search the mini-galley for comfort food, but it has all been spotlessly organised away into locked cupboards. I can find nothing suitable, either in the way of food or utensils. Eduardo keeps a tight rein on his domain. My eyes eventually light on a basket of small pieces of French stick left over from the evening meal. I wrap a few pieces in a paper napkin and creep disconsolately back to my cabin. I had bought some excellent cheese at the Maleny Cheese Factory in Queensland and intended them as gifts for Joan. I look at them longingly, three beautiful cheeses wrapped in wax, one Tuscan, two Wasabi, but I cannot bring myself to open them. I also have some very poor cheese, however, by accident rather than by choice, soft cheese triangles in foil. Bill, who left us at Melbourne, gave them to Maritje. She quite rightly wanted to get rid of them, so she passed them on to me. Sometime earlier, I had inadvertently let out the secret of my nocturnal eating habits and from then on, I became the reluctant recipient of everyone's unwanted food. I hadn't the heart to refuse it or throw it away, not even surreptitiously. The stash had grown to include some savoury biscuits, including rye and wheat crackers, and some Special K mini breaks. I had tried one of these earlier, but decided that I preferred hunger, and the biscuits are too rough for my still very tender gums to cope with. The plastic bread and the soft cheese will have to do, but I wash it all down with red bush tea.

It's time to take to my bed. I miss breakfast. Eduardo is concerned and phones me. His call wakes me from a deep sleep I had just managed to get into, having been awake most of the night.

"It's okay Eduardo. Don't worry if I miss breakfast again tomorrow."

Thank heavens for the 'Lemsip' and the library. There are hundreds of books to choose from. I have just finished *Whispers of Heaven* by Candice Proctor, a historical novel and romance set in Tasmania at the time of slavery there, all about forbidden love across the mistress-slave divide. Gripping and historically interesting. I am now enjoying Paul Theroux's *The Great Railway Bazaar*, a parting gift from Bill. You would have to be very good at recording detailed information very quickly and efficiently, or retaining it and then writing it all up, to be able to write a book like that. An excellent read. I take two valerian forte tablets to help me to sleep.

Hovering on the edge of consciousness, I am woken by unusual quiet. We are rolling gently from side to side, but there is no pitching. Fully awake now, I look out of the window. The floodlights are on. Something is wrong. The ship judders. The engineers must be attempting to start the engines. I go outside and look over the edge onto the black waters below. All is still. No movement at all. I hesitate to go to the bridge as we have been told not to go there at night, but I do so in any case, making sure to open and close the door quickly so as not to let in any light which might disturb the night vision of the Duty Officer. I enter the darkened wheel house and once my eyes have adjusted, see Captain Ivanović sitting huddled in his chair at the controls, wrapped in a blanket. He too has a cold.

"It's cold," he says as I enter, and he smiles a smile of welcome.

"Is something wrong?"

"Yes, it's a gasket problem. The engineers are working on it."

I stay and watch for a while, staring into the inky blackness, trying to find something to settle my eyes on. We are adrift for two hours. We can easily make this up and keep to our schedule for passing through Panama. I retreat to my bed. The ship judders as the engines spring to life. Reassured as the noisy familiarity of their growl is restored, I fall asleep, waking in time to see the sun rise over the eastern Pacific, a hot mug of tea in my hand. The magically still waters have become an almost perfect mirror. It is all a welcome pause from the usual battering from the south-easterlies. I look down into the water and see the sky, clear blue and dotted with small puffs of white clouds. I look up and see it all again. It is a perfect and slightly disorientating reflection. The horizon has all but disappeared. We are sailing under the sky and on the sky, no water, just sky to sail on. Velvety warm air wraps itself round me. This is a day for feeling better, a day for breakfast, my first for two days.

It is the forenoon watch and Third Officer Dragomir is on duty.

"It looks calm," he says, "but there's a strong current out there. Ground speed nineteen knots, but effective water speed just eleven knots."

It's the South Pacific Gyre once more gently encouraging us along, and as we approach the coast of Peru, it sweeps us northwards into the Humboldt Current. There is a massive upwelling of cold water here, part of the deep water circulation of the oceans, and it brings with it vast quantities of nutrients in the form of nitrates and phosphates. At the surface, they interact with sunlight to encourage the growth of enormous quantities of phytoplankton and this in turn gives rise to one of the world's most prolific fishing grounds, of anchovies, pilchards and sardines. Also in the southern hemisphere, there is a similar current off the coast of Southwest Africa, the Benguela Current, whilst to the north the equivalents are the California Current and the Canaries Current. In all these cases, the direction of flow is towards the equator. They are all cool currents and form the eastern extensions of the north and south Pacific and Atlantic Gyres. Their impact on the climates of their adjacent territories is profound, as are the economic spin-offs. For us the immediate benefit is that our land speed is more than double our water speed.

The enormity of the ocean is mind-numbing. Since Napier, we have been sailing non-stop for eight days, twenty-four seven, most of it at the same speed of about twenty knots, in the same direction, sixty-four degrees, and with the southeast trades battering us to starboard. We are still over the East Pacific Rise and are heading towards the Galapagos Islands. Another seven days before we reach Panama.

Up on the bridge, as the afternoon watch is ending, Patrik laughs.

"You got it then."

"I certainly did. Thanks for the Lemsip."

"You're welcome. Nice to see you up and about again."

The enormity of the ocean is one thing. That of the skies is another. In Northumberland, where I live, we have dark skies. There is, over Kielder, an expanse of sky covering a land area of some five hundred and eighty square miles (about fifteen hundred square kilometres) that is so dark, it qualifies for International Dark Sky Park status. It is in fact the largest area of dark sky in Europe. There are no lights to be seen anywhere. I live on the edge of it, where there is a smudge of orange to the south hovering above the city of Newcastle upon Tyne thirty miles away, and looking the other way to the north, I can see the polka dots of people's house lights on the other side of my valley. Even so, I reckon the skies are pretty dark above my house, so dark that on cloudless nights, I can look up and see a sight that kills all words, stills all attempts at description.

The Milky Way, which enfolds planet earth, and indeed the whole of our solar system, appears as a broad swathe of delicately speckled silken sheen winding its way through the universe, trailing across the heavens like an infinitesimally light pashmina draped over the shoulders of the cosmos. This lady certainly knows how to inspire. The statistics that purport to define her dimensions are so vast, so outside the normal parameters of everyday life, that we have no conceptual framework in which to fit them. One estimate is that the Milky Way is one hundred thousand light years wide. I can only cope with such magnitudes by looking for single wonders, the proud thrust of Orion's Sword, the tight cluster of Pleiades on the shoulder of The Bull, the majestic Ursa Major repetitively ploughing the same furrow as she strides from east to west across the heavens. No words are fully adequate either to explain or to describe the infinity of beauty that surrounds and enfolds us. Some have tried, though, and the most poignant I have come across is the Japanese legend of the Husband and Wife stars who, as they journey through celestial space, only get to meet once a year on the bridge that spans the River of Heaven, the Milky Way. The ancient words have been adapted by my friend Graham Stacy and put into a song called simply *Pleiades*.

I loved her like the budding leaves of spring
That weighed the willow branches on the bank
Where we walked while she was of this world;
My life was built on her and now it's blank.
She soared like the morning bird,
Hidden in a mulberry white cloud.
She soared to the setting sun
To where the haze lay like a shroud.
Shine autumn moon.
We watched Orion rise above the fields.
When spring comes again
Farewell the Pleiades.[53]

It is interesting that the most powerful way we seem to have devised to get our minds round the great dimensions of human experience – wonder, joy, awe, beauty, or even horror, terror, evil – is to personalise them. Where were you, asked God of Job,

When the morning stars sang together,
And all the heavenly beings shouted for joy?[54]

And the Son of Man was revealed to St. John the Divine as one who "in his right hand... held seven stars" (the Pleiades)[55].

We never normally get to see the stars. One estimate has it that eighty-five per cent of UK residents have never seen a totally dark sky and have no idea of the majestic, awesome beauty that surrounds us. Sodium street lights have become the new normality; beyond them, we see nothing. We have blotted out celestial beauty.

I have been sailing across the Pacific for twelve days and each night there is a truly dark sky above me. Here it is still possible to see the Milky Way, and Orion is visible in summer, and of course, here in the southern hemisphere, there is the famous Crux Australis, the Southern Cross, and also Carina, the Keel; Pyxis, the Mariner's Compass; and Pictor, the Painter's Easel, all southern constellations, and all unknown to us in the northern hemisphere. I don't know much about these, but I do know that if I go to the Monkey Deck, I look over a sea area of just over six hundred square miles, nearly sixteen hundred square kilometres, with the sky above totally, eerily, uncannily, awesomely black, festooned with minute quiverings of light representing worlds too far away for us to imagine. Each night on this journey, I pass through a dark sky park as big as Northumberland's. Except for coastal areas, where there are ribbons of terrestrial light, every one of the Pacific Ocean's one hundred and eighty million square kilometres, is a truly dark sky area. The Pacific Ocean contains the equivalent of one hundred and twenty thousand Dark Sky Parks, like the one at Kielder. On cloudless nights, the trillions of stars are overwhelming in their magnificence. On moonless, starless nights, the blackness is so intense, it becomes almost tangible, smooth velvet blackness, blackness that you can touch, as black as the inky blackness of the sea.

Perhaps it was the experience of the dark skies that gave rise to early ideas about a transcendent Being, something or someone bigger than ourselves, mightier than we can ever imagine, that holds the universe in his/her/its hands. The theologian Rudolf Otto, in his book *The Idea of the Holy*, suggested that underlying all religions was an experience of what he called the numinous, a feeling that is characterised by a sense of tremendous mystery, a mysterium tremendum et fascinans or, in Robert Winston's words, "a feeling of overwhelming power...a universal experience of fear and fascination ... a mighty presence, something entirely 'other'".[56]

Whatever it was that first gave rise to religious ideas, I can well believe that when primitive human beings first became conscious of themselves as alone in a terrifying universe, or experienced the unimaginable emptiness of the night skies with absolutely no artificial light of any kind to relieve the terror, except perhaps for the occasional meagre fire around which they would huddle for mutual comfort and protection, it must have induced feelings of helplessness, of utter dependency on some great and awesome power totally outside of their control, particularly when confronted with the wanton destruction of storm, lightning, flood, volcano or earthquake, all of which struck so randomly, almost, it must have seemed, maliciously. And perhaps the only way they could have made themselves feel safe, was by personalising those mysterious forces and then seeking to placate them, as they would a fellow human being whom they had inadvertently provoked. Under such circumstances, it is not hard to see how the idea of God, or gods, developed. The God of the Old Testament is often depicted as one who compels worship and humility through the raw power and might of the universe he has made.

> When I consider thy heavens, the work of thy fingers,
> the moon and the stars, which thou hast ordained;
> What is man, that thou art mindful of him?[57]

When I was young, I used to sing a hymn based on these words. It sent tingles down my spine, and whatever my beliefs, or lack of them, today, it still has the power to do so.

> O Lord my God! when I in awesome wonder
> Consider all the works Thy hand hath made,
> I see the stars, I hear the mighty thunder,
> Thy power throughout the universe displayed:
>
> *Then sings my soul, my Saviour God to Thee,*
> *How great Thou art! How great Thou art!* [58]

Extract taken from the song 'How Great Thou Art' by Stuart K Hine Copyright © 1949 Thankyou Music*

At twelve noon the next day, we pass within one hundred and twenty-one nautical miles of the Galapagos Islands, but again the tantalising prospect of catching sight of them, eludes us all. There is a complete cloud cover, the nights are thick black, the days sultry. Shade temperature is thirty, the air still. We are back in the doldrums.

> Down dropt the breeze, the sails dropt down,
> 'Twas sad as sad could be;

And we did speak only to break
The silence of the sea![59]

I take my cabin's fold-up chair and sit outside under the port bridge wing all afternoon, blissfully unaware of the passage of time, reading and dozing, catching up on sleep. Here, there is a light breeze that relieves some of the stickiness and the shade minimises the risk of sunburn, possible even under this continuous cloud.

We cross the equator soon after five the following morning, change our course to zero forty-one and head directly for Panama.

"Now we have another current pushing us a bit more to the east," Patrik says.

"Oh, is that the Equatorial Countercurrent?"

"Yes. I'm impressed."

"School geography," I tell him. "My favourite subject."

CHAPTER 20: Panamax

"Land!" exclaims Jörg as I enter the conference room.

It's where I go every morning just after nine o'clock, when Eduardo cleans my cabin. I join Jörg where he is standing at the window, and gaze with him at the coast of Panama.

"At last!"

It is our first sight of land in two weeks. We stand silently and take it in. Something shifts inside, a reconnection with the familiar world whose absence my body has been adjusting to all this time. Once again, I can see but can't yet touch what once I took for normalcy. My feet itch to sense what it's like to feel the solid earth again without it giving way beneath me, to walk without rolling, without having to rebalance with each step. Side by side, we look and contemplate its strange familiarity, reaching out to solidity.

Still on our course of 041, we are heading almost directly into a fresh breeze from the same direction, the north-easterlies. This gives us a relative wind of thirty-seven knots, gale force. As I climb the outside steps to the port bridge wing, I lose my balance and fall back down. My foot catches between the open steps and harsh metal edges scrape my shins. I reach out for the railing and steady myself, grasping frantically. For God's sake take care, I tell myself. Flimsy footwear is the problem. Sandals are not good in these conditions.

In the evening, we anchor off the port of Balboa, six degrees north of the equator. The air is sultry, temperature thirty-one. It has been a long voyage, Brisbane to Napier, just over three thousand nautical miles, and from Napier to Balboa, six thousand four hundred and forty-five nautical miles (twelve thousand kilometres) taking the rhumb line route. Altogether from Brisbane, we have travelled nine thousand four hundred and sixty nautical miles, or just over seventeen thousand five hundred kilometres. Before us, stretches the impressive Pont des Amériques. Having cut a massive ditch across the Isthmus of Panama to separate the two continents of North and South America, it was then necessary to build a bridge to re-join them.

At two-thirty a.m. we pass under the bridge, and by three, we prepare to enter the first of the two Miraflores locks. It will take three locks to lift us from sea level to Lake Gatun at twenty-six metres above. At five a.m. we enter the second. The sodium lights create a tapestry of yellow and sepia shadows, a world of hushed, methodical, nocturnal busyness. As all operations are the responsibility of the Panama Canal Company, a relief crew comes on board. The ship teems with strangers going about the business of getting us through. A subdued air of grudging acceptance descends as officers and crew reluctantly but courteously give way to these men who invade our living and working space. Below us, snub-nosed mules attach themselves to us and gently guide us through each lock. We seem impossibly big, they impossibly small to pull such a gargantuan beast as ours. We slide through with inches to spare on each side. The lines on which these special engines operate are like a gigantic switch-back, with steep inclines between locks, the central rack rail ensuring there is no slippage.

Down to my cabin for a shower, a shave, a mug of tea. Back on deck, it is now daylight. The Pedro Miguel lock takes us to the level of Lake Gatun. We slip through the Culebra Cut, which links lock and lake. Almost fourteen kilometres long and a hundred and ninety metres wide, it has been progressively widened to allow for the increasing size of transit ships. On curves it needs to be wider, over two hundred metres. Ahead of us the Centennial Bridge, opened in 2004, spans the Culebra Cut. It carries six lanes of the Pan-American Highway, and supplements the already over-crowded Bridge of the Americas. A kilometre long and with a clearance of eighty metres, we pass under it with consummate ease. As we slide through the Cut, I nip down to the Mess for a quick breakfast. Back on deck, the wide expanse of Lake Gatun opens before us.

Massive works have begun as part of the programme of canal expansion to enable it to accommodate the larger ships that are already beginning to eclipse this one. On each side of us, tropical rainforest has been stripped away, exposing the underlying reddish brown clay soils and making them vulnerable to erosion. With an annual precipitation of almost two thousand millimetres, this might very well turn into a major problem for Panama. The muddying of the waters of the canal suggests that the process is already beginning. It is like pushing our way through a brown sludge.

The current maximum size of vessels that can be accommodated is 32.3 metres wide by 294.1 m long and with a draft of twelve metres. These are Panamax ships and their maximum container capacity is five thousand TEUs. But there is a whole generation of ships coming on line that are too big to pass through the canal as it is at present, the post-Panamax generation. The works currently being undertaken are to enable it to handle these monsters, ships with a carrying capacity of up to thirteen thousand TEUs, and measuring three hundred and sixty-six metres long by forty-nine wide. However, the new Maersk Triple-E Class, can carry 18,000 TEUs and is 400 m (1,312 feet) long, too big even for post-Panamax ships. These are the ULCs, the Ultra-Large Container ships. [60]

Just before we enter Lake Gatun, a ribbon of clear steel-grey water enters the muddy brown water of the Canal on our starboard side, from the north-east. This is the Chagres River, described by some sources as one of the most important rivers of the world[61], for it is this river that has made the Panama Canal possible. Without it, the Canal would have been much more difficult to maintain as a viable waterway, and it would probably never have been built. The lower part of the river, which flowed into the Caribbean Sea, was dammed in 1914 to form Lake Gatun, and the numerous islands that litter the lake are the remnants of the hills that once lined its lower reaches. When it became clear that further water regulation would be necessary, another dam was built across the Chagres River, two hundred and fifty feet above sea level. This is the Madden Dam, built in 1935 to create Lake Alajuela, which holds twenty-nine million cubic feet of water and generates hydro-electric power for use in operating the Canal works. The watershed area of this critically important river is protected by the Chagres National Park, created in the mid-1980s.[62]

The wide sweeping waters of this beautiful river, slam into the muddy waters of the Panama Canal and come virtually to a standstill, as if reluctant to get involved. Our water, the water of the Canal, is all churned up, disturbed and made mucky by the continuous passage of ships and the stripping of the protective vegetative cover. They are still, sullen waters, old, spent and weary. Those of the Chagres by comparison are crystal clear in their youthful vigour, dynamic, a joy to behold. The confluence of these two waters is marked by an almost clear straight line separating the two distinctively different waters, and this juncture is spanned by a railway bridge across the Chagres, close up against the small town and forest resort of Gamboa. But it is not the narrow struts of the bridge that prevent them from mixing. These struts are too small and too few in number to achieve that. Rather is it their difference that holds them back, brown and languid our side, steely-grey and energetic the other. In just one or two places, it is possible to make out where the new and the old waters have started to mix, the fresh, young waters forced at last to do the work for which their short span of life has prepared them. Having entered the Canal, this river, uniquely, flows in two separate directions, to the north and to the south, and ends up in two different oceans, the Pacific and the Atlantic, and two different hemispheres.

We anchor in Lake Gatun for four hours, waiting for ships from the Atlantic to pass through. Everywhere as far as the eye can see, is water and tropical rainforest. The islands are covered with forest, so thickly that no land can be seen at all; they are like floating islands of vegetation, subsisting entirely on the water surrounding them. Here on the Monkey Island, I look into the eyes of an eagle hovering on an invisible current, piercing my gaze, waiting, watching. The silence is broken just before 14:00 hours as a cry goes up from one of the pilots.

"Crocodile! Starboard side."

There is a rush of excitement as passengers, pilot, one or two officers and several crew members hurry to the starboard side and look over. There, sunning itself on an islet of sand and stone a couple of metres from the edge of the canal, lazes a large grey crocodile, eight to ten feet long, its stubby legs looking deceptively harmless, the edge of its pale cream belly just visible beneath its massive bulk, the tip of its nonchalantly curved tail some three metres away from its mighty jaws. Earlier in the year, one of these beasts took a man while he was fishing for tilapia with friends.[63]

Half an hour, later the pilot for the second half of our passage, comes on board and prepares to guide us through the lake towards the three Gatun Locks that will take us back down to sea level. The blazing sun shines out of a cloudless sky, shade temperature is thirty-two, but there is a welcome breeze, sometimes uncomfortably strong. At the top of our watery stairway we pause, just as the day is ending, poised between two continents, two oceans, two hemispheres, and look ahead onto the blue-grey Caribbean shimmering in the distance.

CHAPTER 21: Atlantic Conveyor Belt

A ship of unconventional design passes in front of us, cutting right across our bow, almost too close for comfort. This surely is against all the navigational rules of the high seas. She should be giving way to us. It's orange, with what appear to be two white superstructures, one at each end, and a long low-slung main deck from which protrude twelve to fifteen white masts of varying height and thickness. We can read her name clearly through the binoculars, Super Servant, and the name of the company, Dockwise Yacht Transport.

It's mid-morning by the time I get up to the bridge, the middle of the forenoon watch, with Third Officer Dragomir on duty. Everyone is very tired today. All put in long hours yesterday and we calculate the Captain worked an eighteen-hour day. During the night, we docked at Punta Manzanillo, at the northern end of the Canal, offloading three hundred containers and taking on a mere ten, all of them full of pineapples. So we are lighter, much lighter. And we can certainly feel the difference, for although the wind from the north-east is the same as we have been experiencing in the northern Pacific, we are now being thrown about much more. We are sitting high in the water and what is more, we are adrift.

"Problems, Drago?"

"Yes, engine trouble."

"Serious?"

"No, it'll soon be sorted."

"What's that ship doing passing right in front of us?"

"It's ok. I contacted it more than an hour ago to say it could pass on our starboard side. But we've drifted. So that's why it's ok to cut across us like that. They know we're not going anywhere yet."

"Strange looking ship. What is it?"

"It's a heavy lift vessel. I've got the details here from the AIS."

These HLVs are specialist ships, designed to carry cargo that will not fit onto regular bulk carriers or container ships, such as drilling rigs, marine cranes, or even other ships. This one is registered in the Netherlands Antilles, which lies to the south of us, off the coast of Venezuela, and it looks as if it is heading there. It is a flo-flo ship, float-on/float-off. The Super Servant's speciality is transporting yachts. It is semi-submersible, which means it can lower itself into the sea, flood its main deck and so transform itself into a floating marina. Multi-millionaires who want their yachts taken to some other part of the world can then float their pride and joy onto one of these extraordinary ships. Once aboard, the yachts are secured, the ship raises itself, the water is drained away and it becomes a floating dry-dock. This accounts for the curious array of masts on the main deck; they belong to the dozen or so yachts it is carrying. At its destination, the process is reversed and the yachts float away to see if the sea is bluer, the sun shinier in some other marine paradise.

About the same size as the Manet, the Super Servant is one hundred and sixty-nine metres long and thirty-two wide. The superstructure at the stern end holds the gear associated with getting the cargo on board, whilst that at the bow houses the normal set of cabins, offices, wheel house, navigational equipment, etc.[64] If ever we needed a sign to confirm that we are in the Caribbean this is it, playground of the rich and home to some of the poorest nations on earth. Another ship passes us, going the other way. It belongs to Maestro Reefers, a company specialising in carrying refrigerated goods. This time, the AIS is not able to provide further details because our engines are not functioning and neither, therefore, do we have electricity. All systems are down. It's another waiting game.

At lunch, the ship judders as the engines spring to life once more. I go up to the bridge. The contrast with our passage across the Pacific could not be greater. Whereas we went for two weeks with no sight of land at all, now there is an abundance of it. We are heading north-west through the Jamaica Channel. To port, the east end of Jamaica slides past us; to starboard, just off the coast of Haiti, we pass close to the tiny uninhabited island of Navassa, exquisitely close. A mere five square kilometres in area, this island is administered by the United States, but it is also claimed by Haiti. Like a tear drop in shape, it is a flat island, ringed by whitish-yellow cliffs forming a terrace as far as the eye can see. According to the US Geological Survey, the island comprises the remnants of an ancient coral atoll, its limestone surface capped with a stratum of phosphate, which may have been guano originally[65]. The phosphate has been of particular interest to the United States and probably explains why the USA took possession of it in the mid-nineteenth century. A solitary lighthouse, now obsolete, breaks the otherwise completely flat landscape.

Time for my mid-afternoon walk on the Main Deck, but it is still not possible to complete a circuit because of the painting, which resumed as soon as we came out of Panama. This project is a very serious one. Every part of the exposed paintwork on the main deck is being renewed, particularly the railings and deck floor, but also including the clutter of appliances on the f'o'csle and poop decks. I go up to where the men are working then turn round and go the other way. It's not as satisfying as a complete circuit, but it's possible to cover the distance. The men are used to me and Maritje walking this way each day. Whenever I get to them, they greet me with an avuncular air of amused bewilderment. Jörg doesn't get to see this as he doesn't do walking. My quota for the day accomplished, I climb the hundred or so stairs and join Jörg on the starboard bridge wing. He is studying the distance through a pair of powerful binoculars, of which I am envious, his long white hair swept aside by the brisk north-easterly. We've swung directly into this wind now to take us through the Windward Passage that separates Haiti and Cuba. Jörg is studying the coast of Haiti.

"Cap à Foux," he says as I join him. "And there," he adds, pointing, "Le Bahie du Môle."

We go inside and check the charts. Nestling inside the bay is Le Môle-St-Nicolas. It is just possible to make it out with the binoculars. This is where Christopher Columbus is reputed to have landed in December 1492, laying the foundation for so much ensuing history. What momentous events grew from such a serendipitous landfall! On the other side of the Windward Passage to the west of us lies Cuba, and close at hand, the notorious Guantanamo Bay. It feels strange being so close to the one place in the world that, more than any other, generates such strong feeling for or against the American way of doing foreign policy.

Sparkie tells me that a couple of years ago he was going this way on another ship. It called at Port-Au-Prince and a stow-away managed to jump on board and hide in the ship's rudder housing. He had been seen by tug men when they were in the Bahamas and the port authorities there refused to accept him, so the ship had to turn round and return him. This was a very humanitarian thing to do as it would have been enormously costly to the company. They told the culprit that he was lucky, for some ships would have simply dumped him in the sea and left him to die. I was told that this is not unknown. It does happen. Some of these unfortunate men are simply thrown overboard. On the high seas, ships are beyond the jurisdiction of any particular country.

Overnight, we pass the Turks and Caicos Islands and the next morning finds us in the Bahamas. There are more than seven hundred and fifty islands here, nearly all of them uninhabited and made almost entirely of limestone. The surface geography is a product of the submarine geography; what you see are but tiny fragments of the huge formations that lie out of sight below the ocean. The limestone of which these islands are formed, has been accumulating for one hundred million years, perhaps even more, and it is derived from the remains of tiny marine organisms, coral, or those that live in shells, such as foraminifera. Over this time, enormous thicknesses of limestone have formed, sometimes more than four thousand five hundred metres (nearly fifteen thousand feet), and in this way huge banks have formed, of which the largest is the Great Bahama Bank, closely followed by the Little Bahama Bank to the north. The Turks and Caicos Islands were also formed in the same way.

As this limestone was deposited in shallow waters, it seems that they have submerged under their own weight. Even today, the waters immediately surrounding the Bahamas are shallow, often no deeper than twenty-five metres. We keep well away from these shallows. Our route takes us through Crooked Island Passage, between Long Island (which straddles the Tropic of Cancer) and Crooked Island, then between Rum Cay and San Salvador, with little uninhabited Conception Island lying further over to the west of us. Here and along the eastern edges of Cat Island and then Eleuthera, the water is deep, for the edges of the Bahama Banks are exceptionally steep, the equivalent of submarine cliffs. We follow the line of these cliffs, well within deep water, close enough to see the islands, eventually taking our leave of the Bahamas as we pass Great Abaco Island, on the Little Bahama Bank.[66]

It's a cruising paradise here. Passenger liners pass us regularly. Today, we see the Seven Seas Navigator, a cruise ship on which all the accommodation, for just under five hundred 'guests', is in the form of suites rather than cabins, and which is bound for Fort Lauderdale. Later Disney Magic passes us, a huge cruise ship for nearly three thousand passengers and a thousand crew and entertainment staff.

We are now back on a north-westerly course and making twenty-one knots, with a water speed of just fourteen. This time we're riding on the North Equatorial Current, which here transforms itself into the Gulf Stream and then the North Atlantic Drift, without which the British Isles would have the same climate as Labrador, with its sub-polar severe winters and short cool summers. We are saved from that climatic fate by the warm waters of the Gulf Stream and the warm air that clings to it, giving to the UK a warmer climate than is justified by its latitude. North-west Europe is a beneficiary of the climatic mechanism that transfers heat from equatorial regions to higher latitudes. The warm Gulf Stream sweeps all the way up along the east coast of the USA until it meets the cold waters of the Labrador Current coming south.

It is this cold current that is largely responsible for Labrador's cold climate. It could, however, disappear and if this were to happen, it would pose a threat to the climate of the British Isles. One possible scenario for global warming is that continuing melting of the Arctic Ice Cap could release such large quantities of fresh water into the North Atlantic that the overall salinity would be reduced, making it less dense and lighter. This cold water, straight off the ice sheet, would therefore remain on the surface and this would radically interfere with the oceanic conveyor belt to such an extent that the North Atlantic Drift, which transfers much needed heat from the equator to our otherwise cold shores, might cease altogether. If the system did break down in this way, the whole of north-west Europe would freeze in winter and our summers would be significantly cooler and shorter, just like those of Labrador, whose latitude we share. We would then have the paradoxical situation of global warming bringing cooling to north-western Europe! Studies are currently under way to measure whether the North Atlantic Drift is in fact changing in this way[67].

For the time being, however, our ship is definitely benefiting from the way the ocean currents are behaving. The North Atlantic Gyre promises to speed our progress and assist us all the way back to the UK. The North Atlantic is not always kind, though; it's a rough time of year to cross it. Some freight companies won't take passengers across the North Atlantic in the winter months as it is too hazardous. As I study the charts, Captain Ivanović puts the latest weather report for the North Atlantic in front of me. It shows a massive low right in the middle of our route and another one across the British Isles.

"The Atlantic, eh!" he says, with a wry smile.

"Doesn't look good. Any chance we'll hit it?"

"We've mapped four alternative routes – just in case it gets too bad."

We're out of the tropics now and back in the northern and western hemispheres. It feels close to home, the skies lower, the weather more familiar. A familiar chill wraps itself round me. The sun sets before six. Still unable to complete a circuit on deck, I finish off my daily perambulations with a visit to the gym. After dinner, I watch *Finding Forester*. Sean Connery is superb as the ageing novelist brought back to life and vitality by the inspirational enthusiasm of the black teenager Jamal Wallace, played by Rob Brown. An uplifting film and a good note on which to end the day.

CHAPTER 22: Savannah

A thick shroud of fog greets the morning. This forces us to miss our 14:00 hours rendezvous with the pilot. We have to proceed slowly and hesitatingly to our waypoint.

"Now, we'll pick up the pilot at eleven tomorrow, a day behind schedule," says the Captain.

Allowing enough time for the immigration people to come on board and question us, it is doubtful that we will be able to go ashore and see anything of Savannah. Nine o'clock the next morning and still the hours drag interminably by. There's a signal on my mobile and I manage to tell family what is happening. It is now unlikely that I will be able to get back home in time for the last performance of the cabaret show the Amateur Dramatic Society is putting on. It's on St. Valentine's Day - lots of potential for disappointment.

14.30 and there is still no sign of the fog lifting, no traffic on the Savannah River, nothing going in, nothing coming out. Another ten laps round the deck and half an hour on the rowing machine. The men resume the painting. It passes the time.

Meanwhile Patrik and Sparkie have gone fishing. They've dropped a line over the stern end with various bits of squid attached for bait. Two small sharks have been swimming around and they want to catch one and make a curry. It is a bright white fog, not at all like the depressing grey, bleak fog in the East China Sea. Captain Ivanović is scheduled to leave us here at Savannah, but his replacement cannot reach us from Chicago on account of the fog. Patrik, the Second Officer, is also leaving us here. I shall be sorry to see him go. He has been fantastic, informative, friendly, and unfailingly cheerful, even when putting in sixteen and eighteen hour days. He has also been very considerate, always asking after me when I was poorly. Yes, he will be a loss. He doesn't, however, manage to catch the shark and we have to do without the curry.

It is evening of the second day and the fog is receding. I can now see the numerous ships lying at anchor, waiting to berth. It is dark by the time we enter the Savannah River. We glide past the East Riverside area with its multitude of grills, taverns, pizzarias and wine bars. It is bustling with activity. The sound of merriment and laughter occasionally wafts across to us. Riverboats line the frontage, lit up and full of winers and diners. It sounds like party time. The circular lights on the riverside walkway are reflected in the river as elongated beacons, tapering into nothing as they plumb the black depths of the water. Once more I feel the isolation; it would be good to mingle with the crowd, to re-join normal humanity. Some of the crew announce their intention, when we get to the container port, of going to the out-of-town Walmart to do some shopping; cheap laptops seem to be the main attraction. They will need to get a taxi and make it short, swift and single-minded, however. Not my idea of a shore visit.

All the riverside activity abruptly ends as we pass under the Talmadge Memorial Bridge, which links the Riverside area with Hutchinson Island and then continues over the Back River to Jasper County, South Carolina. Then, on the Georgia side, we come alongside an enormous industrial complex that looks as if it is on fire, chimneys reaching into the pitch black sky way beyond the reach of the sulphur lights below. Long, billowing clouds of yellow smoke drift lazily and noxiously away from the nightlife and the gaiety we have just passed downstream, before disappearing into the inky blackness of the night sky. This is three dimensional industry par excellence, occupying every space that catches the eye, the whole of it lit by glaring yellow lights. No corner of this infinity of complexity escapes their searching glare. It is a monstrous inferno. Below us, even the water catches the reflection of this frenzy of activity, setting the river alight, enveloping us in fire. We are like Old Testament Daniel in the burning fiery furnace who survived unscathed, and like him, we pass quietly on our way, unscathed.

The transition from the world of wine bars and merriment to thunderous son et lumière is as astonishing as it is abrupt. This is the International Paper Company, whose products include chemicals and corrugated containers as well as paper and packaging. It is what gives Savannah its vibrancy. Without the wealth it generates, the wine bars would not be possible. We slip past this industrial monster and creep towards the largest single container terminal on the eastern seaboard of the United States. By comparison, this is a flat two-dimensional landscape of orange and yellow lighting stretching to the horizon, another twenty-four seven operation, ensuring the global market place is well stocked. We hear the occasional subdued clang of metal on metal as containers are manipulated, the soft squelch of rubber on concrete as straddle cranes go about their business, keeping American consumers happy.

Welcome to Savannah, Georgia's oldest city, built on cotton and the plantation system two and a half centuries ago, now a major port and industrial centre. It is nine o'clock at night. Paper, chemicals, containers, wine bars and Walmart. I am not inclined to go there. A quick taxi ride, hurried purchases, frenzied acquisitions, a taxi ride back. It is not to my liking. The men, however, want their laptops to take home, for they are much cheaper here. I stay on the bridge and watch as they are whisked away, before turning in at ten, not wanting to miss the downstream journey early tomorrow morning.

It is morning and plans have changed. Overnight, the new Captain and second mate have come aboard, but Captain Ivanović and Second Officer Patrik are to remain in place until Philadelphia, where the two new men will take over their duties. The sky is clear, the air cool when we leave the wharf, but a whiff of downstream chemicals is wafted to us on the breeze. Now, the details of the industrial giant we passed last night become clear, even more complex than I could possibly have imagined; a mass of buildings of every conceivable size and shape – low and squat, tall and dominating, round, conical, perpendicular, horizontal. In this grey, mechanistic world, everything is mind-bogglingly complicated as tubes, pipes, conveyor belts, ladders, holding tanks, elevated metallic walkways, heating systems, cooling systems, interact and integrate to produce such mundane things as paper and packaging.

Opposite is Hutchinson Island, an elongated stretch of land in the middle of the river. A curious piece of ground on this island interests me. It is white, gleaming white. "Saltpans"? I suggest to Jörg. "An outdoor skating rink?" he offers. We draw closer. It's a collection of large white circles, each with a dark brown centre where water rises and spreads out to create white foam, the kind of foam you get at the edge of the sea when waves crash onto the sand. It turns out to be a waste water treatment pond for the International Paper Company, the white circles marking the point where the water is being agitated to aerate and purify it.[68]

Back under the Talmadge Memorial Bridge and the new day has transformed the evening's wine bars into a zone of coffee houses, restaurants and a business district. The Hyatt Hotel slips past, the City Hall, East River Street, lined with restaurants and shops, with their colourful awnings of racing green, blue, white and sunflower yellow. Between shop frontages and the river, is a series of raised beds of soft red brick enclosing shrubs and trees, the walls low enough for a few people to sit on in the warm sun. Shady piazzas and pedestrian walkways declare that this is to be an area for people, not cars. Moored alongside is the Georgia Queen Riverboat, its red paddlewheel matching the red awning of the River Street Sweets Candy Store and, next to it, the dark red of the River Boat Ticket Office. It is an altogether beguiling scene, frustrating because so tantalisingly close to the hustle and bustle of ordinary life and yet so far away, the mundane pleasure of a coffee and a stroll in the sun, but so impossibly out of reach. Passing the glass frontage of the Marriott Riverfront Hotel, I watch the reflection of our ship as we slip away, like a mirage, emphasising the loneliness of this shipboard life, its complete detachment from the exquisite pleasures of ordinariness.

CHAPTER 23: City of Brotherly Love

05:45 hours. The telephone jars me awake. It's the Captain.

"Please report to the Crew's Mess in fifteen minutes."

No explanation. Just a command. I meet Jörg on the way down. We both shrug.

"What's going on?" he asks.

"No idea."

Together, we make our half-awake way down the stairs, totally unprepared for the day, the stale sweat and smell of sleep clinging disagreeably to us. Along the corridors and standing around the open door of the Mess, half a dozen sinister-looking men scatter themselves around, clad in black and grey fatigues, helmets, bullet vests, guns in their hands, guns hanging round their waists, looking for all the world like terminators. They direct us into the already crowded room. We join Maritje, who wears an expression of exasperation. Jörg looks bewildered, the crew ill at ease. I feel intimidated, under suspicion. It is the US Coast Guard. We cram together, around the scattered tables and chairs, officers, crew, passengers, while the Captain hands over our passports, visas, and personnel manifest. Only the First Officer is absent, on the bridge for the morning watch. Four heavily armed men are sent to search the ship, to check that there are no other people on board unaccounted for. The soft squelch of what we used to call brothel creepers, disappears along the corridor. Those remaining question us, the passengers in particular. Why are we travelling on a cargo ship? Why not travel normally, by plane or on a cruise liner? Every passport, every visa, is checked and rechecked. Each name is called out, slowly, deliberately, inquisitorially, and with each response, faces are scrutinised and compared, notes made, eyebrows raised, a smile suggested, the hint of a frown. The measured erosion of confidence. Some of the crew, the most vulnerable, are visibly cowed.

The questioning over, we wait for the search detail to report back. A scattering of quiet conversations take place. It distracts from the feeling of powerlessness and overwhelming authority pressing down on us. An hour and a half later, the squeak of rubber on polished floors and the soft metallic click of tightly held guns, announce the return of the armed men. No one has been found. There are no stowaways. All our papers are in order. There is nothing suspicious. We're given the all clear.

Their departure is as swift and silent as their arrival. Tables and chairs are rearranged. The crew settle down to a hasty breakfast before resuming duties. Officers and passengers go next door to the Officers' Mess, to a breakfast of scrambled egg, toast and marmalade, coffee. It feels mean, unnecessarily hierarchical, to separate ourselves off in this way after such shared angst.

The bridge provides a superb view of several whales sending spouts of water high up into the air. We are close to land now, inside American territorial waters, just off Albemarle and Pamlico Sounds, large lagoons sheltered from the Atlantic by a series of elongated spits and sand bars aptly named 'barrier islands'. Along the whole of the northern half of North Carolina, these sand bars smooth out what would otherwise be a pretty complicated coastline, deeply indented by the estuaries of the Roanoke, Chowan, Pamlico and Neuse Rivers. They owe their formation to the combined effects of the continual deposition of silt from these rivers and the north-south trending winds and ocean currents, particularly our friend the Gulf Stream. Later, we pass Chesapeake Bay into which flow the Susquehanna and Potomac Rivers, whose mouths together make this the largest estuary in the USA, the

Pamlico and Albemarle Sounds complex being the second largest. Further north, we can make out the sky scrapers of Ocean City, Maryland. At 15:00 hours, Cape May Point, the southernmost tip of New Jersey, heaves into view, marking our entrance to Delaware Bay.

Half an hour later and the pilot's boat draws alongside. He is accompanied by a trainee pilot. Before commencing their duties, they join us in the Officers' Lounge for afternoon tea. The trainee pilot is from Lewes, Sussex County, Delaware, which is twinned with Lewes, Sussex, UK.

"That's my old stomping ground," I tell him. "I used to cycle through Sussex as a lad."

"D'you know Lewes, England?"

"I certainly do. I've got a friend living there. Lovely place, but prone to flooding."

Up on the bridge, the pilot points out a lighthouse in the middle of the estuary, a small squat affair on a rock of just sufficient size to support it, with absolutely no room for anything else.

"Someone's just bought it for two hundred and fifty thousand dollars," he says. "Set it up as a bed and breakfast venture."

He's been up and down this river three thousand times, he tells me. It's a long haul apparently, a good five hours. The temperature is down to ten Celsius. We're heading north and into a north wind, making walking on the Main Deck unpleasant, the rowing machine a more attractive alternative. On the bridge, Patrik is on the afternoon watch, probably his last before he disembarks for shore leave. Since Savannah, he has been shadowed by the new second mate, who will take over tomorrow, as will the new Captain, who has been keeping a low profile since he too came aboard at Savannah. He is a personal friend of both the first and second mates and although he spends time on the bridge, he says nothing, just shadowing and observing.

I like Philadelphia and I want to explore on my own. Maritje and Jörg each intend doing their own thing too, so it's a good arrangement. Home of the Liberty Bell and Independence Hall, I am moved by the values and sentiments that strike such a deep chord with freedom-loving people throughout the world, but I am sad that for all the fine words, often religious in origin, that accompanied the founding of the American nation, so much of their subsequent history contradicts them. It's about aspiration and failure, the spirit being willing but the flesh weak, all part of the human condition.

I like to think about the deep complexities of this human predicament and am moved by the inscription on the Liberty Bell: "Proclaim liberty throughout all the Land unto all the inhabitants thereof." It's a biblical quotation[69] whose origin lies in the Old Testament concept of the Jubilee, and that context needs to be known for the full meaning of those words to be understood. The Jubilee was a year of liberty for all households enslaved by debt. It involved the restoration of land to families who had been compelled to sell it out of economic necessity in the previous fifty years. It was devised to protect the viability of households as the basic unit of land tenure and therefore the basic unit of production. Where, out of penury, households had been forced to sell their land, that land was restored to the household. This redistribution happened every fifty years. The institution of the Jubilee was based on the principles of liberty, restoration and compassion. It ensured that excessive wealth and power did not concentrate too much in too few hands. It occurs to me that it would be pretty revolutionary to follow the full spirit of those proud words on the Liberty Bell.

In Liberty Hall, as I sit through the daily presentation with three hundred other visitors from all over the world, I am moved by the nobility of the sentiments that are so eloquently expressed. The proud words: "We hold these Truths to be self-evident, that all Men are created equal..." are recognised throughout the world as lofty aspirations for the whole of humankind in our common pursuit of life, liberty, and happiness. Every day, the message is proclaimed in Liberty Hall, and I think about how easy it is to fall short of our own idealism. The story that is told here in this memorable building is deeply moving and deeply sad. At its core are religious sentiments that are meant to unify but which seem to end up doing the very opposite.

I look for other commentaries on this puzzle of human nature. They are all here in this glorious City of Brotherly Love; the capacity of the American people for openness and self-examination, for ruthless honesty as well as its opposite, the single-minded pursuit of wealth and well-being and the poverty and misery it can so easily spawn. There is ample evidence in the superbly laid out display material in the National Constitution Centre, that the American people themselves recognise that they have not always lived up to their own ideals. I buy a copy of Jon Meacham's book *American Gospel: God, the Founding Fathers and the Making of a Nation.* At a time when religion and politics are deeply divisive issues in the United States, it tells the story of the interweaving of these powerful leitmotifs throughout this great nation's history.

But, it seems, for all the problems religion causes us, we cannot do without it. According to Homer, "all men need the gods." Although we've given ourselves the title *homo sapiens,* or wise men, we are nevertheless perpetually inclined to look beyond ourselves to a supernatural power to provide the answers to life's most intractable questions. It's as if we are incapable of following through on the ideals we set ourselves and yearn for divine help. We are, Meacham tells us, inescapably religious. We are, in short, *homo religiosus.*[70]

Sometimes, however, religion encourages us to find answers within ourselves rather than supernaturally. In the African American Museum, there is a display about religion in ancient Egypt, where the ultimate purpose of life was to understand oneself and the higher powers that each one of us possesses. This is achieved through the daily contemplation of Ma'at, variously conceived of as truth, order, justice, harmony, balance. Sometimes these attributes were personified as a goddess, because that seems to make them more accessible to the human mind. In that sense, the goddess

Ma'at becomes a judge who, when we pass from this life, weighs our souls against a feather in the cosmic scales of justice. If our lives have been marked by harmony, justice and truth, and our relationships by service and reciprocity, by doing to others what we'd like them to do to us, our souls will be as light as a feather. Once again, I am struck by the closeness of these teachings to those of the biblical Jesus. The similarity provides yet more evidence to suggest that during his sojourn in Egypt as a young man, Jesus may have absorbed some of the religious teachings prevalent there at that time. His ideas weren't necessarily all that new.

I wander on and find a series of photographs, *Engulfed by Katrina*, portraying the destruction of the mighty hurricane that ripped people's lives apart a few years earlier. I am impressed most of all by a photograph, amidst all the carnage, of the doorway to Calvary Spiritual Church. Trauma so often leads us back to our religious roots. We should never devalue or belittle the enormous comfort that religious belief provides for frail humanity at times when events occur over which we have no control. We are indeed *Homo religiosus*.

In the evening, before rejoining the Manet, I wander through the Old City neighbourhood to find the Red Sky restaurant on Market Street. Here I enjoy a fine meal: an arugula salad of leaves, candied walnuts, blue cheese and raspberry vinaigrette, followed by pan-seared Chilean sea bass, with shrimp-fried rice and Chinese black sauce. I finish this off with crème brûlée, and wash it down with a glass or two of house red wine.

CHAPTER 24: Mohawk

A couple of weeks before Christmas 1893, a young woman in her mid-thirties and her husband of seventeen years moved into their new home at 304 Grant Avenue, Nutley, in Essex County, New Jersey. Mr. and Mrs. Frank Butler were comfortably off, having spent most of the previous two decades touring the United States and Europe as part of a troupe belonging to Buffalo Bill's Wild West Show. Both Annie and Frank had been renowned for their sharp shooting abilities, but she was the better of the two and had outshot Frank at a marksman's competition to which he had challenged her, hoping to make some easy money. She was the one, however, who had made the easy money with her consistently accurate shooting, and so much had she impressed her challenger, that she also stole his heart. They were married a year after Frank had issued his challenge.

The woman was better known to the public as Annie Oakley, and between them she and Frank had accumulated sufficient funds to buy their splendid new house outright. In December of 1893, therefore, both Frank Butler and Annie Oakley were feeling good about themselves. Their exhausting touring schedule had made them feel rather rootless and they wanted to have a secure base and some kind of stable domestic life. They wanted, in short, to become part of a settled community. Nutley was ideal. A small town, with a population of about three thousand, it had the added advantage that it was conveniently close to New York, which provided easy access to the passenger liners that took them regularly to

Europe, as well as to the theatres and shops of the metropolis. They also enjoyed an active social life and what better way of getting this going in Nutley than to throw a dinner party. They did this within a week of moving into their new home.

Among the guests, was a certain John Wiltshire, Captain of the Steamship Mohawk that had carried Buffalo Bill's Wild West troupe back to the USA from Europe the year before. J. M. Brown, manager of the Atlantic Transport Company, which had chartered the Mohawk, was also present[71]. It was a brand new ship, having been built by Harland and Wolff in 1892, and she had made her maiden voyage later that same year. This was a steamship, however, unlike the Barque Kilemny which, ten years earlier, had been lost somewhere in the Tasman Sea.

Captain John Wiltshire had more reasons than most to mourn the loss of the ill-fated Kilmeny in the Tasman Sea, for its Captain, William Royan, was his brother-in-law, making John Wiltshire my great-great-uncle. The shock of the tragedy of the Kilmeny reverberated throughout the family. They were not unused to the uncertainties and disappointments that seafaring families were subject to, for the sea was in their blood. It was part of our family tradition. William Royan's grieving widow, Mary, had learned how to cope with the long absences of her husband and her father, for both had been Master Mariners. She remembered well how abandoned she felt when her brother John too went to sea and how pride mingled with fear when he had got his first command. But now, she felt utterly alone. Her father had died a few years earlier, and her husband William was in his watery grave. She now knew, of course, that that last vision she had had of William admiring the daughter on whom he doted, was a premonition. She was grateful for that last ghostly glimpse of him, but with no body to mourn over, she felt unable to say goodbye properly, unable to quite accept that she had lost him forever. A flicker of hope still remained. But she had grown to distrust the sea and now feared for the safety of her brother John. She could not bear the thought of losing him too.

Mary consoled herself with the thought that her brother's ship, the Steamship Mohawk, was altogether stronger and more modern than the Barque Kilmeny had been. For one thing, the Mohawk was bigger. Measuring four hundred and forty-five feet long, the Mohawk was more than twice the length of my great-grandfather's ship, seventeen feet broader and ten feet deeper[72]. And whereas the Kilmeny had depended on sail to carry it along, always at the mercy of whatever caprice the wind might throw at it, the Mohawk had its own independent source of power, in the form of six cylinders and two triple expansion engines. It could therefore make its own way independently of the fickle wind. The Mohawk's engines yielded greater power and fuel efficiency than the older double-expansion systems which had hitherto been the norm. Yes, Captain Wiltshire's ship was altogether safer than the Kilmeny. Mary Royan felt reassured. Nevertheless, a shadow of foreboding must have run through the family when, some years later, another ship, the Titanic, built in the same yard as the Mohawk had been built in, had come to grief on its trans-Atlantic maiden voyage.

In one way or another, these three Master Mariners left their mark on my family history. The first such mark was one of pride. When I was a boy, my great-great-uncle John, Captain of the Mohawk, was a star. I knew of him through a family photograph of Annie Oakley and Buffalo Bill that the duo had given to Uncle John on one of the many trans-Atlantic voyages he had captained. We were very proud of our connection with these iconic Wild West heroes.

And then there was the mark of sorrow. The loss of the Kilmeny had been a tragedy whose repercussions reached deep into our consciousness. It brought fear into the family. Ghosts lingered over unfinished business. Nothing, however, could destroy the deeply ingrained love of the oceans that has cascaded down the generations. My father used to tell how when he was on the troop carriers during the Second World War, there was nothing that thrilled him more than to stand high up on his ship in storms and feel the see-saw rise and fall of its massive bulk, watching the bow slice into solid walls of water, shrugging it all off and then doing the same thing again and again. I too have inherited my family's love of the sea, and the fact that this is my sixth voyage across the Atlantic gives this, the last leg of my long voyage round the world, the feel of easy familiarity. I am in home waters.

On board the Manet, the new Captain has now donned his uniform and is sitting in the seat of power on the bridge with the pilot ready to take us downstream. I introduce myself. He has a firm handshake.

"Captain Teodor Vinkovic. Pleased to meet you. You've been on board a long time, I think."

"Since Brisbane."

"You're welcome on the bridge at any time, but please treat it like a church – be quiet, respect the fact that officers are working, and do not hold conversations."

This young man must have something very special about him to have attained such a position by the age of thirty-one. We pull away shortly before breakfast, with First Officer Radimir on watch. It's a slow haul down river and it is 14:30 before we round Cape May Point. Course ninety-two is subsequently amended to seventy-nine, so it looks as if we are taking the Great Circle Route, the best way of avoiding the storms that are still raging over the Atlantic. The new schedule shows ETA for the Tilbury pilot 16th February 01:00 and ETA at berthing 06:00. We're making good time and with the help of a following wind, are making twenty-one knots. The Captain gives instructions to go as fast as possible to try to catch up on the time we lost at Savannah.

"If we keep this up, we'll be back by the fifteenth," says Dragomir.

I'll miss the last night of the Am Dram's performance and Valentine's Day, but at this rate, I might make the annual dinner!

There's something comfortingly predictable about the North Atlantic with its prevailing south-westerlies and the North Atlantic Drift. Harnessing their combined energy to best effect, saves time and money. It can, however, be seriously rough, especially in winter. At breakfast, two new passengers join us, Phil and Gwen, who joined us at Philadelphia. They live in Washington DC and are on their way to Brussels to stay with their daughter. I thought I was the senior, but they beat me by a few years. They promise to be good company.

Overnight the wind drops and we hit a bank of thick fog on the Grand Banks off the coast of Newfoundland. Here, the warm waters of the Gulf Stream and the cold waters of the Labrador Current, mingle to make it one of the most important fishing grounds in the world and one of the most predictably foggy. In line with standard practice at times of poor visibility, Able Seaman Nonilo has been brought onto the bridge as support lookout.

We're still close enough to America to receive good television signals and I am fascinated with a most extraordinary programme I stumble across as I try to get BBC news. It's from The New Jerusalem, Davao City, Philippines, the eighth International Youth Congress, a service to celebrate the fact that Pastor Apollo C. Quiboloy was appointed Son of God on 13th April 2005. It's emotionally powerful preaching, reminiscent of the Billy Graham rallies I attended in my teenage years. Apart from the fact that God now seems to have a new "Appointed Son" in the person of this charismatic preacher, the teaching seems to be basically evangelical Christianity.

"I am sent from the Father to tell you the truth," this new Son of God declares.

There must be a thousand, perhaps two, in the congregation, all dressed in white, men and women seated separately. A huge full-sized orchestra plays – flutes, trumpets, violins, several keyboards, percussion. "Come to me and be saved," the Son of God declares, as violins play emotionally stirring music. I remember it well from Wembley Stadium, when Billy Graham in 1954 invited me to go forward and give my life to Jesus. "Softly and tenderly Jesus is calling," the massed choir sang, "calling to you and to me."

A powerful emotion gripped my soul and I knew I had to do something about it. I couldn't ignore it or I would go straight to hell. It's powerful stuff.

That was in Wembley on hard seats. This, from New Jerusalem, looks like the height of luxury. The floors are carpeted, seats plushly upholstered – a special, purple one for the "Appointed Son", rather like a throne. Occasional tables are scattered throughout, sweeping, regal staircases, backdrops of rustic bridges over idyllic blue streams evocative of the Garden of Eden, suggestive of purity, innocence, bliss. "If you are sick or in need of healing, or have financial hardship, give me your prayer requests, you will be healed."

All over the auditorium, people break down and cry, hands are raised, reaching out to the sky beseechingly, worshipfully, tearfully. "The reign of righteousness has begun," they are told, and there is a great shout of joy. Pastor Apollo's mandate "does not come from any religion or political system, but from God," he declares. He "literally" heard God's voice, just as Moses did, and as the Old Testament prophets before him did. I think, well if they did, I suppose Pastor Apollo can. "When the Father tells me something, I do not have to question it," he tells them. "The Appointed Son of God" is about to expand the King's dominion in North America, where a great "harvest of souls" is waiting for him.

I am transfixed. I spend the whole day drawn to the screen, watching, listening. And so the glorious variety of religious belief goes on. It serves its purpose. People are consoled. They feel their guilt washed away. They have certainty. The fear of death is erased. Heaven awaits them. You make your choice about what to believe. It works for some, not for others. It's not only the love of seafaring that has left its mark on my family; so also has this kind of evangelical belief system. But on this occasion, my journey has been in the opposite direction, from belief to unbelief. I am almost there now, at the end of a long journey, divesting myself of the clutter of religious beliefs that have not proved helpful. I do retain, however, a small, but significant residue –

a belief in the possibility of a just and compassionate society. Beyond that, I have no interest in religion. Geography and the wonders of the natural world are enough. Better than divinity any day.

We're nearly home now. It's a boisterous night. At two in the morning, we hit a force nine gale. Before reaching Savannah, Captain Ivanović had warned about the series of lows sweeping across the Atlantic. It looks as if we are right in the middle of one of them now. At breakfast, there's a letter from the ship's owners on the mess noticeboard. It draws attention to an incident when a man was working on the f'o'csle of another ship and a large wave swept over it. He was swept to his death and a second man received fatal injuries. We are forbidden to go on the Main Deck. The rear of Decks C, D and E are open to us, however. I miss my walk round the main deck, but calculate that yesterday, in walking between bridge, mess and cabin, I climbed seven hundred and twenty stairs. It's as good as a gym. Nevertheless, I miss my regular walk and resort to the rowing machine for exercise. Five hundred strokes seem to be about my limit each day.

The consuming topic of conversation among the engineers over breakfast is about an incident in the engine room. The air gun that is used for cleaning parts of the engine accidentally fired a burst of air and it caught one of the men in the eye. It's not serious but is the cause of much concern and animated discussion. It has to be recorded, steps taken to ensure it cannot happen again.

We altered course during the night in order to avoid meeting the waves head on.

"Good weather," says the Captain, "is what enables us to keep the speed up."

Even so, it is still rough. We are going through the water like a corkscrew. The ship judders as yet another mighty wave hits us. The whole of the front of the ship is covered with white foam. The bow follows a clockwise movement. As it rises, it is pushed over to the starboard side by the wind and the direction of the swell. It then lunges back down into the sea and the automatic pilot pushes it back to port to correct the bearing, before rising again. And so we corkscrew our way through these steel-grey, angry waters. We maintain our course, along a straight line to the Bishop Rock lighthouse, off the Isles of Scilly.

In the afternoon, it calms a little to Beaufort six and it is possible to sit outside on Deck D and read for a couple of hours, occasionally looking up to watch the stern of the ship perform the same corkscrew pattern, but this time, from where I am, counter-clockwise. It is really quite beautiful and distracts me from reading. It is a magnificent sweeping movement, perfectly balancing that of the bow. Gwen joins me and then Phil. It is a companionable silence. Gwen is not feeling good about the rough seas. She hopes the fresh air will cure her nausea. Over dinner, it gets rougher, back to force ten. Gwen is absent. Jörg too cannot eat. Maritje loves it, as do I. Phil takes it in his stride. It is exhilarating. At night, I have to strain to keep myself from falling off the bed.

Phil and I have been doing a jigsaw puzzle in the lounge. I think, and he thinks, that there are two jigsaws here and we set about trying to disentangle them, discarding all the blue sky, the extra house that isn't in the picture and the edge pieces that don't seem to make sense. The one we think we are working on is a scene from the American civil war, all uniforms, horses, guns, mud, flags, tormented faces. It's infuriating to have to disentangle the two puzzles. There's a box for each. Why not use them, for heaven's sake.

"Why do people do this?" I ask.

"Because they are pure evil," he says with a grin.

That afternoon, Phil leaves the jigsaw to look after Gwen and while he's away I manage to complete it, minus one piece that's missing. After dinner, we go up to the lounge to inspect our work, but a giant wave hits us as we climb the stairs, the ship judders, and all our careful work lies in pieces on the floor.

Eduardo is in his element. He now has five passengers, in addition to the officers, to wait on at mealtimes, and he does it meticulously and with relish. At the beginning of every meal, he approaches each one of us individually, tea towel ostentatiously folded over his left arm, and hands us the menu. Of course, he knows very well what we want for breakfast. Apart from Gwen and Phil, we have been on the ship for several weeks and our choices rarely change. This has no bearing on the case, however, for it is his job to wait on us, and he can only do this if he insists on us studying the menu before giving him our order. We must go through the correct procedures. While we enact the charade of studying what we already know to be there, Eduardo takes his notebook out of his waistcoat pocket with professional authority and waits, pencil poised.

"Muesli, please Eduardo, and fruit," says Maritje.

He then licks his indelible pencil and writes it down, laboriously, meticulously, letter by painful letter. Each recording of our wishes has to be verified and when what we say agrees with what he has written, a broad grin stretches across his otherwise sombre face. This is a triumph of the greatest magnitude. It is a true validation of his vocation. Satisfied, he moves on to the next passenger. Removing the menu from Maritje's hand, he passes it to Jörg and the whole business is repeated. "Muesli and fruit please, Eduardo", he says, and this too is recorded.

Very occasionally, I have broken with routine and ordered scrambled egg on toast. The first time I attempted this, was a master class in the pitfalls of linguistic imprecision. First came the toast – flat and on a cold plate. This had the effect of making the beautiful crisp toast soggy, so cancelling at a stroke the whole purpose of toasting it in the first place. I sat and stared at it and waited for the scrambled egg. Eduardo also went away. After a while he came back empty handed, strode purposefully to the table, looked meaningfully at my plate and, seeing my toast still there untouched, retreated to the galley and waited again. I also waited, pouring a second cup of tea to pass the time. Out he came again, this time staring accusingly at the limp cold toast, shook his head despairingly and returned once more to the galley. Eventually Maritje had an idea.

"I think he's waiting for you to eat the toast first," she said, "then he'll bring you the scrambled egg. He thinks they're two separate courses."

It worked. I buttered the toast, put on a thick dollop of marmalade and ate it. This time when Eduardo came back to inspect my plate, he positively skipped back to the galley with glee and came back with the scrambled egg. Of course, it had by now been waiting for some considerable time and so had the consistency of cold rubber, which only a liberal application of brown and very spicy sauce could counteract. It was some time before I plucked up the courage to ask for scrambled egg on toast again, but when I did so, I emphasised the 'on' part, reinforcing the word with all the dramatic skill I have acquired from performing in the village pantomime. We eventually got it right between us and have had no further problems with that particular dish.

Nevertheless I am full of admiration for the Chief Cook and his assistant, also our steward. They work for a pittance, put in very long hours and do not have the same qualifications and experience of fully trained chefs. They do their best to please us and they usually do. On the whole, the food is good and nutritious and there is always plenty of it. It is true that there's a certain amount of predictability about the menu, so that chicken, for example, always appears on a Wednesday. But even so, every attempt is made to vary the way it is prepared. A couple of weeks ago, for example, "Chicken Cordon Blu" was proudly presented on the menu, and it turned out to be very tasty breaded escalopes, with a rather nice lemon and thyme sauce. It was such a success with us that it was repeated the following week as "Chicken Gordon Blew".

Eduardo is also the most conscientious cabin steward it has been my pleasure to know in all my experience of cargo ships. Cabins are superbly cleaned every day. I often encounter him soon after 06:15 when I get up to go to the conference room for my first cup of tea of the day. He attends officers and passengers at every meal, and as soon as breakfast is over, he starts on his round of cabin cleaning. Bed linen and towels are changed every week, carpets vacuumed and the en suite cleaned daily. He even makes the bed if he gets back to my cabin before I do after breakfast. After the last meal of the day, he sets to work with Cook to clean the galley floor and surfaces. There's no let up for these guys, they work seven days a week and their monthly pay amounts roughly to my electricity bill.

We are over the Porcupine Abyssal Plain, which in places is almost five thousand metres below us. This area of the North-east Atlantic, lying roughly between Iceland and the Bay of Biscay, is being closely monitored. The National Oceanography Centre has set up a research programme to collect data over long periods of time to identify changes in temperature, salinity, and the marine ecosystem. Changes in global sea level and vertical land movements are also being studied as part of GLOSS, the Global Sea Level Observing System, set up under the auspices of the World Meteorological Organisation and the Intergovernmental Oceanographic Commission, in which GPS technology is being used to collect the relevant data, some of which will contribute to an understanding of climate change[73].

"That's our nearest land," says Dragomir, "but I guess you don't want to get off here, eh! Let's wait 'til we get to Tilbury."

I am enjoying the delights of the library. Joanna Trollope's *Next of Kin*, Barbara Kingsolver's *The Bean Trees*, Monica Ali's *Brick Lane*. It's an open, evolving library. Passengers donate books they have of their own and take what they have not finished reading. But mostly it grows by donation; it is well stocked and a god-send for filling time.

The first sight we get of England, is the Bishop Rock Lighthouse. What an amazing structure this is, its reassuring two flashes every fifteen seconds visible from twenty nautical miles away. Standing at the extreme edge of the Scilly Isles, just four and a quarter miles west of St. Agnes, it is little more than a rock measuring forty-six metres by sixteen. If ever anyone is tempted to underestimate the power of the elements, the history of this lighthouse should convince them otherwise. When the plans were being made to build the first one here, the Chief Engineer to Trinity House, James Walker, estimated that the wind pressure was capable of exceeding seven thousand pounds per square foot and that thirty gales a yearwere not uncommon. Just before the lighting equipment could be installed on that first lighthouse, it was demolished in 1850 by a heavy gale.

The most legendary tragedy here was in 1707, when Admiral Sir Cloudesley Shovell was on his way back from action in the siege of Toulon in the War of the Spanish Succession. As they approached home waters, Sir Cloudesley Shovell called the Masters of all the other ships in his convoy to a meeting aboard his flagship, the Association, to consider where exactly they were. Most of the Masters were of the opinion that they were off Ushant. One lone voice, however, the Master of Sir William Jumper's ship, the Lenox, said his calculations showed that they were within three hours sailing of the Isles of Scilly. Tragically, Cloudesley accepted the majority verdict and concluded they were off the coast of north-west France. He and half a dozen other ships therefore continued north-east on this assumption, believing they were about to enter the English Channel, whereas in reality they were heading straight into the Scilly Isles. As a consequence, many of his ships were lost, together with about two thousand men[74]. If only the marine chronometer had been invented by then, the story would have been very different.

As soon as storms had demolished the first Bishop Rock lighthouse, work began on the second, which was up and running by 1858. Thirty years later, it had been strengthened and its height increased by twelve metres. This modified lighthouse is still in use today, except that now it is fully automatic and is crowned by a helideck.[75]

Sparkie shows me an e-mail he has just received from the Harbour Master at Tilbury. Ships are queuing up in the

Thames Estuary because of fog. We have been given instructions to drop anchor on Saturday, so there's little chance of berthing before Sunday. The irony is that we had reduced speed overnight because we were in danger of arriving too early for our rendezvous with the pilot. The signal is strong enough to send a text to Joan wishing her a happy Valentine's Day, for which Sparkie tells me there will be no charge.

A miniscule fishing vessel cuts across our bow. I think of myself as a pretty good sailor, but the sight of this tiny craft being thrown about totally at the mercy of the sea, makes me feel ill. More dramatic than a roller coaster, it completely disappears from view as it plunges down the far side of each mammoth wave, only to shoot up to the crest of the next one, like a cork that has just been released from the bottom of the sea. On and on it goes into the far horizon, shooting up and dropping like a stone, so regularly and so predictably it hardly seems possible for it to make any forward progress at all. Allthis to put fish on our tables.

Morning, and it's a bright day. We are out of the storm, and the wind has weakened to force five from the south-east. Able Seaman Jimmy, whom I always think of as Smiley, was waxing stairs last might, all eighty-six of them, as well as the passageways, so as to avoid disrupting the normal movement of people during the day. This morning our shoes squeak as we walk. Maritje was speaking to another crew member the other day who told her that he was working until 02:00 one night and then had to be up to commence his normal duties at 05:00. Of course, they get paid for this overtime, but I don't think they have much choice about whether to do it or not. All these men have been invariably friendly and companionable. We have put together a contribution to put into the entertainment fund, but we have all given something extra to Cook and Eduardo, without whom our lives on board would have been immeasurably poorer.

Jörg tells me he has just got a signal from BBC television, so we settle down to watch a David Attenborough film about badgers. Television has been so infrequent an experience over the past few weeks, it feels like a novelty. There's an air of suppressed excitement as we approach our various destinations. We passengers are all quietly occupied making arrangements for onward travel. There will be no fond farewells. We have been thrown together randomly, have had a good shared experience, and will shake hands and let it go.

Rounding the shoulder of Kent, where my great-grandfather had cast off his tug more than a hundred and twenty years ago, we anchor off Margate for a night and a day waiting for the fog to clear. In the early afternoon of the following day, a light breeze clears all but the last remnants away and at 16:00 hours, we begin our slow crawl back up the Thames to Tilbury. A few miles off Herne Bay, the graceful silhouettes of the Kentish Flats wind turbines rise out of the purple sea. Through the thin remains of the mist, they look like tired wraiths lazily stirring themselves in response to a rising wind. I last saw these three-armed creatures on October 31st, forty-nine thousand kilometres (thirty thousand miles) ago. The sun is low on the horizon, flushing the sky with a defiant red, shading through orange to yellow. Behind us, night has already fallen, the sky is black. We edge cautiously towards our rendezvous with Tilbury, timed for 21:00 hours. We passengers will be off soon to our ordinary lives. Our mood is light. Home, a long voyage completed. For those left on board this is just another port, another day's work.

How To Do It

A few travel agencies specialise in freighter travel. The only UK one of which I have any real experience is The Cruise People, which is based at 88 York Street, London, W1H 1QT, UK (www.cruisepeople.co.uk). Apart from my early voyages from Australia to New Zealand and China, all of my voyages have been facilitated through The Cruise People. I have always found them to be friendly and efficient.

Some passengers I have travelled with used Strand Voyages (www.strandtravelltd.co.uk) and they gave very good reports of the service they had received. I received word a few months ago, however, that this company is no longer handling passenger transits on cargo ships.

The first cargo ship my wife and I travelled on was from Sydney to New Zealand, a short voyage of four days, followed, a few weeks later by our nineteen-day voyage from Tauranga to Shanghai, the subject of chapter 2. We organised these through Hamish Jamieson of Freighter Travel (NZ), at 248 Kennedy Road, Napier, New Zealand (www.freightertravel.co.nz). When we eventually got to Napier, we made our way to Hamish's office on Kennedy Road, where he was waiting with a bottle of champagne to celebrate our first ever freighter voyage and the successful culmination of eighteen months of meticulous planning.

I cannot speak highly enough of the service my wife and I have received through both The Cruise People and Freighter Travel (NZ).

The important thing is always to book early. It may come as a surprise to realise that passenger-carrying cargo ships can be fully booked a long way ahead. I recommend at least a year, preferably eighteen months or even two years advance booking. This way not only are you more likely to get a cabin, but you are also more likely also to get one higher up and out of all danger of having your view blocked by containers. These better cabins are slightly more expensive but not by a great deal, and it is certainly worth paying the extra to get an unrestricted view. Some shorter haul journeys, and voyages on general cargo ships, can sometimes be booked only a few months ahead, but for the more popular routes, especially to Australia and the USA, a longer booking time is required.

It is also essential to be flexible in your arrangements. With cruise ships, you are given a detailed itinerary for every port of call with precise times of arrival and departure. Do not expect this with freighter travel, for which you cannot even be sure of the day of departure, let alone the hour. The best you will be given is the expected day of departure, but you need to be prepared to board several days before or after this. Once, when I was sailing for Chester, Pennsylvania, from Liverpool, I made the mistake of buying advance economy train tickets. Big mistake. The day of departure was set back by a day so that I had the choice of using my cheap tickets and spending a night at a hotel in Liverpool or getting new train tickets. It was cheaper to do the latter.

For that first freighter voyage from Sydney to Tauranga, the sailing date was brought forward by five days, and we were given just two days' notice of this. Everything we had planned to do in that final week had to be abandoned. So, be flexible.

Obviously, this mode of travel is for people who have plenty of time, perhaps for students who want to take a different kind of gap year, or for retired people who simply want to see the world in a different kind of way.

As for cost, my journey on the Alexandra Rickmers from Tilbury to Melbourne, a voyage of 34 days, cost me £2,220, or just over £65 a day, and the voyage on the Manet from

Brisbane to Tilbury, which lasted for 41 days, cost £3,803, or £93 a day. I was at sea for a total of 75 days at an average daily rate of fractionally over £80. These are pretty good rates when you realise that you are not just paying for the journey, but also for your full board and lodging. These prices may be slightly out of date now, but I recently planned another voyage from Ijmuiden to Chicago via the St Lawrence Seaway and the Great Lakes, which sadly has had to be cancelled, but the average daily cost would have been £64.76. That's a good-value holiday. And with this mode of travel, the journey is the holiday. Your holiday does not begin at your destination but the moment you step on board.

As with other types of holiday, there are incidental costs, not the least of which is insurance, which increases with age. I usually manage to get a pretty good rate by shopping around. There is normally a maximum age limit for this kind of travel, and seventy-nine seems to be about the norm. So if you're interested in this type of travel, now's the time to do it!

Endnotes

Chapter 1

[1] Most of this information, apart from what has been passed down the generations in my family both verbally and in a few documents, comes from the following sources: The Evening Post, Wellington, New Zealand, 17 April 1883 and 29 August 1883. New Zealand Herald, 3 August 1883. Lloyd's Register, 1878-79, 1882-1883.

[2] Marlborough Express, Volume XIX, Issue 170, 3 August 1883, page 2

Chapter 2

[3] Arthur Grimble, *A Pattern of Islands*, (Reprint Society, London, 1954), pages 60-66.

[4] James Frazer, *The Golden Bough*, (Wordsworth Editions Ltd, Ware, 1993, First published in 12 volumes in the USA between 1890 and 1915 and in this abridged form in 1922), pages 109-120.

[5] Rosemary Hammerton, 2000, *Spirituality: Alone and Together*, Eremos: Exploring Spirituality in Australia, February, No. 70, pages 19-24.

[6] Storm Dunlop, *Oxford Dictionary of Weather* (Oxford University Press, New York) 2001.

[7] I have used the following sources for most of this material: A film, whose title I have long since forgotten, seen at the Bradford Imax Cinema, 5 July 1997; an excerpt from

the book, Palau, by Nancy Barbour, in *Reader's Digest World Presents The Living Edens, Palau Paradise of the Pacific*, http://www.pbs.org/edens/palau/p_legends2.htm; Flood, Bo, Beret Strong and William Flood. *The Creation of Palau, Pacific Islands Legends: Tales From Melanesia, Micronesia, Polynesia and Australia*, Honolulu: Bess Press, http://metalx.dreamhosters.com/107/R06-creationofpalau.pdf 8-32.

Chapter 3

[8] htpp://www.hamburg-port-authority.de/en/the-port-of-hamburg/facts-and-figures/Seiten/default.aspx.

[9] See Stephanie Draper, *How a few players in shipping changed the world*, The Guardian, 23 June 2011.

[10] Sir Dudley Stamp and S. H. Beaver, *The British Isles* (Longman, 1971) pages 719-720.

[11] See *Port Information Guide*, portofrotterdam.com.

Chapter 8

[12] Referred to as Euroclydon in the Authorized Version of the Bible.

[13] This would be the Gulf of Sirte on the north coast of present day Libya.

[14] Acts ch. 27 v. 13-20, New Revised Standard Version.

[15] From International Database and Gallery of Structures at http://en.structurae.net/structures/data/index.cfm?id=s0001313 .

[16] Genesis ch. 4 v. 14.

[17] I Kings ch. 18 v. 21.

[18] James Frazer, *The Golden Bough*, (Wordsworth Editions Ltd, Ware, 1993, First published in 12 volumes in the USA between 1890 and 1915 and in this abridged form in 1922), page 363.

[19] Joseph Holden, *An Introduction to Physical Geography and the Environment*, Third Edition, (Pearson Education Limited, Harlow, 2012) page 41.

Chapter 9

[20] Exodus ch. 13 v. 20-22.
[21] Exodus ch. 19 v. 16-19.
[22] Deuteronomy ch. 8 v. 15.
[23] Nahum ch. 1 v. 5-6
[24] Exodus ch. 14 v. 21.
[25] I owe this to a quotation in an old geography text I used at college more than half a century ago by S. W. Wooldridge and W. G. East, *The Spirit and Purpose of Geography*, Hutchinson & Co. Ltd, London, 1958), opening acknowledgement.
[26] Jared Diamond, *Guns, Germs and Steel: A Short History of Everybody for the Last 13,000 Years*, Vintage Books, London, 2005.

Chapter 10

[27] The man in Seat 61 at http://www.seat61.com/CO2flights.htm and *The Observer*, 29 January 2006
[28] *Celtic Myth Podshow*, http://celticmythpodshow.com/
[29] *Ireland's Druid School*, http://www.druidschool.com/site/1030100/page/846679.
[30] *BBC Religions Beltane*, http://www.bbc.co.uk/religion/religions/paganism/holydays/beltane_1.shtml; *The White Goddess*, http://www.thewhitegoddess.co.uk/index.asp.
[31] James Frazer, *The Golden Bough*, (Wordsworth Editions Ltd, Ware, 1993, First published in 12 volumes in the USA between 1890 and 1915 and in this abridged form in 1922), page 358-9.

[32] Quoted by Robert Fisk, *The Great War For Civilisation: The Conquest of the Middle East*, (Harper Perennial, London, 2006), pages 177-178.

[33] See Robert Fisk, *The Great War For Civilisation: The Conquest of the Middle East*, (Harper Perennial, London, 2006), pages 175-180; Lewis M. Alexander, *World Political Patters*, Second Edition, (Rand McNally & Company, Chicago, 1966), pages 355-364.

Chapter 11

[34] *Chagos-Laccadive Ridge*, https://en.wikipedia.org/wiki/Chagos-Laccadive_Ridge

[35] Joseph Holden, *An Introduction to Physical Geography and the Environment*, Third Edition, (Pearson Education Limited, Harlow, 2012) page 47.

Chapter 12

[36] Samuel Taylor Coleridge, *The Rime of the Ancient Mariner* (text of 1834), http://www.poetryfoundation.org/poem/173253.

[37] The mixture of imperial and metric measure is brought about because container dimensions are always given in feet and inches whereas every other aspect of shipping uses the metric system.

[38] Joseph Holden, *An Introduction to Physical Geography and the Environment*, Third Edition, (Pearson Education Limited, Harlow, 2012) pages 437-438.

[39] Jared Diamond, Collapse: *How Societies Choose to Fail or Survive*, (Penguin Books, London, 2005) pages 379, 380.

[40] Bruce Chatwin, *The Songlines*, (Picador, London, 1987) page 142.

[41] Jared Diamond, *Collapse: How Societies Choose to Fail or Survive* (Penguin Books, London, 2006) pages 387-8.

[42] Rodgers & Hammerstein's *Oklahoma! The Complete Book and Lyrics of the Broadway Musical,* (Applause Theatre & Cinema Books, Milwaukee, 2010) page 119.

[43] A full version of Chief Seattle's speech appeared in the *Seattle Sunday Star*, Oct. 29, 1887, in a column by Dr. Henry A. Smith. http://www.halcyon.com/arborhts/chiefsea.html.

[44] Bruce Chatwin, *The Songlines*, (Picador, London, 1987) pages 14-16.

[45] *Rangitoto Island*, https://en.wikipedia.org/wiki/Rangitoto_Island.

[46] James Oakley Wilson, D.S.C., M.COM., A.L.A., Chief Librarian, General Assembly Library, Wellington, in *An Encyclopaedia of New Zealand*, edited by A. H. McLintock. 1966. See http://www.teara.govt.nz/en/1966/aotearoa.

[47] *The Restless Land: Stories of Tongariro National Park World Heritage Area*, Tongariro/Taupo Conservancy, Department of Conservation and Tongariro Natural History Society, (Turangi, 1998) pages 18-19; Karen Williams, *Volcanoes of the South Wind*, (Tongariro Natural History Society, [Inc.] Friends of Tongariro National Park World Heritage Site, 2001) page 9.

[48] Exodus ch. 19 v. 18.

[49] James Frazer, *The Golden Bough*, (Wordsworth Editions Ltd, Ware, 1993, First published in 12 volumes in the USA between 1890 and 1915 and in this abridged form in 1922), page 358.

[50] Michael King, *The Penguin History of New Zealand*, (Penguin, Auckland, 2003) page 353.

Chapter 18

[51] I owe some of the information in parts of this section to Joseph Holden (Editor), *An Introduction to Physical Geography and the Environment,* (Pearson Education Limited, Edinburgh, 2012) ch. 3.

[52] Joyce Kilmer, *Mid-ocean in War-time*,
http://famouspoetsandpoems.com/poets/joyce_kilmer/poems/1
7409.html

Chapter 19

[53] Graham Stacy, *Pleiades*, unpublished song written for
the men's folk choir Voicemale, inspired by two Japanese
poems, *I loved her like the leaves,* from *In Praise of Empress
Jitō*, by Kakinomoto Hitomaro (7th century) and *To this world
farewell,* from *The Love Suicides at Sonezaki*, by Chikamatsu
Monzaemon (1653-1725). Quoted with permission from
Graham Stacy.

[54] Job ch. 38 v. 7.

[55] Revelation ch. 1 v. 16.

[56] Robert Winston, *The Story of God*, (Bantam Books,
London, 2005) pages 246 and 453.

[57] Psalm 8 v. 3,4 Authorized Version .

[58] From *How Great Thou Art*, Translation by Stuart K.
Hine, 1953, *Songs and Hymns of Fellowship*, (Kingsway
Publications, Eastbourne, 1987), number 407. Quoted with
permission.

*Adm. By Capitol CMG Publishing worldwide excl. UK
& Europe, admin by integritymusic.com, a division of David
C Cook songs@integritymusic.com Used by permission.

Chapter 20

[59] Samuel Taylor Coleridge, *The Rime of the Ancient
Mariner* (text of 1834),
http://www.poetryfoundation.org/poem/173253.

[60] As I write Maersk has announced that it is to stop
sending its vessels from Asia through the Panama Canal to the
East Coast of the United States. Bigger ships make it more
profitable to use the Suez Canal.

[61] See for example http://coloncity.com/chagres.html; http://www.ecotourismpanama.com/national-parks/chagres.htm.

[62] Sources for some of the information in this section include the following: Chagres National Park, Panama at http://www.ecotourismpanama.com/national-parks/chagres.htm; Madden Dam and Lake Alajuela at http://www.panamahistorybits.com/article.asp.

Chapter 21

[63] Panama-Guide.com: Thursday, May 17 2007 @ 07:03 PM EDT. Contributed by: Don Winner

[64] For more details see the following: http://www.yacht-transport.com/float-on-float-off-service.html; http://www.oceantrekmarine.com/ex-fofo-float-float; http://www.fleetmon.com/en/vessels/Super_Servant_4_57206.

[65] http://coastal.er.usgs.gov/navassa/geology/; http://wikitravel.org/en/Navassa_Island.

[66] Some of this material is taken from: https://en.wikipedia.org/wiki/Geography_of_the_Bahamas.

[67] Joseph Holden (Editor), *An Introduction to Physical Geography and the Environment,* (Pearson Education Limited, Edinburgh, 2012), page 60.

Chapter 22

[68] I owe this information to an email from the US Army Corps Engineers Library Program and Polly Shamy, who researched it for me.

Chapter 23

[69] Leviticus ch. 25 v. 10.

[70] Homer, *The Odyssey*, trans. Robert Fagles, New York, 1996, 109, quoted by Jon Meacham in, *American Gospel:*

God, the Founding Fathers and the Making of a Nation, (Random House, New York, 2006), page 14.

Chapter 24

[71] From a letter from my sister Eileen who sourced this information from Shirl Kasper, *Annie Oakley*, (University of Oklahoma Press, 2000) page 130.

[72] All details taken from Lloyd's Register 1892-93.

[73] National Oceanography Centre, Natural Environment Research Council, http://noc.ac.uk/ocean-watch.

[74] See The Gunroom of HMSSurprise.org, *The Shipwreck of Sir Cloudesley Shovell, on the Scilly Islands in 1707, From Original and Contemporary Documents Hitherto Unpublished*, (Read at a Meeting of the Society of Antiquaries, London, Feb. 1, 1883), by James Herbert Cooke, F.S.A., Gloucester: John Bellows, http://www.hmssurprise.org/shipwreck-sir-cloudesley-shovell#20a.

[75] See *Worldwide Lighthouses*, http://www.worldwidelighthouses.com/Lighthouses/English-Lighthouses/Trinity-House-Owned/Bishop-Rock. http://www.trinityhouse.co.uk/lighthouses/lighthouse_list/bishop_rock.html.